THE AVCA
VOLLEYBALL HANDBOOK

THE AVCA
VOLLEYBALL HANDBOOK

The Official Handbook of the American Volleyball Coaches' Association

Edited by Bob Bertucci

MP
MASTERS PRESS

A Subsidiary of Howard W. Sams & Co.

Published by Masters Press (A division of Howard W. Sams & Co.)
2647 Waterfront Pkwy. E. Drive, Suite 300
Indianapolis, IN 46214-2041

Library of Congress Cataloging-in-Publication Data

The AVCA volleyball handbook.
     1. Volleyball–United States–Coaching
 I. Bertucci, Bob. II. American Volleyball Coaches' Association.

GV1015.5.C63A93   1987
796.32'5   87-31240

Credits:
Cover design by Susan Milanowski
Text design by Anne Shuart

Photo Credits:
p. xvi – University of Florida Sports Information; p. 55 – Joshua Lee; p. 64 – Terri Norris, ISU Photo Services; p. 72 – Dennis Steers; p. 115 (top) – Doug Hoke; p. 115 (bottom) – Susan Allen Camp; p. 159 (top) – Robert Barclay, CMU Media Relations; p. 160 – Susan Allen Camp; p. 192 – University of Pennsylvania Sports Information; p. 193 – Ball State University Photo Service; p. 230 – Doug Hoke; p. 249 – Gerry Vuchetich, University of Minnesota; p. 236 – Garney, Inc.; p. 328 – Jim Spirakis

CONTENTS

Acknowledgements viii

Preface ix

Introduction xi

PART I: THE BASIC ELEMENTS – INDIVIDUAL SKILLS

Volleying Skills

Chapter 1 – Digging   1
Chapter 2 – Setting 19

Net Skills

Chapter 3 – Spiking 57
Chapter 4 – Blocking 65

Service Skills

Chapter 5 – Serving 73
Chapter 6 – Receiving the Serve 87

Tactics and Strategy

Chapter 7 – Tactics and Strategy in Volleyball 107

PART II: THE MORE ADVANCED ELEMENTS — TEAM PLAY

Offense

Chapter 8 – Systems of Play 117
Chapter 9 – Offensive Combinations 143
Chapter 10 – Service Reception 161

Defense

Chapter 11 – Net Defense: Option Blocking 181
Chapter 12 – Floor Defense: Back Court Defense 195

Transition

Chapter 13 – Elements of Transition 231

PART III: THE RELATED ELEMENTS — PROGRAM DEVELOPMENT

Chapter 14 – Administration of a Volleyball Program 251
Chapter 15 – Physical Factors 289
          Shaping Up for the Attack – Bob Bertucci 327
Chapter 16 – Psychological Factors 329

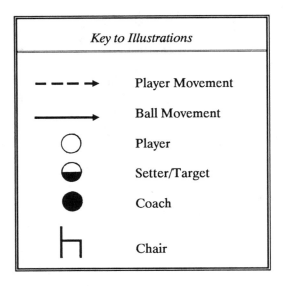

Key to Illustrations

- - - →	Player Movement
——→	Ball Movement
○	Player
◒	Setter/Target
●	Coach
⊓	Chair

CONTRIBUTORS

Authors

Andy Banachowski, *Head Coach, UCLA*
Doug Beal, *Head Coach, 1984 USA Men's Olympic Gold Medal Team*
Jim Coleman, *Technical Advisor, USA National Men's Team*
Frances Compton, *Assistant Coach, Louisiana State University*
Terry Condon, *Assistant Athletic Director, UCLA*
Tony Crabb, *Staff Member, USA National Men's Team*
Vanessa Draper, *Graduate Teaching Associate, University of Tennessee*
Bob Gambardella, *Head Coach, United States Military Academy*
Kathy Gregory, *Head Coach, University of California, Santa Barbara*
Mick Haley, *Head Coach, University of Texas*
Terry Liskevych, *Head Coach, USA National Women's Team*
Sandy Lynn, *Head Coach, University of Tennessee*
Marilyn McReavy, *Head Coach, University of Florida*
Ruth Nelson, *Director of International Volleyball for the Special Olympics*
Bill Neville, *USVBA Technical Director*
Ian Pyka, *Strength Training Director, University of Massachusetts*
Stephanie Schleuder, *Head Coach, University of Minnesota*
Dave Shoji, *Head Coach, University of Hawaii*
Rosie Wegrich, *Head Coach, University of Arizona*
Craig A. Wrisberg, *Professor of Sports Psychology, University of Tennessee*

Editors

General Editor: Bob Bertucci, *Head Coach, Rutgers University*
Copy Editors: Michael L. Keene and Linda K. Blake
Manuscript Editor: Amy E. Wolterstorff

Advisors

Geri Polvino, *Head Coach, Eastern Kentucky University*
Sandy Vivas, *Executive Director, American Volleyball Coaches' Association*

ACKNOWLEDGEMENTS

Assembling under one cover the thoughts, ideas, and convictions of some of the top U.S. volleyball coaches required a great deal of effort and determination from many people. We have been fortunate in having authors and editors who believed in this project from the beginning and nurtured it all along the way. I extend my gratitude to them for their patience, support, and for the quality of their work.

I am indebted to Dr. James Peterson of the United States Military Academy at West Point for the inspiration for this project. Many thanks to Thomas Bast, publisher, Amy Wolterstorff, editor, and the rest of the staff at Masters Press for their insight, creativity, and hard work in seeing the book to its completion. I am also grateful to Mr. Jim Peterson of Sports Camps International for recognizing the value of the project and putting me in contact with Masters Press.

A special thanks needs to be extended to Sandy Vivas, executive director of the American Volleyball Coaches' Association for her continued support and encouragement throughout the project, and to Geri Polvino of Eastern Kentucky University for her professionalism and constructive suggestions during the review of the manuscripts. In addition, I cannot overlook the help received by Herb Benenson in preparing the manuscript and Roxanne Morgan for many of the drawings and illustrations.

Finally, I thank my wife, Tina Bertucci. The encouragement, patience, and guidance she provided made it all possible.

Bob Bertucci
Rutgers University
October 1987

PREFACE

The popularity of volleyball has grown tremendously in recent years. Because of new developments in the game, many coaches have felt the need for an up-to-date and comprehensive guide to coaching volleyball—one which includes information contributed by coaches from across the country. *The AVCA Volleyball Handbook* is a response to that need.

This book is intended for those coaching volleyball at all levels, and provides a fresh review of the sport's various aspects. Included are basic instructions presented in an innovative fashion, as well as information on recent changes in the game. The book is divided into three sections:

    I.   The Basic Elements – Individual Skills
    II. The More Advanced Elements – Team Play
    III. The Related Elements – Program Development

The sections proceed from basic to advanced; in general, from aspects of the game that a novice coach would need to learn to points of interest for more seasoned coaches. Reading the authors' manuscripts for this book brought home to me how much any coach could learn from other coaches' points of view and methods. *The AVCA Volleyball Handbook* will also be useful for the advanced player who is seeking both a comprehensive review of fundamentals and insight into the game's more abstract elements.

Twenty outstanding coaches and educators from around the United States have contributed chapters to this volume. Thus, we hope to provide you not only an overall look at the game, but also the coaching styles and philosophies of a number of successful volleyball coaches. The book contains abundant visuals, including photographs, diagrams, and illustrations. Whether you are a new coach, an experienced coach brushing up, or a player looking for a better understanding of the game, *The AVCA Volleyball Handbook* will add measurably to your success at the exciting sport of volleyball.

Bob Bertucci

VOLLEYBALL: A GENERAL INTRODUCTION

Bob Bertucci

In Holyoke, Massachusetts, in 1895, a YMCA physical education director invented the game known today as volleyball. William G. Morgan originated the game to provide recreation and relaxation for businessmen. The game Morgan developed in the Holyoke gymnasium was called *mintonette*. He borrowed the net from tennis, but decided to raise it 1.98 m (6 ft. 6 ins.) above the floor, just above the average man's head. He asked A.G. Spalding to make the first ball. During a demonstration game, it was remarked that because the men looked to be volleying the ball back and forth over the net, perhaps the game should be called *volleyball*. Morgan accepted the suggestion, and on July 7, 1896, at Springfield College, the first game of volleyball was played.

Volleyball, probably the most popular indoor game in the world, is played in virtually every country. Volleyball is even an Olympic sport, and in the 1984 Los Angeles Games every match was a sellout. In the Olympic Games in Montreal, scalper prices for some preliminary matches were five times the face value of the tickets. In the United States, there are an estimated 22.6 million players of all ages. Data from a 1984–1985 survey by a sporting goods market publication show more female participants than males: 2.1 million in the thirteen-and-under age group, 2.5 million in the eighteen-to-twenty-five age group. The number of male participants is slightly lower: 1.6 million in the thirteen-and-under age group, 1.5 million in the thirteen-to-seventeen age group, and 1.8 million in the eighteen-to-twenty-five age group. Volleyball ranks as the third most popular high school sport. The U.S. National Federation High School Sports poll shows 444 boys' teams (8,616 players) and 11,603 girls' teams (269,498 players).

UNIQUE FEATURES

Volleyball has several unique features. There are twelve players on the court—six per side—in a very small area. Each player must cover approximately 14 sq. m (150 sq. ft.) of the court. Players must play all positions, and each position has different physical and technical demands. Legal contact with the ball is very limited in both time and distance, making precise movement prior to touching the ball extremely important. Volleyball is also the only sport in which a player's maximum force is typically applied while the body is unsupported (in the air). The game is characterized by short, high energy bursts and periods of rest. Unlike most other sports, volleyball games are most often determined by *negative* play—for example, a team failing to control the ball. The volleyball playing environment quickly and constantly changes because of the movement of players, the speed of the ball, the variety of formations and movements of the two teams, and the relationship of the ball to the players on both sides. The movements required of each player change at an extremely fast speed, and the great variety of offensive and defensive maneuvers (for individuals or for whole teams) makes the environment even more changeable. Volleyball also requires a great deal of planned deception on the part of two highly trained teams. Thus, volleyball players require a wide range of abilities, and volleyball training must be broad-based.

THE COURT

Volleyball is played on a court 18 m long by 9 m wide (59 ft. by 29 1/2 ft.). The court is defined by markings called *boundary lines, attack lines, service lines,* and the *center line.* Boundary lines consist of the baselines (at each end of the court) and the sidelines (perpendicular to the net). Attack lines are used as guides for the hitters and are located where the hitter's approach to the ball begins. Extending indefinitely beyond the side lines, these lines are three meters from the center line on each side and parallel to it. There are two service lines, each 15 cm (6 ins.) long and 5 cm (2 ins.) wide, drawn 20 cm (8 ins.) behind and perpendicular to the baseline. These service lines mark the zone (behind the baseline on the right-hand third of the court) where the server must be standing to deliver the serve. The center line lies directly under the net and divides the playing area into two equal parts. Its 5 cm (2 in.) width was developed after the discovery that opposing players' feet went under the net and injuries occurred. The entire court is surrounded by boundary lines that are 5 cm (2 in.) wide and at least 2 m (6 ft. 7 ins.) from all obstructions. The height of the net measured from the center of the court is 2.4 m [7 ft. 11 5/8 ins.] for men and 2.3 m (7 ft. 4 1/8 ins.) for women and children.

THE PLAYERS

Volleyball is played with six players per team on the court at a time. Even though a team is allowed only six people on the court, it usually has twelve people on its roster, especially in international competition. Players start the game in the right, center, and left front positions and the right, center, and left back positions. Each player has a special task. On every team there are one or two *setters,* whose primary responsibilities are to select a teammate who will attack the ball and to direct the ball to that attacker. *Attackers* (hitters or spikers) are players who focus on directing the ball into the opponents' court.

These two main positions — setters and attackers — can be further broken down. Besides setters, there are off-setters, players who usually play the right front position, where they are effective as either setters or hitters. Attackers can be divided into outside hitters and middle blockers. Outside hitters are usually strong, powerful players who can effectively hit a variety of shots around the block posed by the defenders' raised hands. Middle blockers utilize quick, deceptive movements to the set, and hit with more finesse than raw force.

Players can also be front or back court specialists, who play either the three front court or the three back court positions, and then substitute out. Even though only six people are allowed on the court at once, the team usually has twelve people on its roster and these players are used on the substitution principle that pertains to that type of competition.

EQUIPMENT

Playing volleyball requires special equipment. The constant jumping involved in playing makes wearing proper footwear extremely important. Most people use lightweight footwear with strong ankle and arch support as well as good shock absorption. Because volleyball players are constantly falling or diving to the floor, knee pads are essential. Clothing varies greatly in volleyball. For formal matches, most teams wear long-sleeved, collared jerseys. In warmer weather, short-sleeved jerseys are often preferred. Practice attire is usually much different. During practice, most teams wear T-shirts and defensive pants, which are padded in the hip area and extend to the knees, protecting the player from floor burns and bruises.

THE BALL

A standard volleyball has a circumference of 65 to 67 cm (25 to 27 ins.) and weighs 260 to 280 g (9 to 10 oz.). In the United States the ball is usually white, although some imported balls are light tan or yellow. The inflation pressure is stated on the ball and should be strictly observed in order to insure normal feel and ball life expectancy. The pressure should be between 0.48 and 0.52 kg per cm (between 6.8 and 7.4 lbs. per square inch). The players should become familiar with the feel of a properly inflated ball and should strive to maintain that correct pressure. The referee must check the ball before and during the match to be sure it has not become wet or slippery.

The type of ball to select is determined by the type of use expected. Although a rubber ball will outlast even the toughest leather one, players may experience a loss of feeling when using a rubber ball. Consequently, several manufacturers have produced relatively inexpensive, amazingly durable leather balls, which prove to be much better than rubber balls.

THE OFFICIALS

A match is conducted by a referee, an umpire, a scorer, and two or four linesmen. The referee is responsible for the correct conduct of the match. With the blow of the whistle, the referee begins each play and signals service to begin. Each action is considered to be finished when the referee blows the whistle. The referee has authority over all players and officials throughout the match, including any periods during which the match may be temporarily interrupted. Generally speaking, referees should only interrupt play when they are sure that a fault has been committed, and they should not blow the whistle if there is any doubt. The referee has the power to settle all questions including those not specifically covered in the rules. Furthermore, the referee may overrule decisions of other officials when, in the referee's opinion, they have made errors.

The official second to the referee is the umpire. The umpire's position is on the side of the court opposite and facing the referee. Like the referee, the umpire has many responsibilities. At the beginning of the game, the umpire must verify that the positions of the players of both teams correspond with the serving orders listed on the score sheet and with the lineups as given to the scorer. At the time of service, the umpire must supervise the rotation order and positions of the receiving team. The umpire makes calls pertaining to violations at the center line and the attack lines. The umpire also signals any ball contact with the antenna or a ball crossing the net not entirely between the antennae. In addition, the umpire must judge player contact with the net. With the assistance of the scorer at the scoretable, the umpire must keep track of the number and length of time-outs, supervise the conduct of the coaches and substitutes on the bench, and authorize substitutions requested by captains or coaches of the teams.

Unlike the referee and the umpire, the scorer has no first-hand control of the match. The scorer may stop play because of a rotation or point problem, but must do so through the referee. Before the match begins, the scorer records the numbers of the players on the score sheet. As the match progresses, the scorer records the scores, carefully noting the number of time-outs and substitutions. The scorer must also make sure that the serving and rotation orders of players are followed correctly.

THE PLAY

The Serve. A volleyball match begins with a coin toss. The team winning the toss picks either first serve or the side of the court they would like. The game begins with the serve: the right back player hits the ball into the opponents' court. If the serve is good, an ace or a *point* for the serving team may result. If the player serves the ball into the net, a *side out* occurs and the service goes to the opposing team. The first service alternates with each game. If play goes into a deciding game, a second coin toss determines who will serve.

Defense. The most basic defensive movement in volleyball is the underhand pass, or *dig*, in which the ball is contacted with the upper surface of the forearm. The player receives the serve in the defensive position, then digs the ball toward the setter. The setter passes the ball overhand to a hitter. The setter also has the option of passing the ball backward (a *back set*), or executing a set while airborne (a *jump set*).

Offense. There are many ways for hitters to get the ball into the opponents' court. The hitter may direct the ball diagonally, inside the blocking team's hands and toward the far sideline of the court, resulting in a *cross-court spike*. In a *line spike,* the hitter directs the ball outside the blocker's hands and down the near sideline of the court. The spiker could also make a *wipe-off spike* by intentionally directing the ball to rebound off the defender's block and fly out of bounds. Another trick is changing the speed at which the ball is contacted. For example, the spiker might either hit a *half-speed shot* or tip the ball. A *tip* is an attack shot that lobs the ball over the net into a vulnerable area of the defending team's court. Any time the defending team is unable to return any type of a spike or tip, a *kill* is recorded in the statistics.

Blocks. The first line of defense against a hitter is the *block.* One or more front line players jump and reach above the net, intercepting the attack by deflecting the ball into the opponent's court. Blockers may block solo, in pairs, and even in threes. When setting up the block, players may intentionally position themselves to take away certain areas of the court, as in *line blocks* (the blockers attempt to stop all shots down the line) or *cross-court blocks*.

Rallies. During a volleyball *rally,* each team is allowed a maximum of three successive contacts of the ball in order to return the ball to the opponents' side. The ball is out of play when it touches the ground, goes out of bounds, or contacts the net or the antenna on either side of the net. Many rule infractions can occur during a rally which also terminate play. The ball may not be held too long, and it may not be played by two players at the same time. Also, the ball cannot make a double contact with any player's body or be unnaturally lifted or thrown in any way. During play, no one is allowed to make contact with the net or cross over the center line. Furthermore, servers are not allowed to step over the service line when serving. Finally, no back row player is allowed to hit the ball in front of the attack line (sometimes called the 10-foot line). If any of these rules are violated, play is stopped and a side out is rewarded to the opposing team.

1
DIGGING

Kathy Gregory

Everyone familiar with volleyball knows that the best offense depends on a sound, consistent defense. After the initial attack — the spike or the service — defense is the first element involved in scoring points in volleyball. Your team's desire to be fearless and tenacious on defense often makes the difference between winning and losing. Power volleyball can become a very one-sided affair unless each member of your team has this commitment to defense.

The underhand pass, or *dig,* is the most basic defensive movement in volleyball. Before we get into the essentials of digging — the various kinds of digs including the roll, dive, and sprawl, as well as the common defensive situations — we should look at the mental and physical attributes of the athletes we teach these skills to. By way of introduction to these chapters on individual skills, we can show how one basic physical drill — the foot patter drill — unites both mental and physical training to make our players more injury-free and more effective on the court.

MENTAL QUALITIES

Certain mental qualities are essential to a good defensive player. As coaches, we all recognize that teaching the physical skills presented in these chapters is an obvious part of our mission. But we also need to pay attention to the amount of *motivation* (in the form of desire and courage) we pass on to our players. A player with only average skill but intense motivation can play good defense. Another mental quality required for good defense is *willingness* — especially the willingness to overcome both the natural fear of falling and the natural tendency of ducking hard-hit balls. I look first for athletes with these mental qualities and then for the gifted volleyball player.

Good defensive players have to learn three lessons which call for *instinctive* behavior:
    1.   Always hustle after every ball; never give up on any ball.

2. Anticipate plays and move quickly; never hesitate. To execute a dig, you have less than half a second, which is *half* the time it takes to decide what to do. Thus, your responses must be pure reaction.

3. Go to the floor for a ball as naturally as you play any other phase of the game.

Practicing these and other fundamentals develops quickness, accuracy, smoothness, and consistency.

Because time for decision making on defense is so limited, the players' responses need to be as nearly automatic as possible. Thus, athletes who excel at defense rely on following their coach's instructions to the letter. When the coach says a certain situation calls for a particular response, that situation should evoke that response automatically. There is too little time to *decide* what to do about an attacked ball.

The goal of techniques such as *game simulated training* — making the practice drills resemble actual game situations as much as possible — is to train instinctive reactions. For example, athletes who automatically go for all balls in their area of responsibility (rather than thinking about it and going for some balls while letting others drop) not only play better defense, but also reduce their chances of injury. And the unthinking, instinctive dig and follow-through are automatically done with correct technique. Nearby teammates do not have to guess the instinctive defender's movements and coverage. Such spontaneity is found only in defensive players who have the right mental qualities: motivation to be intense on defense and willingness to retrain their instinctive reactions.

PHYSICAL QUALITIES

Using game simulated training to convince your defense to react automatically provides a good bridge between mental and physical qualities. Your players must be convinced that the physical skills you teach them are important for both greater defensive effectiveness and greater safety. The goal is for your defensive players to react automatically, physically as well as mentally. The key to good defense is reaction, not anticipation.

The Foot-Patter Drill

The *foot patter drill* is just one example of how your athletes can learn to respond to the opponent's action (based on instinct) rather than their own anticipation (based on thinking). Have you ever watched a good tennis player prepare to receive serve? The player does a little hop, or a side-to-side step followed by a hop, just as the opponent serves the ball. This movement, the foot patter or pre-hop, is designed to break the player's physical and mental inertia. The player crouches a little (with head and arms lifted, elbows relaxed) and lifts one foot, then the other — all without leaving a stationary position. The foot patter serves the same purpose in volleyball as in basketball and football warmups: it gets the athletes off their heels and ready to move to the ball.

2

Getting the athletes off their heels and ready to move is important because many players make the mistake of reaching with their arms on defense, rather than getting their bodies into position behind the ball. Usually this mistake happens because the athlete's body and mind have not been geared toward *reaction*. A player who lunges with the arms and body, rather than moving first with the feet, has less control of his or her center of gravity, and hence less control of how and where the ball is struck. With the pre-hop, the player gets in position by moving the feet first and thus has center-of-gravity control, body control, and ball control.

This game-simulation drill teaches the foot patter: have your players take their defensive positions and practice the foot patter. Then, to simulate the hitter's angles, stand on a chair or table on the other side of the net and follow these steps:
1. In rapid succession, alternate hitting harder, then softer balls at your athletes to help them break the habit of anticipating the speed of the ball.
2. Hit the balls higher, then lower to get the players used to adjusting their stances and the height of their crouches.
3. Keep surprising your players; do not let them think about what they are doing or start guessing what you are going to do next in these drills.

To re-emphasize, reaction — not anticipation — is the key to this and other game simulation drills. Players need to *react* to the ball's height, its velocity, the hitter's arm angle, and even the sound of the hitter's hand against the ball.

Practicing defense develops mental toughness, concentration, and desire. It perfects footwork, improves speed and reflexes, and establishes coordination with adjacent players on the court. These physical and mental attributes contribute not only to strong defense, but also to the offense. The remainder of this chapter covers basic elements of defense: the basic ready position; low, medium, and high digs; the sprawl, roll, dive, and running dive; and some important defensive situations and defensive tips.

BASIC READY POSITION

Defensive players always start in the basic ready position. Figures 1.1 and 1.2 show front and side views of the basic ready position. Note the elements of this position:
- Knees: slightly ahead of toes, bent at 100–120 degrees.
- Waist: bent forward, so that shoulders are in front of knees.
- Arms: relaxed, ready to come together to dig the ball.
- Head: up, eyes following the ball.
- Center of gravity: keep it low!

Figure 1.3 shows the forearms and hands in position to contact the ball. Note that for digging, the contact point on the forearm is lower than the contact point for passing: just above the wrist on the inside, soft tissue area of the forearm.

3

Fig. 1.1   *Fig. 1.2*

Reminder: Your players should listen to the sound of the ball and watch the attacker's arm swing. They must see the ball and react. Do not let them plant their feet, even in this low position. Get them to use the patter or pre-hop instead. This low stance may be awkward initially, but make sure they crouch low and keep their heads up. Keep these points in mind:

- Body position must be kept low.
- Foot patter or pre-hop is the key to maintaining mobility.
- Wrist/hand/arm action must be strong and accurate.

DIGS: LOW, MEDIUM, AND HIGH

Players defend — or dig — the ball at three heights: low, medium, and high. I recommend specific defensive techniques for each height. Let's take a quick look at these heights, then a longer look at the low position, the position used most often.

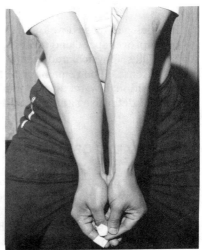

Fig. 1.3

Low Digs

Players execute 70 percent of the defense from the low position. Seven of every ten balls will be received below the defender's knees and within one meter of the athlete's ready position.

Medium Digs

Balls received between the knees and the shoulders are in the medium range. These digs occur most often in the player-up defense (explained in Chapter 12) in the mid-court area. Traditionally, players take the ball in front of their body, jumping so as to meet the ball on their forearms. I suggest a different technique: train your athletes to move to the side of the ball and take it as shown in Figure 1.4.

High Digs

A few times during a match, your setters (and other players as well) will get caught off balance behind the blockers. In these situations, they have to take the ball high above their shoulder — the high position — and use a "rebound" action. The thumbs should be "webbed" so they are out of the way. Figures 1.5 and 1.6 show the

Fig. 1.4

front and back views of the high dig. In this high position, the elbows and wrists compress backward and downward upon impact to give better control, especially for harder hit balls. Although setters are the primary users of this once outlawed technique, it is now common to see any player caught out of position using this technique. A ball hit with two hands above the waist — other than a set ball — used to be "quick whistled" by officials. They felt it was impossible to contact a harder hit ball simultaneously with two separated hands; thus an illegal "double contact." With recent rule changes, though, this maneuver is not as much a concern.

Fig. 1.5

Fig. 1.6

5

LOW POSITION VARIATIONS: SPRAWL, ROLL, DIVE, AND RUNNING DIVE

Because over 70 percent of all attacked balls will be defended below the defender's knees, techniques for low position variations should be practiced much more than techniques for the other reception heights. First, let us take another look at the basic low position dig (Figure 1.7).

There are several techniques all power players must have in their defensive repertoires to use either after the dig or as part of it: the sprawl, roll, dive, and running dive.

Fig. 1.7

The Sprawl

The sprawl is fast becoming the most widely used technique for digging low balls beyond the defensive player's one-step range. Proper execution of the dive (explained later in this chapter) takes much greater arm and shoulder strength than the sprawl. For a player who may not have quite so much upper body strength, the sprawl is far more comfortable both for digging and as a recovery move. Players should use two arms for harder hit balls and one for dinks. The ball can be in front or to the side of the player. Changing directions in the sprawl is easy, making it especially effective.

Sprawl Progression. Figures 1.8, 1.9, and 1.10 show the sprawl progression. Use the sprawl when the ball is too low for a rolling recovery. Keep these points in mind:
- Do not let the feet leave the ground (as in diving).
- Try to use two hands on the ball.
- Shift your shoulders around the ball.
- Keep the shoulders relaxed to absorb the ball's impact.

Arm and Hand Action. In the sprawl (and the roll, explained later), the hands have a unique function that may be new to many coaches. The defender can contact the ball very low to the floor with the soft tissue on the top of the fist (Figure 1.11). With the *wrist flick,* the wrist snaps upward, and the sprawl (or roll) is executed (Figure 1.12).

Scoop. The scoop, in which the player uses the back of the hand as a scoop under the ball, is still very popular, especially in combination with the dive. The wrist flick simply offers another option. Women, especially, may find it more comfortable.

Barrel Roll. From the sprawl, the athlete may simply push up to his or her feet in a crouch position to get ready for the next movement, or barrel roll, to his or her feet (Figure 1.13).

Fig. 1.8 Low position, move toward the ball.

Fig. 1.9 Dig the ball, catch yourself with extended free hand.

Fig. 1.10 Slide forward until the entire body absorbs the momentum.

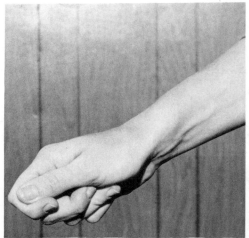

Fig. 1.11

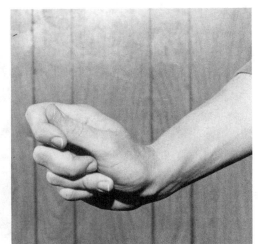

Fig. 1.12

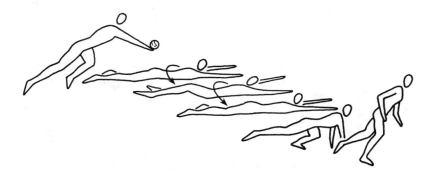

Fig. 1.13

Remember, in the barrel roll the elbows and knees must be kept in such a position that the roll is done over the middle portion of the back. The barrel roll can be used as recovery after a dive as well. It allows the player to stay focused on the ball after executing the pickup move, whether a wrist flick or a scoop.

The Roll

Since the Japanese introduced the roll in 1964, it has quickly become a standard element in volleyball defense worldwide. For medium- to low-hit balls that are to the side of the athlete, the roll is the most widely accepted technique for digging and recovering. The roll is also used for certain tips, deflections off the block, and chasing down balls. Figures 1.14–1.17 show the roll in step-by-step progression.

Teaching your athletes to roll properly results in greater coverage of the defense area and less chance of injury once the defensive attempt has been executed. The properly executed roll allows the player to execute a defensive move and be ready immediately for the next demand. Whenever possible, athletes should use two arms with the roll for greater control and accuracy. Often, the roll only uses one arm. Remind your athletes to bend the elbow of the non-involved arm while rolling over the shoulder of that arm. These maneuvers will help prevent injury and aid in stability on recovery.

The Dive

Players use the dive to pick up tips and short hits in front of them. Mats and hip pads are highly recommended when this technique is first introduced. Take care to keep the chin high to avoid injury by contact with the floor. Figures 1.18–1.21 show the dive.

The Running Dive

The running dive allows the player to cover greater distance than the standard dive. The technique is popular with players who are capable of a move that takes great strength to execute. The athlete runs and leaps toward the ball, using the wrist flick to get under the ball with a clenched fist, and recovers on the abdomen. The athlete slides, absorbing the shock after contacting the ball. For the most advanced players, the running dive could be a good emergency tool.

COMMON DEFENSIVE SITUATIONS: DEFENSIVE TIPS

Volleyball strategies in many textbooks assume the defensive player is behind a perfect two-person block (Chapter 12). In reality, this degree of protection rarely occurs. This section outlines some of the common situations that face the defensive players (other than the blockers) and explains how each position responds. As these pointers illustrate, volleyball is a game of angles. The major point to note concerning adjustment to hitters is that defen-

Fig. 1.14 *Move to the ball, arms out, shoulders square behind the ball.*

Fig. 1.15 *Dig ball with two arms, shift weight forward until back leg is fully extended; use hands for balance. Let the side of the body cushion the fall, then extend.*

Fig. 1.16 *Kick top leg over the same shoulder and upper back for the roll; use arms to push up and help establish balance.*

Fig. 1.17 *Keep head to the side; don't roll up the back of the head.*

sive players must adjust to their own blockers' formation: Are there one, two, or three blockers? Where are the holes in the block? A hole is created when blockers are late to their assignment at the net, leaving the left or right side blocker in a solo blocking position.

Trouble Sets

Trouble sets are situations in which the defense needs to recognize that because the ball has been set a certain way, a particular defensive reaction is immediately required. The following paragraphs describe some of the most common trouble sets and explain how the defense must react.

Down Balls. A down ball is one that is set off the net, and thus usually hits with less velocity than a normal attack. The defensive player knows that the back court defense will usually be the first to handle the attack.

Trapped Sets. In a trapped set, the ball has been set very close to the net, so that the hitter has little room to hit the ball with much control and effectiveness. These sets usually result in dinks.

Sharp Cross-Court Sets. A ball set outside the antenna will usually result in a cross-court shot because of the angle needed to hit clear of the antenna.

Contact Height. The higher the attacker can contact the ball in the air, the greater the options for direction and velocity on the ball. The lower the ball is to the net, the fewer the options. Consider the advantage taller tennis players have when serving: their angle of contact point relative to the net is higher than that of shorter players, increasing the options available with the serve.

Ball Direction. Teach your players to watch the attacker's approach angle and the position of the ball relative to the attacker's shoulder (Figures 1.22 and 1.23). The approach angle largely determines the ball's final destination. A 30 degree angle approach dictates a certain destination, a 90 degree angle a different one. From the attacker's point of view, the 45 degree approach is most effective because it gives the most options for the ball's final destination. Similarly, the ball-to-shoulder proximity helps determine the attacker's options of where the ball will go:

- Ball inside the shoulder: If the ball is contacted high, the attacker has the most options.
- Ball in line with the shoulder: The attacker still has some good options — though not as many — including good cross-court and line shots.
- Ball outside the shoulder: There are fewer options for the attacker, because the attacker will not cross the body with his or her shot.

Fig. 1.18 Low position.

Fig. 1.19 Move to the ball, arms out.

Fig. 1.20 Dig the ball; use legs to dive under the ball. Dive outward, not upward; arch back, chin up.

Fig. 1.21 Cushion fall with hands, chest, and abdomen. Extend through to let the body stop the momentum.

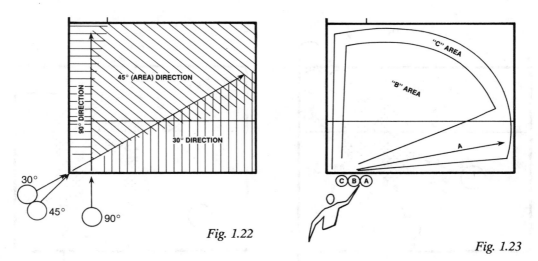

Fig. 1.22

Fig. 1.23

Hitter's Tendencies. Many coaches chart the hitting tendencies of the opponents prior to competition. Consequently, defensive players should know their opponents' favorite and most effective shots.

Defensive Position Responsibilities

The traditional defensive alignment was predicated on a total contact allotment of three per side, including the block. Now there are three contacts allowed after the block, and the coverage possibilities and responsibilities have changed accordingly. Figures 1.24 and 1.25 show the differences that have resulted. This section discusses these changing defensive responsibilities, position by position.

With the old style, deep dinks and surprise shots over the heads of the defenders were unmanageable. The new style allows one player to back up another in whatever formation necessary to cover the hit.

Each player must know the specific responsibilities of each position for each attack possibility. Figures 1.26–1.30 show those responsibilities. Note first the numbering system for players on the court shown in Figure 1.26. Because positions 1 and 5 mirror each other, as do positions 2 and 4, these diagrams are combined.

In general, train your players to roll left and right. When playing a left side position, the player should have the left foot forward; vice versa on the right side. This foot position helps to square the shoulders to the ball, in effect creating a platform from which to keep the ball in the court. If your players start in the correct positions and roll left or right as needed, they will only be penalized during a game if they are not capable and confident of going to the floor for a ball.

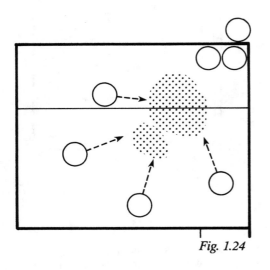

Fig. 1.24

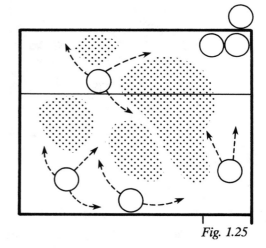

Fig. 1.25

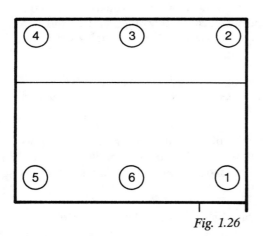

Fig. 1.26

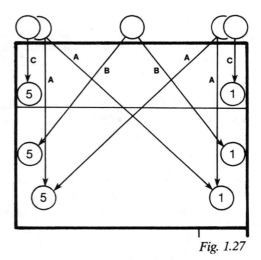

Fig. 1.27

Fig. 1.28 The solid line represents the path of the ball; the broken line indicates player's movement to defense position assignment.

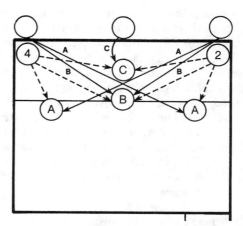

Fig. 1.29

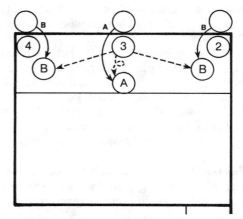

Fig. 1.30

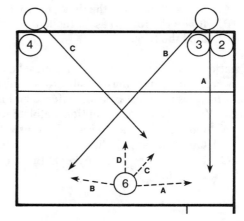

Positions 1 and 5. The responsibilities for positions 1 and 5 are identical, but on opposite sides of the back court. Position 5 is the left back; position 1 is the right back. A special note about position 5 is warranted here. The majority of first attack hits come to this player, and handling the initial attack is critical to success. Thus, you need to have a very good defensive player at this position. This player must be able to roll, dive, and sprawl—without stopping to think about these movements. Remember, the left side player has the left foot forward in the ready position, and vice versa for the right side player (Figure 1.27: A, B, C).

    A. Hard line spike or cross-court spike: The player should stand 1.5 m (5 ft.) from the endline, and .3 m (1 ft.) from the sideline.

    B. Middle attack: The player should stand 4.6 m (15 ft.) from the endline, and .3 m (1 ft.) from the sideline.

    C. After getting to the ball: The player will usually need to roll and to remember to stay low.

Positions 2 and 4. The responsibilities for positions 2 and 4 are identical, but on opposite ends of the net. Position 4 is the left front; position 2 is the right front. The players are primarily blockers, but when the ball is set to the end of the net opposite them, they pull off the net to help either behind the block or with sharp-angle hits in the front court (Figure 1.28: A, B, C).

    A. The player starts at the net, but when the ball is set to the far end of the net away from this player, the role changes from blocker to defense player. The player backs off the net to spot A and waits to help with hits coming to that area, if necessary.

    B. If player 2 or player 4 did not have time to get in position to block, they must move toward the attack line area in the middle to help with tips.

    C. If there is a dink in the middle, the middle player must be able to roll or sprawl to recover after playing a ball in position C.

Position 3. Even the middle blocker has defense responsibilities to think about as an attacker is approaching to hit the ball. The middle blocker in position 3 must be one of the quickest and, if possible, most experienced players on the team. This player must be able to "read" the approaching offense and adjust quickly. He or she must move to help block with the left and right blockers as well as cover the quick attack in the middle (Figure 1.29: A, B).

    A. Block, then cover the dink behind, if necessary.

    B. If late to move to assist the left or right blockers, this player covers the dink behind the block.

Position 6. The player in position 6 must be ready to move laterally (left and right) as well as forward. This player must be able to roll, dive, and sprawl with equal ease. This position usually handles the most balls on defense and is considered to be the most critical position to staff. You will need an exceptional athlete to play this position well (Figure 1.30: A–D).

    A. On the line spike, position 6 helps with the deep line.

    B. On a cross-court shot, position 6 helps with position 5's responsibility deep.

    C. If there is only one blocker at the net, position 6 cuts off the angle by moving up on the ball.

D. If there are no blockers at the net, position 6 moves up into the court for sharper angle hits.

CONCLUSION

Without defense, your team cannot score points in volleyball! Thus, volleyball begins with sound defense.

Every defensive player on the court has a responsibility for every situation. Situations arise so quickly and vary so greatly that there is too little time for complex decision making—players must simply react. If they have practiced and practiced, relearning the necessary responses to balls hit at them, they will know what to do.

Defensive techniques are complicated and possibly the most difficult aspect of volleyball to master. The ball must be defended within half a second of being hit, and the defender must be quick and confident in order to meet the ball before it strikes the ground. Your athletes must understand that offense and defense are indistinguishable: a rally combines and interchanges them so that one is as important to the final outcome as the other.

Your players will point out to you that practicing defense is not as much fun as practicing hitting. But defensive drills build more than good defensive techniques—they build the fight that excellent athletes need in order to win long rallies as well. Practicing defense develops mental toughness, concentration, tenacity, and desire. The physical benefits are countless: footwork is perfected, speed and reflexes are improved, and coordination among adjacent players on the court is increased. And all of these attributes carry over to the offense.

The women's game in particular uses a variety of shots combining skill and finesse, producing longer rallies than in the men's game. Longer rallies put a special emphasis on the ability to prolong a point with outstanding defense. But both men's and women's teams must train long and hard to be able to achieve the final result of entertaining, safe, and competitive volleyball.

2
SETTING

Terry Condon and Sandy Lynn

The setter is one of the most valuable assets any team can have. Your setter is your quarterback — how your team performs usually depends on how well your setter performs. A good setter can convert a potentially precarious situation into a stable one; a weak setter cannot. Because setting must be decisive and accurate, the setter must be capable of reacting to situations that require speed, agility, coordination, intelligence, and technique. Thus, for coaches, the development of the setter should be a priority consideration.

There are many great setters with different styles and techniques. The techniques discussed in this chapter originate from a simple philosophy: a setter must be trained with solid fundamentals. As the setter gains experience, an individual style will inevitably develop.

As a coach, you must be willing to spend that extra time necessary to develop your setter. The minimum time per day specifically devoted to your setter (or setters) should be thirty minutes. If you can arrange an hour, the setter's progress will increase rapidly, and so will your team's success. Neglecting your setter is neglecting your team. Results take time and repetition, and you as a coach must initiate this directed workout.

If training a setter is one of your weakest areas, take extra time to study this chapter. But possibly the most important education can be gained simply by watching. Find a great setter and watch every move that setter makes on the court. Successful setters have spent numerous hours watching, imitating, and practicing.

IDENTIFICATION OF A SETTER

Your ability to place players in positions that enhance their talents is the first step toward your team's success. Even if your team is perfectly trained, how well you use your personnel on the court will determine the end result. Before you can begin to apply all of your knowledge to training a setter, you must have the right person. You may be choosing your setter from hundreds of players or from fifteen. The following is a basic checklist for your initial search.

Physical Qualities

- Height — The setter needs to be 178 to 183 cm tall (5 ft. 10 ins. to 6 ft.) and possibly left-handed. Although there are many great small setters, height added to the qualities listed below is certainly an advantage.
- Speed — The setter must have the ability to move the feet quickly, enabling him or her to get to the ball fast.
- Eyes — The setter must demonstrate quick eye movement and good peripheral vision.
- Ambidexterity — The setter must be able to hit the ball with either arm. This is a trainable skill if the player already has good upper body strength.

Mental Qualities

- Personality — If a player's off-court personality shows leadership, independence, and self-motivation, then that player will probably demonstrate the same qualities on the court. A setter must be the kind of person who keeps his or her head when others are losing theirs.
- Intelligence — Your setter should be able to make quick, smart decisions, always working with the hitters.
- Responsibility — Because of a setter's leadership role, the setter must be strong enough to accept more responsibility than any other player, even the responsibility of a loss.

TEACHING TECHNIQUE

Thorough instruction in correct methods is the most important factor in developing the setter's basic skills and in furthering the setter's progress. Consequently, setters need special attention during the initial stage of instruction, when mistakes can be corrected most easily. There are many different styles and techniques to setting. To better explain and suggest a style you can use in training your setter, we next outline a traditional method for teaching body position and footwork. In the *basic body position,* the setter's shoulders, hips, and toes face the target. The right foot should be slightly in front of the left, with the feet shoulder width apart. Ideally, the setter should move quickly, set the feet, and square the shoulders to the target. No matter where the ball is passed, the setter's first priority is to beat the ball to position, square off, and then set the ball. This one element of technique will take time and repetition to develop. The following sections explain other fundamentals in detail: movement, starting position, ball contact and hand position, releases, and integration of body and foot position.

Movement

It is immensely important to train setters in proper movement. The setter must be able to make all kinds of movements in all directions and at the same time get into proper position to set the ball. Patterns of movement encountered by a setter include the following:
- Moving left and right, forward and back (Figure 2.1).
- Turning left or right, 180 degrees (Figure 2.2).
- Running, stopping, and jumping (Figure 2.3).
- Moving and rolling to recover (Figure 2.4).

One of the most important movements of setters is the initial movement to the ball. They must first get to the proper position at the net, and then adjust to the pass. The setter should be standing at the net waiting for the pass, then seeing and making a movement to the ball.

Starting Position

The starting position should be the same for all the sets so as not to advertise where the ball is going to be set. For that same reason, the place of contact with the ball should be the same for every set. As the ball begins its descent, the player should assume a starting position with feet comfortably spread and body weight equally distributed. The knees are bent and ready to make minor adjustments as the ball approaches. The heels of the feet should not carry much weight. The wrists are cocked so that the angle between the forearms and hand is 135 degrees or less (Figure 2.5). The hands are cupped and relaxed. This relaxation is very essential to smooth setting.

Ball Contact and Hand Position

Ball contact is made above the face or forehead on the pads of the fingers. The ball is not batted, but it actually remains in contact with the hands for an instant. The fingers must form a cup between both hands. The thumbs are directed up and back, never forward and down. The greatest amount of contact is on the first three fingers, but some contact is made with all the fingers (Figure 2.6). Most importantly, the ball should sink well into the hands.

A technique used to find the correct hand position is to place the hands in a praying position at the forehead. The player opens the hands to form the correct position. Figure 2.7 shows the correct technique, while Figure 2.8 shows hand position too far from the forehead. The major force applied to the ball is not that of wrist snap, but more of a coordinated body action through the ball. The line of force extends from the feet (or trailing foot) through the center of gravity toward the ball. Neither the set nor the follow-through should be a quick, jerky motion; it should be one smooth, coordinated motion, with arms fully extended upon release (Figure 2.9). A flowing follow-through from ankles, legs, and arms is very important to a smooth flight of the set. If the movement of the body is abrupt, then the flight of the ball will be uncertain, not deliberate.

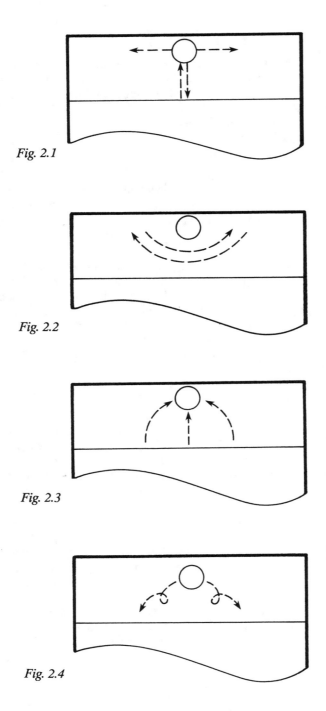

Fig. 2.1

Fig. 2.2

Fig. 2.3

Fig. 2.4

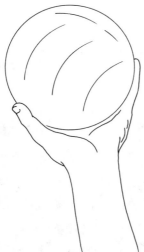

Fig. 2.5

Fig. 2.6

Fig. 2.7

Fig. 2.8

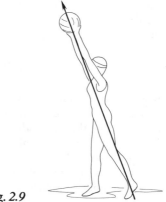

Fig. 2.9

Releases

The *full-extension release* is used for high (or long, distant) sets. The ball contact utilizes the same basic position — off the forehead — but the arms extend through the ball. This same technique will be used by all players when they set to a hitter. Figure 2.10 shows first contact; Figure 2.11 shows full extension.

Fig. 2.10   *Fig. 2.11*

The *quick release* is used in more advanced systems of play. Do not let the word "advanced" persuade you to eliminate this technique. This release is used for the shorter, quicker sets. The hands contact the ball at the forehead and return to the forehead with no extension, a technique that allows better ball control for the play sets. Figure 2.12 shows the first contact, and Figure 2.13 shows the quick release.

Integration of Body and Foot Position

Integration of movement and footwork is fundamental to developing a setter. This integration normally involves the following sequence:
1. Movement to the estimated area of interception based on the flight of the ball.
2. Body alignment to intersect the path of the oncoming ball with the intended path of the set.
3. Orientation with intended target; foot positioning.
4. Final adjustments and execution.

Fig. 2.12   Fig. 2.13

REVIEW

Basically, the important fundamentals to be observed when setting the ball include the following:

- The midline of the body should correspond to the path of the ball and the desired direction of the pass; the feet should be in a front-back stride position to allow for weight transfer (see Figure 2.9.).
- The longer the distance of the pass, the greater should be the force contributed by the legs.
- The hips should face in the direction of the pass, and the body should follow through in the direction of the set.
- The setter should remember that passes made over a short distance require relatively minimal use of the entire body.
- The setter should move forward into the oncoming ball and never in a direction away from it.

TYPES OF SETS

There are many types of sets that may be used effectively in volleyball today. Discussed in the following sections are some of the most common: the back-court set, the back set, the play set, the save set, the forearm set, and the jump set.

The Back-court Set

Any ball set from behind the 10-foot line is designated a back-court set. The full-extension release will be necessary because the ball will be set higher, and the distance of the set will be greater. The body position is the same as that explained previously. This set is one that all players should be able to perform with accuracy. Drill work and repetition are necessary to increase all players' consistency on the back-court set.

The Back Set

A back set occurs when you set the ball over your head to a spiker behind you. The beginning position for the back set is the same as in the front set. The hands are at the forehead with fingers spread. Immediately after the ball is contacted, the wrists rock back slightly. The amount of arm extension will depend on the distance and height of the set. The hips should be loose to push through the ball. The amount of hip thrust and arm extension will determine the height and distance of each set. As seen in Figures 2.14 and 2.15, it becomes important for the hand position to remain the same. If the hands reach above the head, the back set becomes less deceptive. Figure 2.14 shows the incorrect position; Figure 2.15 shows the correct one.

The *back-set body position* most common among setters is with the back squared off to the right front. The set is then sent directly overhead back to the right front position. The problem with this technique is that it alerts the blockers to where the ball will be set. Yet many coaches still prefer to use this technique because it makes it easier for a setter to develop consistency.

A body position that can increase the deception of the back set is the one previously discussed as the *basic body position*. The back set does not change this position unless the ball is being set from an extreme back court position. The setter should get to position quickly and set the feet with the hips, shoulders, and toes facing the left front. The only motions that change are the extension of the arms and the follow-through. After the ball comes in contact with the hands, the hands and arms extend to the right and back to push the ball to the right front. Figures 2.16 and 2.17 depict the two back sets: 2.16 the traditional back set, and 2.17 the deceptive backset. Note that the direction of a set should not affect the change of the body position unless the set is from a deep back court position.

The Play Set

It is important to use the quick release on all play sets to establish consistency. The setter must be able to set a consistent ball to each offensive position. Many techniques are employed to designate the type of set. The setter may call out a number to each hitter or may give a one-hand signal, which tells all hitters what set they will hit. Since this chapter does not deal with offensive systems, you only need to know that your setter must be able to set all sets consistently.

Fig. 2.14

Fig. 2.15

Fig. 2.16

Fig. 2.17

The Save Set

The save set is used when the setter is unable to get the correct body position to the ball. This incorrect position could result from an off-dig or a deep pass. In this instance, the set-ter must be flexible and acrobatic in order to get hands on the ball and set a nice, high set. The most effective method is the set with a half roll, which allows the set-ter to get underneath the ball with hands at the forehead and set with a full-extension release.

Figures 2.18 through 2.20 illustrate how to teach the set and half roll:
1. The knees should be in front of the ball, with the right foot forward.
2. The hands begin at the forehead.
3. After ball contact, the arms extend through the ball.
4. Momentum will push the body into a half roll.

The Forearm Set

When it is impossible for your setter to get hands on the ball, the setter must use the forearm set. The body

Fig. 2.18

must still be in the full-squat position. When the ball is contacted, the arms will follow through and the player will return to an upright position. Figures 2.21 and 2.22 show this set.

Fig. 2.19

Fig. 2.20

Fig. 2.21

Fig. 2.22

The Jump Set

The jump set should be added for any advanced offense. It increases the setter's options, thereby increasing the hitter's options. The position of the hands and body is important in the effectiveness of this set. The body position is the same as with a regular set, and the hand position remains the same as in all other sets. If the setter broad jumps through the ball, the hitter will have difficulty in his or her approach angles. It is very important to keep the hands at the forehead. The ball is contacted at the peak of the jump. The setter jumps, hangs in the air, and sets the ball. Figure 2.23 illustrates the jump set.

SECOND-BALL PLAY

Setters must be able to hit and tip the second ball, preferably with either hand. They must also be able to make split-second decisions on when — and when not — to tip or hit the second ball. In any hitting or tipping situation, it is the setter's responsibility to know what the blockers are doing. If the setter is blindly hitting away or tipping, the options will not be as effective. Figures 2.24, 2.25, and 2.26 show the left-handed tip, right-handed tip, and left-handed hit, respectively.

Fig. 2.23

Fig. 2.24

Fig. 2.25

Fig. 2.26

The Tip or Dump

The tip (or dump) may be used with a jump set or from a regular standing position. The setter's hand position is the same as for a regular set. Only one hand contacts the ball. Use a left-handed tip when you want the ball to be placed off the net. If you want to tip the ball close to the net, the best method is to use the right hand, with the palm rotated back toward the face. Tight passes make this tip very effective. To make the tip more deceptive to the blockers, train your setter to keep both hands in the setting position.

Times to Tip

There are five situations in which it is appropriate to tip:
- When opponents are switching position during a rally.
- After a long rally.
- When a weak spot in the defense has been determined.
- When the left back player is serving. (Many times teams do not cover this position, and the server is slow in switching into position.)
- Against a player-back defense (Chapter 12).

Hitting the Second Ball

If your setter is left-handed, then you are fortunate. If not, start training your setter to hit the second ball with either arm. If you run a 5–1 offense, such flexibility is a valuable tool when the setter is in the front row. The setter now has the option to jump set, jump tip, or jump hit. A well-trained setter can keep the blockers guessing by using all three of these options. The best time to get a good swing at the ball is on a medium-high pass close to the net. Again, the setter must first put the hands in setting position as if preparing to jump and set the ball. Immediately, the non-hitting arm drops and the hitting arm swings.

EYE CHECKS

After training your setters in the proper techniques, you must not forget to train their eyes. The more comfortable and experienced the setter becomes with basic setting, the more he or she will be willing to look away from the ball and at the total court. Many setters focus their eyes only on the ball, unaware of what their opponents are doing. This one skill — being able to look away from the ball to see the entire court — takes many hours of practice through eye-movement drills. The more efficient the eye movement becomes, the more successful your setter will be in the total team effort. It will be easier to get one-on-one situations for your hitters, or to tip and hit at the most opportune time, if the setter has total-court awareness.

Eye checks may be incorporated into most of your setting drills after your setter becomes familiar with basic setting skills. The following eye check progression is taken after the pass and before the set:

Step 1: Eye check to the left front. This check will also help in preparing the body to square off toward the left front.

Step 2: Eye check to the opposing right front blocker.

Step 3: Eye check to the opposing middle blocker—this one is critical.

Step 4: Eye check to the right front hitter.

Step 5: Eye check to the opponent's back court defense.

Training in each of these eye checks will prepare the setter for any given situation. Peripheral vision also becomes important because there are many times when the setter needs to see the blocker—the middle blocker especially—immediately before setting the ball. For example: Your setter is jumping to tip or hit, and a blocker jumps also. With good peripheral vision, your setter can turn and set the ball. Consequently, you need to broaden your setter's court vision through eye training.

SETTER RESPONSIBILITIES

Here is a summary list of the setter's responsibilities:
1. Set the best possible ball in all situations.
2. Set the most desired set according to each hitter. (Know your hitters.)
3. Take responsibility for hitting errors.
4. Make all passes look good.
5. Know your opponents! Be able to make the best possible choices.
6. Know the high-percentage and low-percentage sets.
7. Be able to recognize a "hot" hitter.
8. Keep a cool head and be a good leader.
9. Be aware of weak blockers and gaps in the defense.
10. Be in control of the game's rhythm.
11. Take responsibility to make things happen on the court!

TRAINING THE SETTER

Great setters are few and far between, usually because of inadequate coaching. A setter is like a quarterback on a football team or a director of an athletic department—no one could be successful in these positions without proper training and experience. Put in the time to provide the direction necessary to mold your setter into the director of your team. A setter's technical development requires time, patience, organization, and effort. Following is a guideline for this development.

Mobility and Technique

Work with your setter on:
- speed, agility, coordination
- types of footwork
- posture
- basic overhand pass: technique

Sets from the Back Court

Your setter needs practice on:
- set after moving forward
- set after moving to the side
- set after moving backward
- set from a jump

Sets from the Near Net

Your setter needs to practice these basic sets:

1. **The Basic High Set**
   - set after moving forward
   - set after moving to the side
   - set after moving backward
   - set from neutral position
   - set with forearms
   - set with jump

2. **The Back Set**
   - set after moving to net
   - set after moving away from net
   - set after moving forward or backward
   - set from a jump

3. **The Jump Set**
   - set after moving in different directions

4. **The Quick Set**
   - set after moving in different directions
   - set from different positions after moving
   - set from a jump after moving

5. **The Side Set**
   - set while facing the net

- set from a jump while facing the net
- set after moving different directions while facing the net
- set from a jump while facing the net after moving in different directions

6. The Shoot Set
- set after moving
- set from a jump after moving

7. The Play Set
- set after moving
- set from different positions and postures

8. The One-Hand Set
- set from a jump after moving

DRILLS

Hand Position Drills

Here are some drills for teaching your setter(s) the proper hand position:
1. Kneeling on the floor: Place hands on the floor in the correct hand position for an overhand pass: thumbs 3 cm (1 1/8 in.) apart, forefingers 5 cm (2 ins.) apart, with the thumbs pointing away from the body very slightly. Stress that the outsides of the thumbs contact the floor. Keep one hand on the floor and with the other lift the thumbs off the floor, working for flexibility.
2. With the ball on the floor: Place the hands on the ball in proper position — remove, replace, remove.
3. Standing, bend over at the hips: Drop the ball, and catch it in front of the face after the bounce.
4. Standing, bend over at the hips: Continuous bouncing, contact the ball as it is descending; then repeat, only contact the ball as it is ascending.
5. Partners stand 2 to 3 m apart (6 ft. 6 ins. to 9 ft. 10 ins.): Bounce the ball back and forth, and catch it with the correct hand position.
6. Rest the ball on the fingers in front of the face, and vary the body position: Bend down, turn, jump, run forward and backward, shift sideways, skip, kneel, sit, and lie down. Stress holding the ball 7 cm (2 3/4 ins.) in front of the eyes and nose.
7. Toss the ball to self 2 to 3 m straight up (6 ft. 6 ins. to 9 ft. 10 ins.), and catch it in front of the face, stressing proper hand position on the ball.
8. Same as number 7, only increase the difficulty by making the player move before catching the ball: Toss the ball forward, to the sides, and backward. Stress that the player must get under the ball. When the ball is low, the player must catch the ball by placing one foot in front of the other, bending the knees and dropping the hips below the knee of the lead foot.

9. Same as number 8, only make the player catch the ball in a low position by varying the toss: Toss from under one leg, from back between both legs, and two hands from behind the back.
10. Increase the difficulty of the ball/body orientation by having the player catch the ball in varying positions: Toss, then catch while kneeling, then while sitting. This forces the player to predict the path of the ball.
11. Toss the ball, let it bounce, and catch it in proper position. Stress getting under the ball.
12. Same as number 11, only force the player to get to the ball late, and therefore low, by adding movement after the toss: Touch the floor with the fingertips, kneel, sit down, lie down, forward roll, backward roll, turn 360 degrees.
13. Toss the ball at the wall: Shift behind and under the ball and catch it in proper position; add movement.
14. Partners: A tosses, B catches in proper ball-body relationship with correct hand position.
15. Same as number 14, only progress from no movement to movement: A tosses the ball so B has to shift forward, backward, left, and right. As the player becomes proficient, vary the direction of the tosses from predictable to unpredictable.

Basic Back Set Drills

Here are basic back set drills to use when training your setter(s):
1. Toss and catch the ball behind your head, look at the ball.
2. Toss and back set high in the air, follow through the ball in the direction opposite the set.
3. Toss and let the ball bounce, then back set. Turn, let the ball drop to the floor again, and then back set again.
4. Pairs, one person passing to another: back set to the wall, catch, and repeat.

Elementary Drills

The following drills can be used for either front or back setting. Jump setting can also be used for these elementary drills.
1. Partners, sitting on the floor 2 m (6 ft. 6 ins.) apart: Throw and catch the ball back and forth as quickly as possible.
2. Individual: Volley to self in different body positions—squatting, kneeling, sitting, and standing.
3. Individual: Volley 3 to 5 m in the air (9 ft. 10 ins. to 16 ft. 5 ins.), let the ball bounce, move underneath the volley, and set up again. Stress extending the legs so that the body is moving up into the ball.
4. Individual: Toss to self and volley at the wall. Stress movement into the ball and follow-through.
5. Individual: Volley at the wall, let the ball bounce, and volley at the wall. Stress moving behind the ball before contact and moving forward into the ball prior to,

during, and after contact. This is a very difficult drill to perform correctly as it requires quick, continuous movement.

6. Partners: A tosses to B, B volleys to A, A catches the ball in proper position.
7. Partners: Continuous volleying, 1 m apart.
8. Partners: 3 to 5 m apart (9 ft. 10 ins. to 16 ft. 5 ins.), continuous volleying. A volleys to self, A volleys to B; B volleys to self, B volleys to A. Stress moving forward in direction of the pass while passing to partners.
9. Triangle: A passes to B, B passes to C, C passes to A; continuous volleying, both directions (Figure 2.27).
10. Triangle: Same as number 9, only return the volley in the direction it came from, and then pass to the next player (Figure 2.28).
11. Triangle, four players: Same as number 9, only after making the pass, continue forward to replace the player who received the pass (Figure 2.29).
12. Square formation, five players: A volleys to B, then follows the pass to replace B after B volleys to D; D volleys to C, then C volleys to E (Figure 2.30).
13. Square formation, large group: Follow the pass as shown in Figure 2.31.
14. Square formation, group of seven: Follow the pass as shown in Figure 2.32.
15. Square formation, maximum of eight players, two in each corner. Follow your pass; increase the difficulty by adding another ball (Figure 2.33).

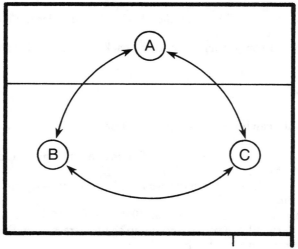

Fig. 2.27

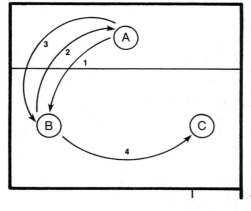

Fig. 2.28

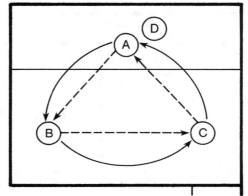

Fig. 2.29

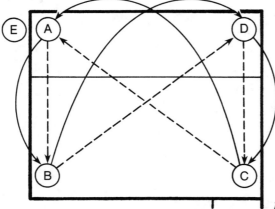

Fig. 2.30

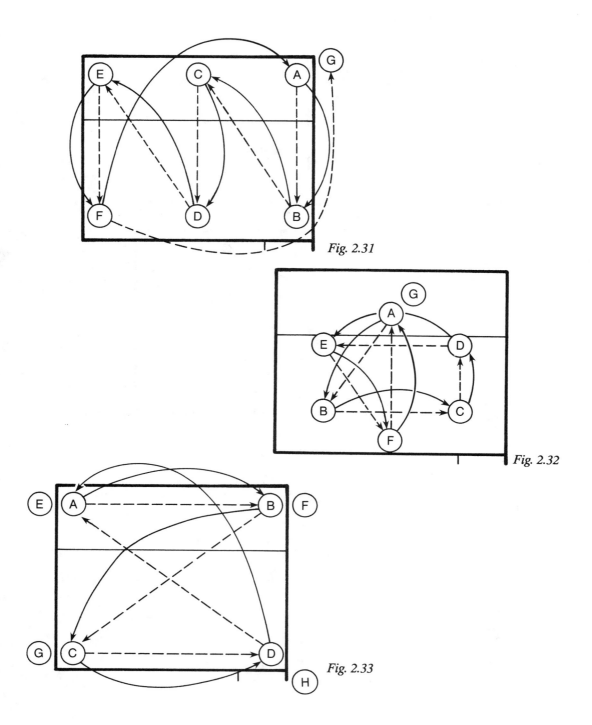

Fig. 2.31

Fig. 2.32

Fig. 2.33

Intermediate Drills

Here are sixteen intermediate drills for your setter(s):

1. Individual: Volley the ball straight up, volley it forward 3 to 4 m (9 ft. 10 ins. to 13 ft. 1 in.) and run forward under the ball; volley straight up and then volley it forward.
2. Individual: Same as number 1, only pass the ball backward, then straight up; sideways, and then straight up.
3. Individual, 2 m (6 ft. 6 ins.) from wall: Continuous volleying at wall while shifting back and forth along the wall; also move closer to and further away from the wall.
4. Individual, 2 m (6 ft. 6 ins.) from wall: Volley the ball straight up, run and touch the wall, and volley the ball straight up.
5. Partners: Each player volleys to self, then volleys to partner. Add movement which must be done during the time when the ball has been passed to partner: jump, turn 360 degrees, jump and turn, sit down, lie down on stomach, lie down on back, forward shoulder roll, backward shoulder roll, run up and touch partner's knee, run around partner, be parallel and near wall (2 m or 6 ft. 6 ins.) and run to touch it.
6. Partners: A and B stand 3 to 5 m apart (9 ft. 10 ins. to 16 ft. 5 ins.). A passes the ball straight up, B runs forward and passes the ball 3 to 5 m in front; meanwhile A moves back and under the ball to pass straight up (Figure 2.34).
7. Partners: A and B stand 2 to 4 m apart (6 ft. 6 ins. to 13 ft. 1 in.), facing each other: A passes the ball 2 to 3 m (6 ft. 6 ins. to 9 ft. 10 ins.) to B's right, B shifts under the ball and passes it 2 to 3 m to A's left. Stress to your players that they should be stopped and facing the direction of the pass before making the volley (Figure 2.35).
8. Partners: Set moving forward and backward; one player advances and the other retreats to a spot, alternately (Figure 2.36).
9. Partners, consecutive sets with a roll: Partners take turns rolling and tossing.
10. A sets over the net and runs under the net, then retreats and sets again; consecutively performed by both partners (Figure 2.37).
11. Your setter is between two partners: The setter alternately moves from the attack line to the net and turns 90 degrees to set to partners (Figure 2.38).
12. Your setter is between two partners: The setter runs under the net and back sets over the net (Figure 2.39).
13. Group of three, give and go: After passing, the players must run outside the sideline before making the next pass (Figure 2.40).
14. Partner, short then long: Partner at the net passes the ball short then long; B must move short then long (Figure 2.41).
15. Shuttle drill, group of three: After the set, run under the net to the end of line; work for a consecutive number without a mistake (Figure 2.42).
16. Group of four: A passes to C, C passes to B, B passes to D, D passes to B, B passes to C, C passes to A. After passing, A and D run to the baseline and return to make the next pass, B and C only run after passing to each other; then increase the difficulty (Figure 2.43).

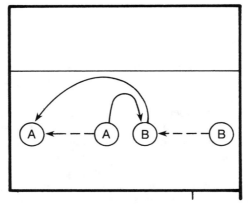

Fig. 2.34

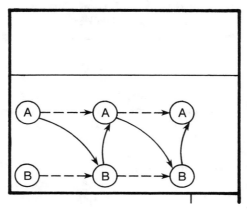

Fig. 2.35

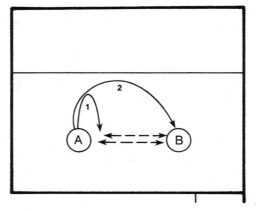

Fig. 2.36

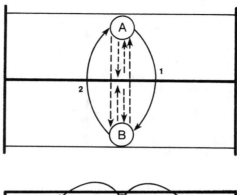

Fig. 2.37

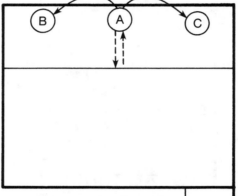

Fig. 2.38

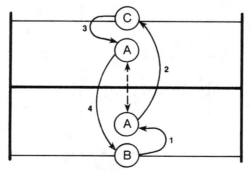

Fig. 2.39

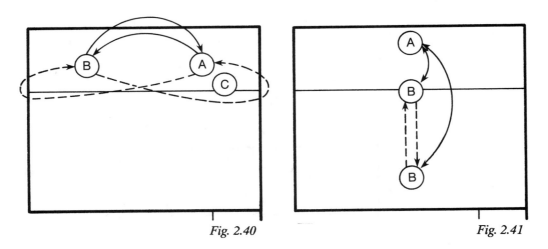

Fig. 2.40

Fig. 2.41

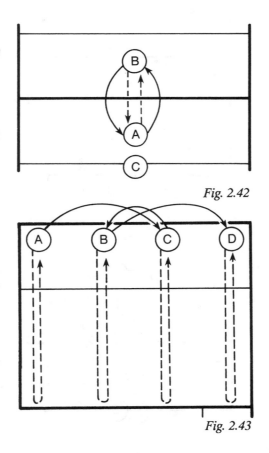

Fig. 2.42

Fig. 2.43

Advanced Training

Players who have progressed to this point of training have mastered the individual techniques of overhand passing. These exercises are designed to orient your players to setting the ball along the net and to give your players experience in situations that demand ball control and mental discipline. Your setters should be able to execute the different sets and implement the following fundamental tactics:

1. Make pre-attack observations and be aware of the positions of attackers and opposing blockers.
2. Know who the strongest spikers are.
3. Know the types of sets each spiker prefers.
4. Know the types of sets each spiker prefers least and has the greatest difficulty with.
5. Direct the majority of the sets to the strongest spiker.
6. Be able to set deceptively; do not telegraph where the sets will be directed beforehand.
7. Recognize emergency situations and make the most appropriate set for that situation. For example, if a spiker digs the ball with a roll, your setter must see that and set one of the other hitters.
8. Be able to determine where the block is being set and direct the set to an area or position where a successful spike is more probable. For example, if the blocker is up for the one set in the middle, the setter must see that and set a different hitter.

Once players become familiar with the pattern of movement involved, the drill should become more goal oriented. Some minimum standards of performance could be:

- Play the ball a certain number of times in succession.
- Play the ball from within the attack zone; players cannot touch the net or go over the center line.
- Keep the ball in play for a specific period of time.
- Require a proportion of the sets to be jump sets. For example, play the ball thirty times nonstop, of which fifteen sets must be jump sets.

Setter Movement Drills. These drills are advanced and must be preceded by basic fundamentals. All tosses may vary in height and in placement on the court. The set direction can be predetermined by the coach. All sets—jump sets, tips, hits, set/half roll—can be implemented as any part of the drill. A heavier ball or a basketball may be used. The coach should move around and toss from every position on the court.

Note: Any time a chair appears in the following diagrams, it indicates a serve-reception drill. The coach slaps the ball, signaling for the setter to break to setting position. The toss is directed away from the setting position, which will require the setter to move, face the left front, and set. A shagger is helpful in all drills and makes for a more efficient practice (Figures 2.44–2.66).

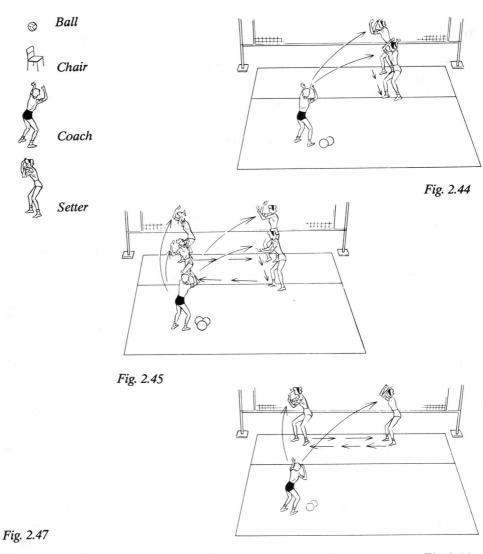

Ball

Chair

Coach

Setter

Fig. 2.44

Fig. 2.45

Fig. 2.47

Fig. 2.46

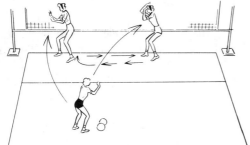

Fig. 2.48

Fig. 2.49

Fig. 2.50

Fig. 2.51

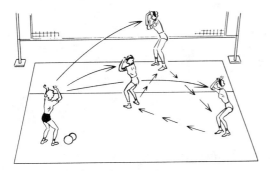

Fig. 2.52

Fig. 2.53

Fig. 2.54

Fig. 2.55

Fig. 2.56

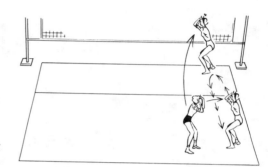

Fig. 2.57

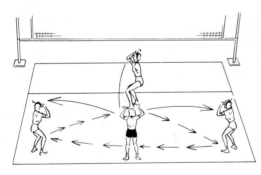

Fig. 2.58

Fig. 2.59

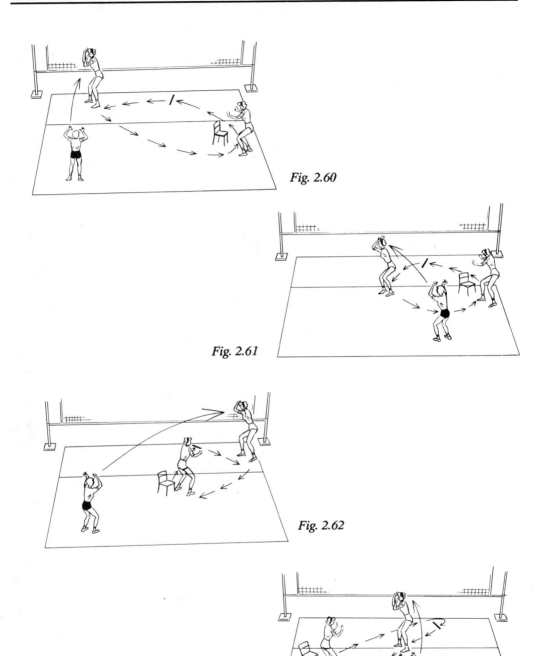

Fig. 2.60

Fig. 2.61

Fig. 2.62

Fig. 2.63

Fig. 2.64

Fig. 2.65

Fig. 2.66

Setting Attackers. These drills are designed to improve your setter's accuracy and consistency in a game-like situation. It is also important for your setter to develop timing and rhythm with your team's attackers to enhance their effectiveness.

1. You toss the ball to the net. The setter runs in from the 10-foot line and you yell out a type of set to be set. The setter must wait for the call. For example, you toss the ball and the setter runs in, you yell "back," and your setter sets a back set. Then increase the difficulty. For example, the player must jump set every time (Figure 2.67).
2. You toss the ball at the net. The setter runs in from the 10-foot line. If the blocker jumps, the setter sets outside. If the blocker does not jump, the setter sets middle (Figure 2.68).
3. Sets with outside hitters: You toss a ball to the net, and the setter runs in and sets the ball. Work on consistent sets: set forward and behind, short and deep, all varieties of sets. Penetrate from the middle and left positions (Figures 2.69 and 2.70).
4. Set with the middle hitters, and vary the location of the toss along the net: The setter puts the ball the same distance in front of self; when the setter must go to the left of center court, the middle hitter comes behind for a back set (Figures 2.71–2.73).
5. Set with middle hitters: Similar series as number 5, except the pass from you is more than 2 m (6 ft. 6 ins.) back from the net.
6. Set with two or three hitters: You toss to the setter, who must now choose among three hitters (Figure 2.74).
7. You lob over an easy serve that one of the three passers receives. The setter sets; setters and hitters change positions each time (Figure 2.75).
8. Simulate a free ball: You bounce a ball on the floor, the players drop off the net, and the setter penetrates. You underhand toss the ball over the net; set, hit, etc. (Figure 2.76).
9. Same as number 7, except you add blockers. Your setter should attempt to prevent a two-player block from forming (Figure 2.77).

When you are at the right stage of training for an advanced setter, you can change these drills by adding little items to make them more difficult. For example, the setter must jump set every ball, must look across the net before setting the ball, and must know if your hitters are early or late. Most importantly, the setter must first get to the net, then react to the pass and/or situation, and set the ball. Also, the position for each set, no matter what, must be the same each time so that no one will be able to determine where the ball is being set.

SUMMARY

The development of your setter must proceed according to sound teaching principles, starting with the basics and progressing systematically to the advanced techniques. Selection of a particular player to be trained as a setter should include the need for above-average athletic ability and intelligence. As the training process begins, the primary objective must be to develop superior execution of the overhand pass. The training sessions must emphasize correct hand position, body posture, and technical performance. The setter in training must practice setting from two locations on the court: along the net and from the back court. Once the set is performed with relative consistency (75 percent accuracy), the training program can progress.

The need for repetition must be emphasized. An athlete training to become a setter must make many correct contacts with the ball, whether passing it alone to a wall, or to targets, or with a partner. There is no substitute for practice, and both the coach and the athlete must realize the importance of volume — the sheer number of repetitions. They must keep performing the skill over and over.

BIBLIOGRAPHY

Canadian Volleyball Association. *Level I – Coaches Manual.* Dollco Printing, 1978.

----------------. *Level II – Coaches Manual.* Dollco Printing, 1979.

----------------. *Level III – Coaches Manual.* Dollco Printing, 1979.

Ejen, Miloslaz, Jaroslav Buchtel, and Karen Johnson. *Contemporary Volleyball.* Newport Beach: Volleyball Plus, 1983.

Gozansky, Sue. *Championship Volleyball: Techniques and Drills.* West Nyack: Parker Publishing Co., 1983.

FIVB Coach Training Course. *Textbook for Volleyball Coaches.* 1971.

Keller, Val. *Point, Game and Match.* Hollywood, California: Creative Sports Books, 1968.

Peppler, Mary Jo. *The Fifteen Minute Setter.* Intervol Interprises, 1986.

Scates, Allen. *Power Volleyball.* Allyn and Bacon, Inc., 1969.

Selinger, Dr. Arie, and Joan Ackermann-Blount. *Arie Selinger's Power Volleyball.* New York: St. Martin's Press, 1986.

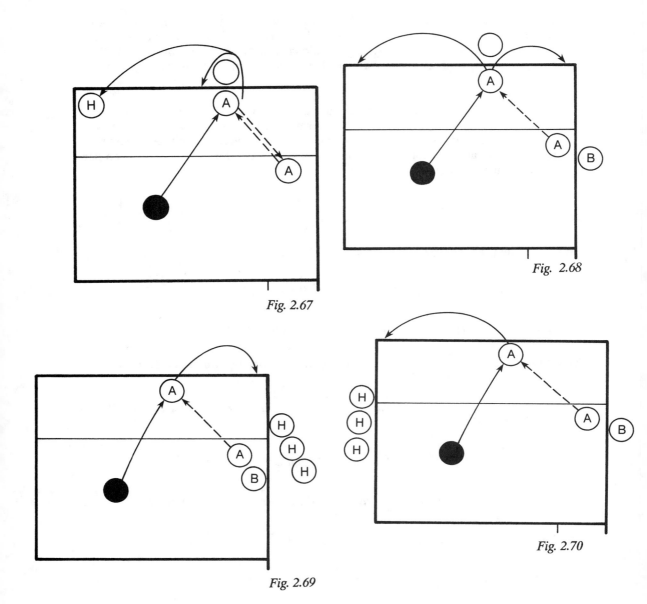

Fig. 2.67

Fig. 2.68

Fig. 2.69

Fig. 2.70

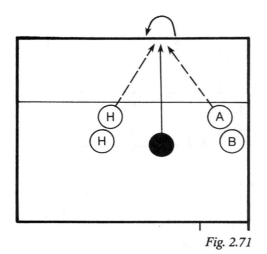

Fig. 2.71

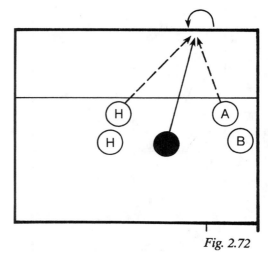

Fig. 2.72

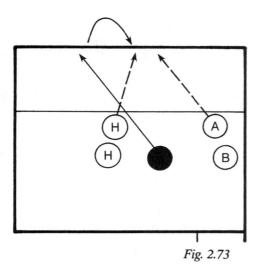

Fig. 2.73

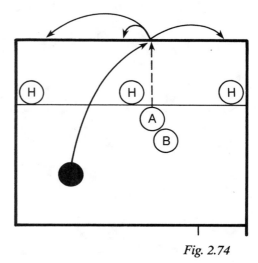

Fig. 2.74

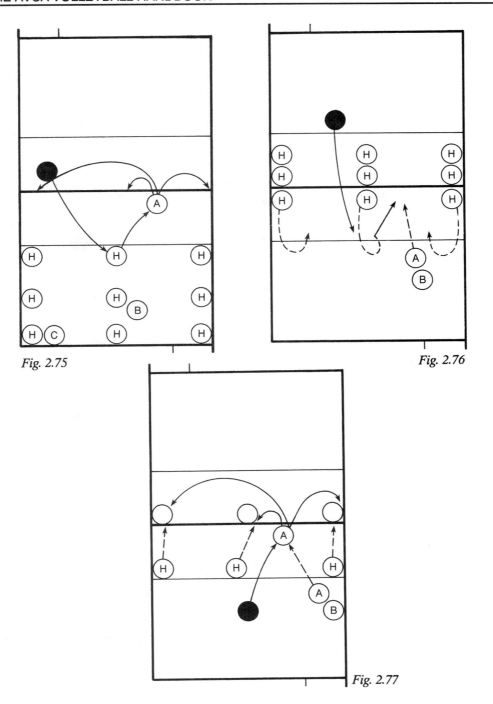

Fig. 2.75

Fig. 2.76

Fig. 2.77

3

SPIKING

Mick Haley

A *spike* in volleyball is the act of hitting a set ball from above the level of the net into the opponent's court. It consists of an approach, jump, arm swing, follow-through, and landing. Spiking is probably the most difficult individual skill to master in volleyball because it requires a great deal of body control and coordination while the spiker's body is airborne.

All the spikers on your team should be able to hit the ball high and hard. They should also be able to hit with top spin at half to three-quarter speed, or to open-hand tip—all at various positions on the court. This chapter presents the important basics of spiking: the approach, the jump, the spike, and the landing. Also included are teaching techniques and general learning concepts.

THE APPROACH

The spiker begins an approach approximately 3 to 3.6 m (10 to 12 ft.) from the net. The exact approach distance will depend on each athlete's stride length. The angle of approach varies depending on what the spiker wants to accomplish with the attack. Generally, the correct angle to the net will be between 45 and 60 degrees for a right-hander on the left side, and between 60 and 90 degrees for a right-hander on the right side. For left-handers, the angles are reversed, as shown in Figure 3.1.

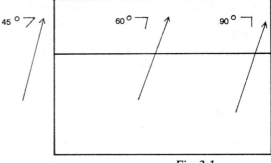

Fig. 3.1

The speed of the approach should be from slow to fast, building momentum. The spiker should take at least three steps, and probably no more than four. The approach begins with either the left or the right foot, depending on the number of steps in the approach and whether the player is right- or left-handed. Many right-handers start with the weight on the left foot for a four-step approach. Thus, the first step is taken forward with the right foot, followed by the left foot (sometimes called a directional step, since it is in the direction of the ball), then a right-left closing action (sometimes called a hop or step and close).

All of the foot movements must stay within 5 to 13 cm (2 to 5 ins.) of the floor, as opposed to a hopping action where the feet go up in the air 30 cm or more (12 or more ins.), and then come down to the floor. Such a hopping action will disrupt the spiker's ability to accelerate during the approach.

Each foot should stay on the floor for as short a length of time as possible. Thus, the spiker's transfer of weight during the approach strides needs to be as efficient as possible. The center of gravity must move *forward*, not up and down, and must be low to the floor (so at the jump it only has to come up, not down and then up).

The length between steps depends on the kind of jump the spiker desires and the spiker's leg strength. The distance between each of the last steps is critical. In the traditional kind of approach jump, each step of the approach progresses in length and speed until the hop or step-close phase. The first step of the approach for right-handers in a four-step approach is taken with the right foot. The second step, the directional step, is taken with the left foot and should be twice as long and fast as the first step. The third step is taken with the right foot, twice as long and fast as the second step. To this point, the steps increase in distance and speed, increasing the spiker's momentum toward the ball. At this point, the traditional approach requires a great deal of strength, possibly limiting its effectiveness for some players. The last step of the traditional approach is taken with the left foot. It is a very short, quick step that plants the foot in a blocking action to stop forward momentum and convert it into a vertical jump. The combination of the plant of the right foot on the third step and the block by the fourth step is termed the step-close or hop step.

For the highest possible vertical jump, regardless of strength, the second of the four steps that most people take should be the longest. In this step the left foot goes forward and plants. Then the third, or next to the last, step is taken with the right foot and is either as long as or shorter than the second step. For maximum vertical jump, the third step should be shorter than the second, but not so short that the momentum toward the net slows down. This slightly shorter length allows the last foot (the left) to get down and plant almost simultaneously with the right, and the feet are on the floor the least amount of time. Using this foot position allows the body to rise upward for maximum height with very little forward drift.

To travel a greater distance — to get the ball in a broad jumping kind of approach — the third step could be as long as the second. The last step is the step that makes the difference. It is not so short and quick as in the more vertical approach. The result is more forward momentum and a slight loss of vertical height. The transfer is toward a point out away from where the feet are planted (a broad jump) as opposed to a point above where the feet are planted (a vertical jump). This broad jumping technique sacrifices a little height but allows your spiker to jump *to* the ball, thus creating various judgment and timing problems for the blockers. The ultimate broad jumping approach and the most radical change in the approach to spiking is the one-legged takeoff, like a layup in basketball. Common thirty years ago, this takeoff's reccurrence has been made exclusively to increase broad jumping approach advantages. In contrast, a spiker who maximizes vertical jumping ability presents the blockers less difficulty in setting the block, but actually makes it harder for the blockers to contact the ball.

The vertical jump style approach is what I would recommend teaching first. In the two vertical approach styles, the speed of the last step is critical. For maximum vertical height, the spiker's last two steps need to be such that the time both feet are on the floor is as short as possible. The last foot and the next-to-last foot go down simultaneously. The distance between the second and third steps may also be a key factor because it controls the distance the left foot has to travel. The longer that distance, the longer the right foot stays on the ground and the greater the loss of momentum and dissipation of forces.

The next-to-last foot planted should be the right foot, and it should point toward the net at about a 45 degree angle. The last (left) foot planted should be somewhere between parallel and 45 degrees (Figure 3.2). One school of thought holds that rotating the toe at slightly more than a 45 degree angle will create a blocking action that transfers the weight quicker and forces the body to leave the floor quicker. This rotation will also stop some natural drifting common among younger players, and it will open up the spiker's hips (make them more nearly perpendicular to the net) to increase power upon contact with the ball.

Fig. 3.2

THE JUMP

During the approach, your spiker's arms should move the same way as if he or she were running or walking. At the third step both arms should be behind the body, no more than 45 degrees back, and the upper torso should remain as nearly perpendicular to the floor as possible. If the arms are back more than 45 degrees, the upper torso bends too far forward at the waist, decreasing the efficiency of the jumping action. The spiker's arms should then be whipped forward so that they arrive at or above the top of the head before the feet leave the floor. This whipping movement starts with the arms being thrust straight below the waist, then up in front of the body with the elbows bent and next to the body so as to get them above the head quicker. This arm thrust is essential for assisting the jump, and the key to the arm thrust is in the movement from the 45 degree back position to the front side of the body slightly above the waist. From there on it is a fight to get the arms above the head as quickly as possible, and the arm action from that point on does not increase the spiker's jumping ability.

The spiker's hips and shoulders must be open (toward the setter) while leaving the floor. Although some people can jump strongly enough to be able to leave the floor with their shoulders and hips parallel to the net and still remain open and hit the ball, such jumping is not recommended either for younger players or for advanced players trying to maximize their efficiency.

As the body leaves the floor, the spiker's hitting arm is drawn into one of the two most widely used positions: one for maximum height and strength, the other for a little less height and more quickness.

Maximum Height

To achieve maximum height, as the arms ascend above the head, the hitting hand is drawn back with the elbow high toward the ceiling. The arm is drawn back, arching the back only slightly. This is a strength position and usually can be accomplished only if the arm swing up to that point has been efficient. As the forward arm swing begins, the player is simultaneously reaching for maximum height. Thus, the arm swing must begin as the body is moving upward. Contact with the ball thus occurs at maximum height or just prior to it (Figure 3.3). If the arms do not get to head height before the spiker leaves the ground, arm swing problems usually result.

Fig. 3.3

Maximum Quickness

The other arm swing is more like shooting a bow and arrow. The arms are not brought up as high — just somewhere near the top of the head — and the hitting hand is turned out to rotate the elbow high. The arm is drawn back as if drawing a bow, allowing for a much quicker, snapping action in the spike (Figure 3.4). The disadvantage is that the bow position many times does not allow a maximum reach upward to contact the ball, something that is especially a consideration for younger players.

Both arm swings serve a specific purpose. The high power position is a little bit more efficient and allows for maximum reach. The bow technique, for the most part, creates a faster arm swing.

Fig. 3.4

THE SPIKE

Contact with the ball should be made in front of the spiker, preferably closer to the center of the top of the head, but at least somewhere in a position between the shoulder and the top of the head — not outside the line of the body. The hand should contact the ball slightly above center (Figure 3.3). Contact at this point gives a top spin. Contact above center and on the right side gives a right top spin; contact above center on the left gives a left top spin. If the ball lacks top spin, it usually means the spiker is not getting the wrists behind the elbow on the arm swing. (This happens more with basketball players who are new to volleyball because of the elbow lead they use for the jump shot.) The wrist should snap upon contact. For less velocity and more control, attackers should open their hands more and spread their fingers slightly. For more velocity, they should bring their fingers closer together and slightly cup the hand. After contact, the hitting arm bends at the elbow and follows through, coming down toward the midline of the spiker's body. For a coach, the most important thing to watch is the elbow rotation or elbow snap — before, during, and after the spike. Train yourself to look at each part of the spiker's movement, and be especially sure that the elbow action is efficient.

For right-handers, the arm speed can be improved by lifting the left knee just prior to contact. This movement increases the speed of the arm action and allows the spiker to hit the ball with a slightly quicker arm speed. The opposite action works for left-handers.

61

THE LANDING

The spiker should land on both feet simultaneously whenever possible. The knees should be slightly flexed, the feet should be shoulder width apart, and the weight should be evenly distributed.

TEACHING TECHNIQUES

Make sure your teaching techniques are consistent with sound learning concepts. Try using only three or four key words to teach each skill, and never change them. For example:
1. First key word: "ready" or "ready position."
2. Second key word: "feet" or "feet to the ball."
3. Third key word: "explode."
4. Fourth key word: "swing" or "snap high."

Define the words at the beginning, and do not add new ones. Do not become a sportscaster with your language, and do not create situations that could disrupt your players' concentration.

Remember this learning sequence:
1. *Picturing.* Your players need a positive picture of what they are supposed to do, and they need to see it numerous times.
2. *Trying.* Your players need to try the skill, then see it again, then try it again, over and over.
3. *Evaluating.* Your players need to be evaluated on whether they are doing the skill properly. The evaluation should be short and quick.

The sequence outlined above is important in teaching any physical skill. Consistent with this sequence, following are some guidelines for teaching young players and beginners:
1. Provide a picture of the skill, with emphasis on just one point at a time. Do not confuse the mental process by giving too much information at once. And remember that for young players and especially for beginners, the attention span for earning new skills is usually no longer than twenty minutes.
2. Have the players repeatedly practice the skill.
3. Provide constant re-evaluation. Keep the evaluation brief. Be positive and make sure the players understand exactly what you want them to do.
4. Make sure that any tossing of the ball is done accurately and consistently. Tossing is a skill that must be practiced. During these drills it is important for players to learn to track and strike a *moving* ball. Stationary situations are not game-like and do not enhance your players' abilities.

Providing plenty of positive examples is probably the most important key. Make sure the examples are mechanically efficient and technically correct, because new players may copy all the wrong things. The most efficient process for teaching physical skills in this situation probably involves using key words, miming the skill, and providing plenty of visual imagery.

Finally, you need to organize your teaching so as to develop confidence and stimulate motivation in your players. For example, you need to make sure that all training sessions end on a successful note, even if (especially with beginners) this means adjusting the situation by lowering the net and using foam balls or balloons.

SUMMARY

Spiking is probably the most difficult individual volleyball skill to master. In teaching the components of the spike, it is important to incorporate sound teaching principles, and to begin, the vertical jump style is a recommended technique. In order to learn the spike, players must work on their timing, footwork, and arm and body positioning, and they should pay particular attention to their elbow rotation. Coaches should teach the spike by helping players choose key words, mentally go through the learning sequence, and practice. In addition, coaches must provide constant evaluation.

4
BLOCKING

Doug Beal and Tony Crabb

Blocking is one of the necessary elements of winning volleyball. Blocking has two functions:

- To *stop* the ball from coming across the net (to *block, roof,* or *stuff* the ball). This abrupt end to the action will result in a point or side-out for the blocking team.
- To *deflect* the ball up into the block team's court so that the three contacts can be used to mount an offensive strike.

As a preliminary overview, here is the sequence for your players to use when blocking:

1. Identify the attackers and their probable options.
2. Watch where the pass is going and assess the setter options.
3. Follow the person you are blocking and call out to teammates what that person is doing.
4. Get into position to block according to your assigned responsibility.
5. Jump while facing the net and scanning the attacker from shoulder to hand.
6. "Seal" the net with your arms on the way up, and then extend as they penetrate over the net.
7. Just before the attacker hits the ball, press your midsection back. This action is sometimes called *piking on the block* because of the resulting body position, or *turning the ball into the court*. Do not lock your elbows until after the attacker has committed to a direction of attack.

This chapter presents the basic elements of blocking in terms of the eight blocking skills, key transition ingredients, and blocking principles. Each coach must carefully determine what role the block has on his or her team. Furthermore, the coach must determine how important blocking is at that team's level of competition. At the level of the USA Men's or Women's Teams, for example, blocking is critical.

BLOCKING SKILLS

Effective blocking depends on your players' mastering these eight skills:
- Recognition of when to block.
- Proper footwork.
- Correct body position.
- Correct hand and arm position.
- Reading visual keys.
- Good timing.
- Smooth coordination among multiple blockers.
- Careful study of the opposing spikers.

Recognition of When to Block

Players should block only when they can successfully perform one of the two blocking functions listed at the beginning of this chapter. Here are some keys for making that judgment:
- How well does the opponent handle the first ball? The worse the control of the first ball, the less the chance the setter has for accurately setting the second ball, and thus the less need there will be for a block.
- Where is the attacker relative to the set? If the attacker is in poor position (for example, by being under the ball, too late to the ball, or if the ball is coming from behind the attacker), then the blocker should give the unfortunate attacker the opportunity to make a spiking error rather than jumping up and presenting the attacker a potential tool (a target off of which to hit the ball).

Footwork

There are two types of footwork: the slide step and the cross step. The slide step should be used when the lateral distance to be covered is 1.8 m (6 ft.) or less, or when the ball is set high and there is plenty of time to get into position. The cross step is mainly used by the middle blocker to get to the outside in a hurry on a low set. A lateral move of more than 1.8 m (6 ft.) usually requires a cross step.

In the cross step, the weight is on the foot opposite to the intended direction. You step out with the foot on the side of the intended direction, cross step with the opposite foot in front of the body, plant that foot so that your toes point toward the opponents' court, and swing the other foot around so your shoulders are squared to the net—then jump. If a high set comes to the outside, your block should be performed with care so that this footwork aligns you next to the outside blocker. For optimal body position, it is important that your toes be pointed toward the spiker, and that the outside foot (the one on the side in the direction of the set) is well planted to be the base of the main force of the jump. An outside blocker should actually jump to the inside of the court.

Body Position

Eighty percent of all spikes are hit in the direction of the spiker's approach. Therefore, the blocker must first identify the spiker's angle of approach and the point where the spiker will intercept the ball, and second, get to the right spot on the continuation of the spiker's approach angle to block the shot. The blocker must have good balance and must be no more than 36 cm (14 ins.) from the net. The blocker must be able to jump with control, avoiding dismantling the net, and always penetrating for the ball.

Hand and Arm Position

When the blocker is in the correct body position, the hands are above and in front of the shoulders. The jump rockets the blocker straight up, and the hands penetrate the top of the net immediately. The jump must be straight up, not floating to the outside. The arms should not be fully extended until the spiker makes a final move. When the spiker's final move occurs, the blocker, stretching all the way up from the abdomen, extends arms, hands, and fingers (thumbs pointing toward each other).

For outside blockers, the hands must not reach beyond the outside shoulder. Instead, the hands must be moving in. The blocking motion is pressing to the center of the back line, with the outside hand reaching over and out, across the net, perpendicular to the outside shoulder. Therefore, the blocker's outside arm and shoulder extend over the net slightly farther than the other half of the body. Prior to contact, the blocker extends forward from the shoulders, with the deltoids touching the ears. The blocker seals the net with the triceps and pushes tension from the abdominals through the fingers upon contact with the ball.

Middle blockers use basically the same technique, with some minor adjustments for blocking the quick attack. The middle blocker positions with his or her head aligned with the extension of the quick attacker's arm. On the quick attack, the middle blocker jumps when the set occurs, not waiting for the hitter to hit the ball. The jump must be high enough for the middle blocker to place his or her hands on the ball. If possible, the middle blocker spreads the arms and then closes them after determining where the quick attack is going. Otherwise, the middle blocker should stay spread and cut off the angles. There is no chance for any pike action; the tension in this maneuver is primarily from the shoulders. The quick shot must be pressed back into the middle of the court. These same tips also apply to forming the block with the outside blocker outside on the high ball or slow play set.

Visual Keys

In order for the physical moves of blocking to be correct, continual practice in mastering the evaluation of information must be stressed. Here is the sequence of information to be given to the blocker:
1. Be aware of the score and game tempo. Since these factors will often indicate who the setter will set, awareness of them is critical.

2. Review the tendencies of the spiker you must face.
3. Evaluate the quality of the service reception. How good or bad it is will affect where, what, and how well the setter can set the ball.
4. Note what kind of set is on its way.
5. Watch the spiker's legs, determining the attack angle and what position the spiker is in to hit the ball.
6. Once the blocker has moved to cut off the attack angle, watch the spiker's hand and wrist. Then make the final hand adjustments to stuff the ball.

Timing

Other blocking skills become mere exercise if the timing is off. Here are two timing basics:
- If the ball is set within .5 m (1 ft. 8 ins.) of the net, then the blocker begins to jump as the spiker's hand is crossing in front of his or her face on the back swing.
- If the set is high and more than a meter off the net, the blocker jumps as the spiker's hand is coming forward to contact the ball.

Blocking Responsibilities

The keys to successful blocking are always the same: *talk — work hard — analyze — penetrate.* The specific responsibilities for blocking change depending on whether one is a right, left, or middle blocker, or blocking the multiple attack.

Left Blocker. The left blocker plays the opponents' number 2 position attacker (right front). The left blocker calls the offensive crossover or switch (against the crossing play or X) and helps on the quick attack if number 2 runs the X play. The left blocker also takes the hitter if number 2 flares out for a back set and sets the block for the middle person.

Right Blocker. The right blocker plays the opponents' number 4 attacker (left front), takes the number 2 opponent on the X play, takes the number 4 attacker coming in for an inside set, and sets the block for the middle person on the left side.

Middle Blocker. The middle blocker must block the quick hitter and always let the outside blockers know what to expect. The middle blocker must identify the attackers and get in on all blocks.

There are some slightly different responsibilities for blocking the *multiple attack:*
- Each blocker should block person-to-person, being responsible for the person directly across the net.
- The right blocker comes over to take the number 2 hitter who is crossing when the left blocker calls the X. The right blocker always plays person-to-person and helps on the quick attack when possible.
- The middle blocker takes the quick hitter, then helps on the X.

- The left blocker helps on the X if that blocker's person is Xing. The left blocker calls the X if the left blocker's person is going, then "NO" if that person flares back. The left blocker must eliminate certain variables (especially against an offensive system in which the number 2 attacker calls where he or she is going to the setter) by intentionally overplaying and then coming back after that attacker.
- If the left and middle blockers are on the X, they take away number 5. If the middle and right blockers take away number 1 they also need to cover tips.

Study of the Opposing Spikers

Here are the key variables for your players to study when considering the opponents:
- How far off the net is the set?
- In what zone is the ball set?
- What is the height of the set?
- What is the position of the spiker's body and arm in relation to the ball?
- What hand does the spiker hit with?
- What type of swing does the spiker use?
- What are the habits of the spiker?
- What is the design and intention of the play?
- What is the spiker's attack angle?

TRANSITION POSITIONS

There are important things you must teach about blocking that do not come under the heading of skills. These things mostly concern transition positions when there is a free ball or a down ball.

Free Ball

The front row drops straight back to the 10-foot line, and the outside hitters stay in the court. The center hitter stays in the middle of the court, while the back row defenders split the court and face the place where the ball is coming from.

If the free ball is coming from deep in the opponent's court, then the defenders must play deeper. If it is coming from inside the 10-foot line, the blockers must move up and encourage the remaining team members to work over the blockers' heads. The setter must release as soon as a free ball is called.

All free balls should be played with an overhead pass. No one should leave the court until the free ball is passed. And everyone, absolutely everyone, should call "FREE BALL" — everyone!

Down Block

In the down block situation, the two blockers at the net see the hit and cover the half-speed shots and tips. They stay close to the net. The four primary defenders form a semicircle facing the attack, playing deeper on the line and shallower cross-court. The setter must think *dig* first, and release to set only after making sure the hit is not going to his or her area.

BLOCKING PRINCIPLES

Finally, here are five principles to remember for good blocking:

1. *Block offensively.* Under virtually every situation, the blocker's goal is to stuff every ball.
   - Force the hitter to hit a secondary shot.
   - Never give up a straight down kill.
   - Always penetrate the net.
   The goal should be to instill in your blockers a philosophy of intimidation.
2. *Do not block or jump* if you perceive that the hitter cannot score (hitter is out of position, ball is very deep, ball is outside antennae, hitter is standing). Knowing when to block is critical.
3. *Seal the antennae.* If the ball is set to the pin or beyond, the outside blocker insures that the ball cannot be hit between the pin and the block. This is an important rule.
4. If the ball is set tight, *surround the ball!* Never allow the hitter to hit straight down in front of the back row.
5. Know the *keys to blocking:* See the hitter making contact with the ball, see yourself block the ball. Follow the ball with your eyes, then head, then body. Here is the sequence:
   - See the pass.
   - Watch the setter set the ball.
   - Pick up the hitter's line of attack.
   - Follow the ball with your eyes to its apex.
   - Shift your primary focus to the hitter, centering on the shoulders.
   - Watch the attackers make contact.
   - Follow the ball's direction.
   - Verbalize the path of the ball.
   - Keep your eyes open and see the block; make contact with your hands.
   - On most normal sets (approximately 1.5 m or 4 ft. 11 ins. from the net), the timing is for the blocker to jump when the attacker's hitting arm clears his or her eyebrows on the ascent. This is a key point!
   - Position your block in front of the extension of the spiker's arm.
   - The outside blocker's primary responsibility is to establish the position described in number 9, then stuff the ball.

— The middle blocker's responsibility on outside sets is to attempt to close on the outside blocker; the middle blocker's primary responsibility is to block the cross-court angle.

SUMMARY

Blocking is used to stop the ball from coming across the net and to deflect the ball into the blocking team's court. Players should go through a seven-step sequence and should master eight skills in performing a successful block. Skills include knowing when to block; proper footwork; body, hand, and arm positioning; reading visual keys; timing; coordination; and studying opposing spikers. The keys to successful blocking are always the same: *talk— work hard—analyze—penetrate*. The responsibilities for the right, left, and middle blockers differ somewhat, and blockers should know the responsibilities for their positions. In addition, players should also know how to block the multiple attack, and they should know about transition positions for a free ball and for a down ball. It is also important that players be aware of and remember the principles and keys of blocking.

5
SERVING

Bob Gambardella

(Photo Credits: James Holman)

In the fifth game of the match, the score is 15–14 your favor. The majority of the fifth game has been side-out volleyball, and the opposition calls their last time-out. After the time-out, your server gets to the endline, the referee blows the whistle, and your player serves the ball into the net for a side-out.

This situation has happened to all coaches at one time or another. It can break the momentum of your team and give your opponents a boost to get fired up. Now let's turn the tables and think about how the entire team feels when a member serves an ace. It always puts a spark of enthusiasm in your team's play.

Coaches look at serving in one of two ways: serving for points, or serving to get the ball over the net and relying on the team's defense either to stop (block) the ball at the net or to play tough transition and score points. I believe we should train our players to serve for points.

SERVING TOUGH = GETTING POINTS

It takes time to learn how to serve for points. First, you must work on the mechanics of serving with all your players so that each player's serving efficiency is at the same level as the rest of the team's play. Along with that, tactics must be taught. Different serve reception formations warrant different serves and serving strategies. A good serving team will force its opponents to make critical errors throughout the entire match.

This chapter deals mostly with serving techniques and tactics. The first step toward becoming a good serving team is for the coach to develop a philosophy of serving that best suits that particular team. With younger players you might want to focus more on mechanics, whereas with older players or more experienced players you would focus on teaching different types of serves that are tactically advantageous to the serving team.

SERVING TECHNIQUES

As a rule, better volleyball teams usually use a wider variety of serves, hitting different parts of the court with different trajectories, spins, and speeds. This section presents the techniques for the overhand float serve, the round house floater serve, the top spin overhand serve, the underhand serve, and the jump serve.

The Overhand Float Serve

The overhand float serve is the most widely used serve in volleyball. "Float" means that the ball has no spin and no predetermined flight path; air currents and other factors can affect its flight. Approximately 90 percent of collegiate and international volleyball players use this serve. It requires a sufficient amount of upper body strength along with coordination of all body parts. This is a good serve because of its combination of placement and a floating action. Figures 5.1–5.5 show this skill in detail.

Lower Body. The server's feet are almost perpendicular to the net, shoulder width apart. There is a slight flex in the knees. The weight is mostly on the back foot. If younger players find this stance difficult, they can adapt it to suit their more limited abilities.

Upper Body. The waist is open (almost perpendicular) to the net. The hitting arm is up just about shoulder height, bent at the elbow, and slightly cocked away from the ball. The hand tossing the ball is 38 to 50 cm (approximately 15 to 20 ins.) away from the body, depending on the individual.

Serving Action. The toss is in front of the server, approximately 50 to 75 cm (approximately 20 to 30 ins.) above eye level. The hitting arm should be drawn back as the ball is making its ascent and should start to move forward as soon as the ball starts its descent. The exact nature of the toss depends on the quickness of each player's arm swing. The lower the toss, the quicker the arm swing. Contact is made in the middle of the ball with the lower third portion of the hand (the heel of the hand). During the contact phase, the upper body moves into a position parallel to the net. There is a minimal amount of follow-through with the hitting arm. The lower body starts the transfer of weight as soon as the ball is tossed, and the transfer ends immediately after the contact. The wrist remains stiff throughout the contact phase. Players should avoid putting a spin on the ball. Younger players especially will have a higher tendency to snap the wrist upon contact. Making quick contact with a stiff wrist will yield a higher percentage floater serve.

Fig. 5.1

Fig. 5.2

Fig. 5.3

Fig. 5.4

Fig. 5.5

Problems associated with this serve are usually caused by a lack of upper body strength, improper weight transfer, incorrect toss, or incorrect hand contact. Following are some specific serving problems and their causes:

- *If the ball is served into the net or out of bounds wide,* improper footwork is usually to blame. Check to see whether the server is actually picking up the rear foot; doing so tends to tilt the upper body in a downward position. When the serve is wide, it usually means contact with the ball was off center. Concentration in serving is the key.
- *If the ball has a slight spin,* the server is snapping the wrist upon contact. The wrist must remain rigid throughout the contact phase.
- *If the ball is out of bounds past the opponent's endline,* there is usually too much force on the ball. The server should think about placement on the court rather than trying to contact the ball as hard as possible.
- *If the ball drops before it reaches center court,* either the player is not strong enough or the ball was hit incorrectly. Beginners and young players often do not have enough upper body strength to get the ball over. Such players may need to resort to another serve until they are able to master the floater. For example, the round house serve may show better results because there are more upper body muscle masses involved.

The Round House Floater Serve

Most coaches are not comfortable teaching this serve, so they never introduce it to their teams. Instead, they feel that a player who cannot serve an overhand float should use an underhand serve. Using the underhand serve guarantees getting the ball over the net; however, its action or float is nonexistent. As a result, the opponent gets an easy ball to pass.

The Japanese developed the round house serve (or Asian floater) for their women to compensate for a lack of upper body strength. The serve uses more muscle groups than the overhand float serve to give players a ball that will float. The serve has a very unpredictable flight (float) path, as does the overhand floater, but moves much more quickly than any floater type serve. In addition to its float, this serve when correctly performed has a flat trajectory and at any given moment will quickly drop toward the floor. Figures 5.6–5.13 show the round house serve in detail.

Lower Body. The feet are about waist width apart, positioned almost perpendicular to the net. Legs are straight, but not locked at the knee. The weight is evenly distributed between the balls and toes of the feet.

Upper Body. The torso is slightly coiled. The hitting arm is extended out in front with the elbow locked when touching the ball. The tossing arm is about waist high, and grasps the ball mostly with the fingertips. (Note that tossing the ball with the fingertips, rather than the palm of the hand, gives a more precise toss.)

77

Fig. 5.6

Fig. 5.7

Fig. 5.8

Fig. 5.9

Fig. 5.10

Fig. 5.11

Fig. 5.12

Fig. 5.13

Serving Action. The toss has to be precise. It must be made directly above the server's head, approximately 75 cm to 1 m (approximately 30 to 40 ins.) above eye level. If the ball is contacted in front of the server, it will have a downward trajectory (winding up in the net). Contact behind the server will cause an upward trajectory (winding up out of bounds). Remaining straight and locked at the elbow, the hitting arm starts to draw back toward the buttocks. As the arm reaches its preparatory phase, it will then start to move up and over the server's head, where contact with the ball is made. Remember that the actions of the toss and striking arm have to be synchronized. If not, the serve is difficult to execute. The contact is made with the lower third part of the hand striking the middle of the ball while the upper body uncoils. There is a minimal amount of follow-through in order to insure the correct action (float) on the ball. The weight transfer happens during and after the contact phase.

These problems are associated with the round house serve:

- Because of lack of knowledge in the coaching profession, coaches do not feel confident in teaching this serve.
- There is often a lack of repetition. Not enough time is spent on training players to serve.
- An imprecise or improperly timed toss hurts this serve even more than most serves.

Top Spin Overhand

The top spin serve is another serve that is not used enough in competition. I would not recommend this serve for beginners. Instead, it is for the more experienced players who would like to add another dimension to their serving game. USA Team member Beverly Robinson, the present record holder of the NCAA Championship for most service aces in one match (eleven), presented a fine illustration of the execution of this serve.

This serve incorporates the same mechanics as the spike, except that the serve is done on the ground. It is a great serve to use as a changeup (as in baseball). If the opponent is not ready for the top spin, it usually yields a point or gives a more predictable play for the blockers to block.

The top spin serve has a trajectory that travels in a direct flight path, but at a faster velocity than the float serve. The server's timing and coordination are very important because the slightest deviation from proper execution can cause an errant serve. The top spin has a higher percentage of efficiency (aces) than the floater; however, it usually has a higher incidence of errors as well. Figures 5.14–5.20 illustrate the key components of the top spin serve.

Lower Body. The feet are almost parallel to the net, approximately waist width apart. There is a slight flex in the knees. The weight is distributed equally on both feet with a flat-footed stance.

Fig. 5.14

Fig. 5.15

Fig. 5.16

Fig. 5.17

Fig. 5.18

Fig. 5.19

Fig. 5.20

Upper Body. The waist is open (coiled), approximately 30 to 40 degrees in relation to the net. The hitting arm is extended and relaxes when touching the ball. The tossing arm holds the ball at the level of the waist with the fingertips and fingers approximately 20 to 25 cm (approximately 8 to 10 ins.) from the body.

Serving Action. The toss varies from 90 cm to 1.5 m (approximately 36 to 60 ins.) above eye level. The toss is thrown up in a direct line with the hitter's arm, off center (left or right) in relationship to the hitter's sagittal plane. When tossing for this serve, the server should put a forward spin on the ball. With a higher toss, this spin helps to keep the ball in a straight line in its pre-contact phase. The spin initiated by the toss also makes the contact phase easier to perform. Contact is made below the center of the ball: first, with the heel of the hand; and second, by snapping the wrist to initiate a whole-hand contact with the ball. The two-part contact phase starts the two actions of the ball. The heel contact dictates the *speed* of the ball, and the snap of the wrist and follow-through will dictate the *quickness* of the spin. The faster the spin, the quicker the ball moves towards the ground. The follow-through is the same as in spiking, with a good range of motion throughout the serve.

Underhand Serve and Jump Serve

Two other serves worth mentioning are the underhand serve and the jump serve. The underhand serve has been with the sport since its beginning. It is an easy serve to execute, and the level of success in getting the ball over the net is very good. However, using this serve in collegiate or other higher forms of organized volleyball is probably detrimental to the serving team. Because of the nature of the serving action, the serve causes the ball to travel in a parabolic flight path, which resembles a free ball situation for the opponent. Since it is easy to execute, the underhand serve is a good serve for very young players or beginners, because the emphasis at their levels is on keeping the ball in play.

Although the jump serve was the exciting addition to the 1984 Los Angeles Olympics, its use has been traced back to the 1960s. The jump serve is rather difficult to master because of all the variables involved in it. Strength, coordination, and proper movement are prerequisites to the mastery of the skill. The jump serve produces more points, but at the same time it can cause lots of errors. (Such errors were witnessed with Brazil in the USA-Brazil finals of the 1984 Olympics in Los Angeles.) This serve will become even more popular in the future because of FIVB's rule change prohibiting blocking serves. A team that is only an average passing team will make more errors when confronted with this type of serve. Presently, we see the jump serve filtering down into the collegiate men's game with much success.

The start position for the jump serve varies from 3 to 4.6 m (10 to 15 ft.) from the endline, depending on the server's stride. The jump serve has a pre-contact approach, as in spiking, which leads into a vertical jump. Once a start position is established, the toss and approach should be learned. The toss is initiated with two hands. The toss has to be high enough and moving sufficiently in the direction of the server's endline to allow enough time for the server to make an approach and takeoff. After the coordination and timing of the toss are mastered, the height of the toss is the biggest problem for proper execution of the jump serves (as it is for all serves). The mechanics of spiking also apply to jump serving with one exception: the contact with the ball. Contact should be the heel-snap contact, but it needs to occur below the midpoint of the ball, ensuring a curved trajectory that passes well above the net.

After your serving technique has been developed, one other factor needs to enter your training: serving under pressure. You must use your imagination to set up situations that are game-like. For example, imagine that the score is 14–14, or the score is 14–2, or the team-mate before you has just served into the net. The more your training can place the server in game-like situations, the more that training will pay off in actual games.

SERVING TACTICS

Before considering tactics in serving, the coach has to set guidelines for the team's performance. An example would be: first, get the ace; second, force the opponents to give you a free ball; and third, serve a ball that cuts down on the opponent's offensive options, thus making it a more predictable set to block. Depending on what those guidelines are for your team, you should teach your players to employ these tactics:
1. *Always* serve to the opponent's weakest player, and do not ever let up.
2. Serve to a player who has just made a mistake.
3. Serve to a player who has just substituted into the game.
4. Serve to the weakest spot(s) in the receiving formation so as to force the opponents to make major adjustments to cover those weak areas.
5. Serve to areas in between players (hit the seams).
6. Use their setter as a key for placement of your serve. For example, when their setter is penetrating from the left back position, serve cross-court short.
7. Use the Pavlovian serve (developed by the USA Men's Team), a serve that is contacted *immediately* (without thought) after the referee's whistle.
8. If in doubt, serve to the deep corners, especially cross-court deep.

Directional Serving. It has been said that a coach has only a limited number of moves he or she can make (time-outs and substitutions) during a game. *Directional serving* gives the coach an additional, important way to stay directly involved in the game. Every time the team serves, the coach can decide where the serve should go. With the court divided up as shown in Figure 5.21, this decision can be signaled in from the bench. When the coach wants the player to serve area number 1, the coach holds out one finger; area number 2, two fingers; and so on. Area number 6 is represented by a fist. Serving to different areas can be very effective in attacking weaknesses of an opponent's serve reception formation, thus reducing the opponent's quick attack potential.

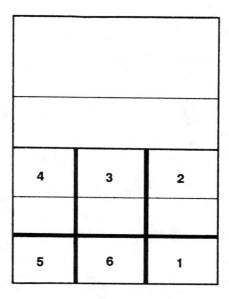

Fig. 5.21

SUMMARY

In order to serve for points, coaches must work on teaching players the mechanics of serving, serving tactics and techniques, and the various types of serves. Types of serves include: the overhand float serve, the most widely used serve in volleyball; the round house floater serve, developed by the Japanese, a serve with an unpredictable path but the fastest floater type serve; the top spin overhand serve, a serve for experienced players that incorporates the same mechanics as the spike; the underhand serve, an easy serve to execute; and the jump serve, a serve that is difficult to master. Players must be able to serve under pressure, and to learn to do so, must train in game-like situations. It is important for coaches to teach serving tactics, but they should do so only after setting guidelines for the team's performance. One way for coaches to stay directly involved in serving is by implementing directional serving during games.

6

RECEIVING THE SERVE

Rosie Wegrich

Receiving the serve is a critical volleyball skill, one that must be mastered before any team attains a high level of play. Without the pinpoint passing accuracy that results only from effective serve reception, there can be no multiple or quick attacks. Good serve reception requires a system of responsibilities achieved mostly through synchronized movement and communication among all six players on the court. The prerequisite to any such system, however, is mastery of the necessary individual skills. These skills include early movement to the ball (anticipation) combined with proper technique (efficiency), both accomplished while tracking a moving object (the ball) that is subject to sudden direction and velocity changes. Adding to the difficulty of the skill, the pass that results from serve reception must be controlled and directed to a given area of the court at least 80 percent of the time. As the level of play in volleyball rises, the serves increase in difficulty and the target area shrinks in preciseness.

Effective service reception begins with each player assuming the proper ready position (made up of lower and upper body position, shown in Figure 6.1), proper movement before and during contact, accurate side passing, good training, and teamwork. These components of effective service reception are the organizing points of this chapter.

LOWER BODY POSITION

The components of the lower body position are the feet and the knees. With those in proper position, your players can reap the advantages of correct lower body positioning.

The Feet

I prefer to teach foot position by stressing the stance with the right foot forward and the feet slightly more than shoulder width apart. This position assumes the offense is initiated

Fig. 6.1

from beyond the right of center court. In this way, the player can draw impetus from the left leg to push through the ball and direct it toward the right. The player's feet are rotated slightly inward to properly distribute the weight on the inside balls of the feet. This position readies the player to move in a split second. Coaches should remind players to avoid sitting back on their heels as the server strikes the ball.

The Knees

The knees are slightly flexed in a medium position level (120 degrees flexion). Thus the passer is allowed to move efficiently to the oncoming served ball. The knees must be kept slightly ahead of the toes in order to aid the player's speed, especially the starting time. To develop a habitual pattern of proper positioning, a player should repeat this ready position in the learning stage. Full extension of the knees for service reception should be avoided. A full deep squat position level (defensive posture) should also be avoided. Both of these body positioning levels will inhibit the kind of movement speed-effective serve reception requires.

UPPER BODY POSITION

The two key elements in proper upper body positioning are the trunk and the arms.

The Trunk

The trunk or spine should be flexed forward at the hip joint and waist and curved slightly down. You can describe this as "roll the shoulders down and forward." This position distributes the center of gravity over the balls of the feet, further preparing the player to move forward into and through the ball during contact.

The Arms

As the player prepares to pass the serve, the arms are apart and ahead of the body, and slightly flexed at the elbow joint. The elbows should not be extended, because such extension promotes a tightened, restricted shoulder joint. As the player arrives at the pass position, or if the player is not able to stop and the ball must be contacted at this moment, the hands are grasped together simultaneously as the elbows extend. Players who have their hands grasped together may lose their balance, but there are times when a receiver has no choice but to prepare the arms to receive while still moving. A good training rule for readiness discipline is to have the arms ready and presented to the ball before it penetrates the vertical plane of the net.

In the correct upper body positioning, the trunk leans forward so the player's center of gravity is over the balls of the feet. The player's head must face the server during service. This time period is used to evaluate the server's unique cues (body language). Simple evaluative cues include the server's body positioning (line or cross-court), the server's location behind the endline (deep positioning or shallow), the type of toss, and the server's direction of focus. Your player's movement will be quicker if he or she can anticipate the serve first, and then get to position before the ball arrives.

MOVEMENT PRIOR TO CONTACT

The important elements before contact with the ball are court position and anticipation.

Court Position

I prefer my players to start deep in the court, about one stride in from the endline for the two primary receivers (right and left back). This positioning gives the receivers added time to track the oncoming served ball, and it promotes the idea that the player must have forward movement into the ball. In addition, it protects the receiver from having to back pedal to pass a deep served ball. It also eliminates the risky turning movement (side pass) to play the ball that the player has allowed to get too close to his or her body. Generally, then, players should start deep and always move forward to pass the ball. They should then stay deep until they have evaluated the depth of the serve so as not to let the ball get too close to their bodies.

Anticipation

Many receivers move forward before they have made a complete evaluation of the depth of the serve. The resulting reception often produces a shanked pass or one that requires an off-balance contact, thereby increasing the potential for reception error. Remind players that "you play the ball, do not let the ball play you." In more precise terms, fine adjustments of movement *before* contact with the ball in order to have a balanced posture *at the time* of contact with the ball will reduce the failure rate of service reception.

Gaining position *prior* to contact should be the goal of every player when learning how to pass a serve. To me, gaining position means to remain facing the ball as long as possible (maintain the ball-body relationship). Later, as they become more proficient in basic ball control, your players can learn the turning movement to receive serves off one side of the body (the side pass).

CONTACT WITH THE BALL

Critical points of ball contact include hand position, eye contact, proper contact for a slow serve, and proper contact for a high velocity serve.

Hand Position

Early presentation of the arms to the ball enhances the passer's potential to execute the pass successfully. At this time, the receiver has tracked the predicted location of the serve and is now ready to grasp the hands together (Figure 6.2). The hands are interlocked just past the first joint of each finger. The thumbs are parallel and next to each other and the wrists are hyperextended down toward the floor (Figure 6.3). This wrist joint positioning keeps the ball from contacting the hands, which make a poor passing surface. The ball should rebound off both arms simultaneously, just above the wrist bone. The shoulders are flexed and curved forward to reduce the distance between them. From a biomechanical viewpoint, the scapulae move away from each other to a more lateral position.

Fig. 6.2

Fig. 6.3

Eye Contact

During contact with the ball, the receiver should complete the sequence of focusing on the ball not only as it travels through the air, but also as it contacts and leaves the arms (Figure 6.4). Many passing problems occur because players have not disciplined themselves to sustain that complete focus of attention. Often the passer will look at the passing target during contact and make an errant pass because the ball contacted one arm of the platform. A good motto to go by is to "get a picture of the ball as it leaves your arms." Keep the head down as the ball leaves the platform. During partner passing drills, each player should keep eye focus on the ball but should not move his or her head until the ball reaches the partner's arms. Then, as the ball rebounds back, the player brings the head up and focuses on the oncoming ball. This simple exercise will help to train the receiver's proper attentional focus.

Contact for a Slow Serve

As the receiver makes contact with the ball, the arms should be positioned well out in front of the body. The movement arc of the platform (arms) will vary with the speed of the served ball. For slow moving serves, the arc is increased. In this case, the receiver begins the arm action starting from a right angle relationship between arms and body. The arms move forward and up to slightly below shoulder level (Figure 6.5). If the style of pass trajectory for the team's offense is low and flat, then the contact with the ball is more on the back of the ball, and the receiver stabilizes the torso in a more forward flexed position (Figure 6.6). If the desired pass trajectory is high and loopy, then the contact will be from under the ball and the receiver will straighten (extend) the torso and open the joint angle at the waist (Figure 6.7).

Fig. 6.4

Fig. 6.5

Contact for a High Velocity Serve

When attempting to receive a high velocity, flat trajectory serve, a passer must first be sure to present the arms early to the ball. Next, the passer should use one or two of the following techniques to improve control of the rebound. One option is to use the arm-drop motion after contact with the ball. This arm motion is toward the receiver's body, in the same direction as the oncoming ball. This causes a cushioning effect and will result in a slower, more controlled rebound. The passer should hold the torso in a fixed position with relation to the legs and lower body and remain in a forward trunk lean position (Figures 6.8 and 6.9). The second option to consider when passing a high velocity serve is to contact the underside of the ball and put underspin on the ball. The resultant pass trajectory will be slightly more vertical and higher. This will give the setter added time to arrive at the set position.

ARM CONTACT
ON BALL
(FLAT TRAJECTORY)

Fig. 6.6

ARM CONTACT
ON BALL
(REVERSE SPIN)

Fig. 6.7

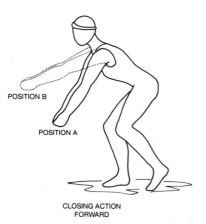

POSITION B

POSITION A

CLOSING ACTION
FORWARD

Fig. 6.8

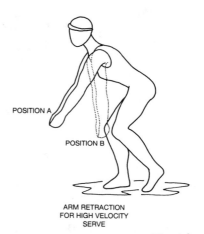

POSITION A

POSITION B

ARM RETRACTION
FOR HIGH VELOCITY
SERVE

Fig. 6.9

The goal for all receivers when faced with passing a high velocity serve should be to (1) keep the ball on your side of the net and not trap the setter against the net, and (2) control the rebound speed by slowing it with arm retraction or giving it underspin in its trajectory for added height. As Figures 6.8 and 6.9 show, by moving the arms through the ball smoothly, the player has a prolonged contact time with the ball, which results in more potential ball control.

SIDE PASSING

During those unpredictable game situations when a receiver has positioned too close to the ball, or is late arriving to the predicted passing position, he or she must pass the ball by turning to the side. The ball contact point is outside the player's center of gravity, the result of the body positioning after the player has pivoted toward the direction of movement. When turning toward the left, the player pivots on the left leg and draws the right leg forward directly ahead of the left (rear) leg (Figure 6.10). The lead shoulder (right) should be lowered by means of flexing the trunk down and forward. This angles the platform (arms) correctly toward the ball. This process will assure simultaneous contact of both arms with the ball. The movement is reversed when turning toward the right.

The initial action of the arms begins behind the center of gravity, and then follows forward in an upward-sideward rotation of the trunk. The specific cues coaches should give when teaching this skill are first to remind players to drop the lead shoulder and raise the back shoulder, and then to remind them to close through the ball (horizontal arm action and trunk rotation) in the direction of the target. The platform is the last body part that will give the

Fig. 6.10

rebound the desired direction. At the moment of contact, the ball should be played off the lead leg. If the ball is contacted off the rear leg, the rebound will most likely be out of bounds, making it extremely difficult for the setter to get to the ball to set it. Coaches should also insist that their players discipline themselves to complete eye contact with the ball during the entire execution of the pass. This is even more critical to the success of the side pass than it is when the ball is perfectly in front of the midline of the body. One last point concerning side passing: during the follow-through phase, the elbows and wrist may bend in order to give added direction to the pass.

TRAINING MOVEMENT PATTERNS

One of the most basic elements of successful serve reception is the speedy movement patterns you teach your players. The efficiency and the form of movement should be of prime concern to all coaches and players. These movement patterns need to be thoroughly learned, until they become so habitual that the players do not have to think about how to move to pass any serve. Only thus can players become able to extend their focus on the ball while moving to gain the best passing position. The best passers are those who can anticipate the flight of the serve and can be at the passing position before the ball's arrival. Attention to these cues on a subconscious level will promote positive serve receptions.

The important elements of movement patterns include side movement (side shuffle) positioning, the step-crossover close motion, the forward run step, the sprawl pass, the turn and run, and the back pedal.

Side Movement (Side Shuffle) Positioning

The most basic pattern is the movement to the side, known as the *side shuffle*. The movement is initiated by pushing off the leg opposite the direction you want to go. For example, if you wish to move right, then the left leg initiates the movement. The feet should remain rotated slightly inward and pointed straight ahead during the movement. The trunk is held in a stabilized forward flexed position, which keeps the center of gravity over the soles of the feet. Any movement up and down should be eliminated because of the time it takes to move the trunk due to the redistribution of the center of gravity that such up and down movement requires (back on the heels when the trunk is raised, onto the balls of the feet when the trunk is lowered). The knees are rotated slightly inward, which keeps the hips and shoulders facing straight ahead during movement (Figure 6.11)

A common error I see when teaching this skill is that many players open the lead leg (rotate the leg outward) in the direction of movement. This rotation forces the hips and shoulders to turn in the direction of movement, and the player passes from an off-centered ball-to-body relationship, which increases the chance of an unsuccessful pass. During the side shuffle, the player keeps the head erect and looks up at the oncoming served ball.

The side shuffle has its limitations. First, it is one of the slowest movement patterns (along with the back pedal). Therefore, it should be used to cover only short distances of less than 1.8 m (6 ft.). High, flat serves can find the player caught too close to the ball when he or she has used the side shuffle pattern to gain passing position. A turning movement at times would be the more logical method of reception in order to get the body further behind the ball. In

Fig. 6.11

Fig. 6.12

Figure 6.12, the player has had adequate time to play the ball in front of the body. If receivers can gain position around the ball, their chances of executing a perfect pass are improved.

Step-Crossover Close Motion

Another method of moving and getting around the ball is known as the *step-crossover close*. This is how it works: If moving to the right, the first step is taken with the right leg, which is pointed in the direction of movement. The trailing leg (the left) crosses over in front of the lead leg. As the left foot is planted, it is rotated to face straight ahead. In the third step, the right foot draws forward and swings around next to the left foot. This closing action closes the body (feet, hips, and shoulders) to face the oncoming served ball. The player should face the passing target position at the moment of contact.

The advantage of this method of movement is that more distance can be covered in the same amount of time it takes to execute the side shuffle. The important emphasis in learning this is on the second step, the realignment step. Be sure the players understand that there is a simultaneous pivoting on the second step as they plant. Failure to complete this pivot will result in a poor body alignment, and the players will find themselves facing away from the passing target.

Forward Run Step

The most often used method of movement is the *forward run step*. This step is used when the serve has lost its momentum and drops short at the deep receiver's feet. The ability to move forward in a flexed trunk position requires excellent quadricep and lower back strength. This is a situation in which players will have to grip their hands together during movement. It is the last chance to prevent the ball from hitting the floor. Also, the players' arms may bend at the elbow so that they may get their arms under the ball. A rushed pass will require the players to continue their movement forward past the point of contact in order to give underspin to the ball. This will prevent the ball from going tight to the net, or — worse — across the net, allowing the opposing blockers to spike the ball straight down. During extreme cases, if the receiver is very late in getting to the served ball, a sprawl pass may be the only remaining choice of reception. The player strides (lunges) forward with the outside leg (the left back would stride with the left leg). This brings the body (trunk and platform) into a horizontal position. As the player contacts the ball, the arms move in an upward arc through the ball. I refer to this action as "closing through the ball." The arms slide along the floor during the follow-through phase of the contact.

Turn and Run

The *turn and run* method of movement is used either to go a long distance very rapidly or to go a short distance when the player needs to get somewhere as quickly as possible. Simply, the player turns or pivots in the direction he or she wishes to travel and sprints to the ball. During movement the player should stabilize the trunk in a forward flexed position. A low trunk position will give the receiver added time to get under the ball due to the lowered level of contact. It will also give a more vertical trajectory than would a high platform (which will drive the ball low and flat, and therefore quickly toward the net). The main goal when passing on the run is to retain ball control in an off-balance posture. The setter at the net just needs a settable pass in this type of situation. Figure 6.13 illustrates the way the ball will spin toward the passing target from each side of the court.

Figure 6.14 shows the correct body posture as the player completes contact. It shows the post-contact phase, as the player continues with arms up and through the ball. The photograph was taken during a reception from the left side of the court, with the passing target located to the right of center.

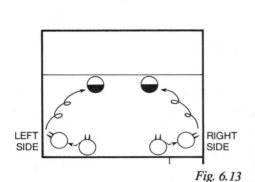

Fig. 6.13

Fig. 6.14

Back Pedal

The final method of movement is the *back pedal*. This movement requires the player to keep the trunk forward over the base. This body posture is necessary because it keeps the player's center of gravity on the balls of the feet as they move backward. If the player draws the torso up, the center of gravity will shift to the heels, which will promote stumbling and awkward movement. The player must get well beyond where the ball will land in order to pass at a level between the knees and the waist. Getting caught halfway ready to pass, that is, too close to the ball, creates a body posture of trunk extension and an upward trajectory pass. In this situation, the player should turn and pass the ball off one side of the body. This will allow the ball to travel a longer distance before it has to be contacted, giving the passer more time to prepare for contact.

The back pedal should be used only for short distances of less than 1.5 m (5 ft.). It is a slow but necessary method of moving backwards. For longer distances, a side shuffle or turn and run is more adequate than the back pedal. These last two methods should not be needed if the reception pattern is such that most player movements will be to the side or forward.

Teaching Movement and Communication

Movement in volleyball is an essential building block in developing a team that can play with speed, safety, and communication. Each player should make an aggressive move toward the ball to communicate his or her state of readiness to play. A player who turns a shoulder and "opens the lane" for the person behind him or her communicates that he or she in fact does not intend to play that ball. Late, tentative movement causes confusion, especially in the passing lane.

From a teaching perspective, a progression starting with the side shuffle, followed by the step-crossover close, and finishing with the turn and run step, will prepare your players to move sideways. The back pedal step should be taught in conjunction with the forward run. Once the form is correct, add a ball and require the players to catch it, emphasizing proper body posture with the ball. Try to reduce any subconscious stress that may develop when players are unable to pass and move simultaneously for the serve. Once movement and balance are solidly established in their repertoire, then you may combine movement and skill. Remember never to skip the progressions of learning; always assume your players need review and repetition. This will make your practice time more satisfying, especially when you put the team together on the court for the first time and they all know how to make that sure, confident movement to the served ball.

SELECTED DRILLS FOR FOREARM PASSING

All receiving drills should begin at an easy level, with all serves coming from half court. A specific target, such as a Catch-It apparatus or a setter, should be present during all drills to provide direct feedback to the receivers of their forearm pass skill. I also believe that players will learn better if they are allowed to do just one facet of the skill (such as receiving the serve to the right of the passer) repeatedly and are allowed to stay in the drill for a consecutive number of repetitions, such as ten attempts. When the skill shows improvement and consistency, the coach should then set a success goal for the receiver to achieve. If you have players who have consistent serves, then have them run the drill. Competition can be set up between the server and the receiver. For example, the server scores a point if the receiver is aced or passes the ball over the net. At the collegiate level, as the skill is more established, a point can be scored if the pass does not arrive in a designated area. All such games, however, have to be constructive, not destructive, during all practices, or they become a waste of time in terms of learning. The coach's explanation of the objectives of the drill should be well thought out.

Drill #1: Half Court Serve (Slow Speed) Directed at the Player. Practice receptions from the RF and RB. Emphasize squaring off (facing toward the inside of the court) to target. Progress to the CF, LF, and LB. Note: When passing from the left side of the court, remind the player to lower the inside (right) shoulder and laterally flex the trunk, dropping the right half of the torso slightly. Impetus from the lower body should come from the outside (left) leg.

Drill #2: Movement Receptions. Helpful Hints: The coach should initially inform the receiver where the ball will be served. Short range movement (side shuffle) will be used. Coaches should emphasize proper body alignment to the players. Next, emphasize as early an arrival to the passing position as possible. Figures 6.15, 6.16, and 6.17 show some of these drills.

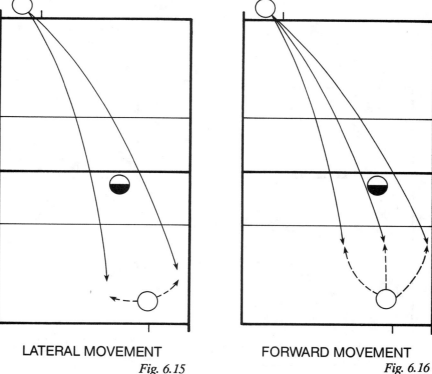

LATERAL MOVEMENT
Fig. 6.15

FORWARD MOVEMENT
Fig. 6.16

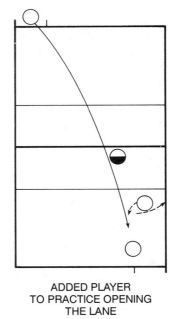

ADDED PLAYER
TO PRACTICE OPENING
THE LANE

Fig. 6.17

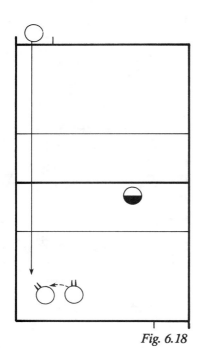

Fig. 6.18

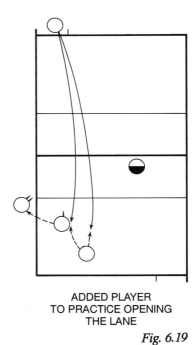

ADDED PLAYER
TO PRACTICE OPENING
THE LANE

Fig. 6.19

Drill #3: Receptions From LF And LB. Helpful Hints: Side passing requires the player to lower the inside shoulder, and the player should play the ball ahead of his or her body. Usually, if the player faces the sideline at about a 45 degree angle, the proper ball-body relationship will be achieved. Figures 6.18 and 6.19 show these drills. Note for Figure 6.19: Added player to practice opening lane. The left front player should repeat the approach jumps if required to open the lane to let the left back pass. Remind LB receiver to maintain focus on the ball at all times. The player in front should not be a source of distraction.

Drill #4: Trash Can Run. Directions: The coach gives a signal to a player to start movement (such as side shuffle, turn and run, back pedal, forward run). As the player makes the first turn, the coach serves the ball in the direction of the player's movement. Note: Tell players that they cannot leave their starting positions until they receive your signal. Emphasis: Receivers must practice patterns of movement at a maximum speed, and must maintain body balance as they pass. Figures 6.20–6.23 illustrate this drill.

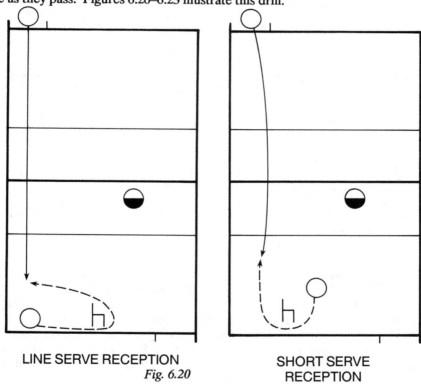

LINE SERVE RECEPTION

Fig. 6.20

SHORT SERVE RECEPTION

Fig. 6.21

103

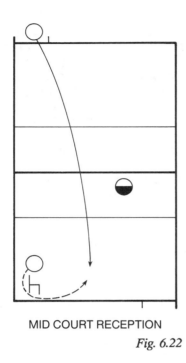

MID COURT RECEPTION

Fig. 6.22

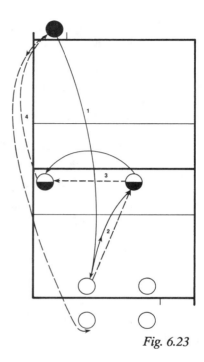

Fig. 6.23

Errors/Corrections

Error: The player shanks the pass out of bounds.
Correction: *Check to see if the player is sustaining complete eye focus when the ball leaves his or her arms. Check the receiver's head level. Is it up — looking ahead at the passing target — while the ball makes contact with the receiver's arms?*

Error: The pass only goes to mid-court from a back row reception.
Correction: *The player's level of platform is too horizontal during contact. The player's torso may have extended (straightened) before contact, causing a redistribution of the center of gravity backward. Also, the hip joint angle may have opened too much as a result of the torso extension. Keep the angle closed and the body flexed forward. If the level of serve caught the player by surprise, the passer's body may be too close to the ball. Suggest to the player that he or she utilize the turning movement and pass the ball from the side. Remind the player to lower the inside (lead) shoulder and rotate the trunk through the ball. Also, side spin on the ball should be into the court.*

Error: The pass goes across the net to the opposing blocker at the net.
Correction: *Stabilize the arm action during contact, use a drop motion of the arms during contact, or try redirecting the arms under the ball and giving the ball underspin.*

Error: The server serves a top spin serve which drops on the floor in front of the back row receiver.

Correction: *The player has failed to recognize the type of toss the server executed. Most top spin servers will hit under, and then up the back side of the ball. Receivers should notice the ball spinning for the first 9.1 m (30 ft.) of distance and move forward to meet the ball. This serve gains its momentum in a dropping action, much like the hitter's wrist action as the ball is spiked. If you are prepared for this serve, you should begin two or three steps behind the place where you predict the ball will land. Then as you read the serve's trajectory, you move forward to meet the ball with a hop to position.*

Error: The front row receiver passes the ball over the net.

Correction: *The level of the platform should be slightly raised when receiving in the front court area. Players should attempt to give underspin to the ball and respond with more of a vertical trajectory pass. This will allow them to pass, then attack either a quick play or a semi-quick play. A good server who has the ability to stand 6.1 m (20 ft.) behind the endline and serve the front row a dropper can cause severe reception problems. By putting underspin on the pass, the contact time is lengthened, allowing for more potential ball control.*

SUMMARY

Proper service reception is achieved through synchronized movement and communication between players, but the prerequisite to this is the mastery of individual skills. Skills involved include: anticipation, proper technique, and tracking the ball. Effective service reception begins with the proper ready position and proceeds to proper contact with the ball, including contact for a high velocity serve and side passing. In addition, movement and movement patterns must be well learned. Important elements of movement patters include side movement positioning, the step-crossover close motion, the forward run step, the sprawl pass, the turn and run, and the back pedal.

7

TACTICS AND STRATEGY IN VOLLEYBALL

Marilyn McReavy

Every sport has strategies so common that they are applied almost automatically. These expected forms of play are used in response to various recurring sport situations. Like other sports, volleyball has certain such strategies which, when properly executed, improve the soundness of your team's game and increase the chances for success. Volleyball's basic strategies can be seen clearly in terms of the sport's six basic skills — digging, setting, spiking, blocking, serving, and receiving the serve.

DIGGING

Centered around digging, sound defensive play requires lots of coaching involvement and teamwork. As in each of the other five basic skills, there are certain strategies each individual player must have. First, each of your players must learn to form the prescribed defensive pattern(s), that is, to get into the correct position *before* the ball is hit. A catch-and-throw method of teaching can help your beginners, especially, learn the necessary defensive patterns.

For successful digging and defense, each player must get ready to play the ball *before* it is hit by the opponents. The only way to be prepared is if every player expects to be hit with the ball every time it is attacked. Thus, every player assumes a defensive ready posture in anticipation.

Another key point for successful digging and defense is that your players must *try* for every ball; they should never allow a ball to hit the floor without at least being touched. Secondly, they must commit themselves to trying for every ball with two hands.

Good defensive training begins with giving your team many repetitions in the basics described here. Although these patterns may seem simple, effective use of them will bring your team greater defensive success.

SETTING

Setting the ball for the attack is strategic at even the simplest level of play. Depending on the quality of the pass, you must be able to rely on your setter to make sound, consistent decisions. Here is a list of strategic demands on your setter, in ascending order of difficulty.

1. The ability to set the ball to the left front position is the most important skill for the setter to acquire. You can develop this ability by emphasizing that fact and by constant drills in practice.
2. With any set, the ball should be delivered well. Good delivery means that the ball is touched legally, set high enough, and positioned properly relative to the attacker.
3. After becoming consistent in the skills outlined in numbers 1 and 2, your setter's primary goal should be to set a good set *to a good attacker.* This goal requires your setter to know who the right attackers are, something that must be emphasized in practice. Your setter should be especially aware of the primary attackers, those who score high statistically.
4. A poor set should never be made to a secondary hitter (a statistically lower attacker). What becomes a *poor* set when made to a secondary hitter may well have been a *good* set, or at least an acceptable one, if it had been made to a good hitter. In other words, often it is the hitter's ability that makes the difference in whether a particular set is poor, acceptable, or good. Secondary spikers require good sets.
5. When setting a good set to a secondary hitter, your setter must have a specific shot planned for that spiker. Obviously, this requires a good deal of thinking by the setter (as should be expected in better intermediate and advanced play). Planning for a specific shot depends on observing the block positioning of the opposition and specifically setting for either a line or a cross-court attack. By paying attention to which attackers the opposing blockers are keying on, your setter can often get the secondary attackers in one-on-one situations. With one blocker versus one attacker, the attacker has a decided advantage. Simply notifying secondary spikers of open shots on the opponent's court before the set is made to that spiker will often result in a successful shot. This kind of communication should occur when the ball is dead before service. Because opponents often place the least effective blockers opposite the secondary attackers, your setter can look for these switches, being especially aware of size mismatches, and communicate the situation to the spiker prior to the next volley.
6. At a critical time, your setter should not set a cold hitter (one just coming into the game, or one who has not been set often throughout the game) or an unsuccessful attacker.

7. Neither critical, high-risk sets nor trick sets and plays should be used at the end of the game, and especially not at game point.

8. When your team is making points, continue to use the sets that are working. Change strategies in the game only when opponents are successful at stopping the attack.

SPIKING

When plays and advanced attack systems are developed along with setting ability, the spikers have less pressure to incorporate individual spiking strategy because deception is planned into the system. Nonetheless, at every level of play each attacker must develop some individual competence, especially to use in less-than-perfect situations. The strategies described here will give even beginning attackers statistical success. Once again, this list is in ascending degree of demand upon the spiker.

1. The ball must be hit into the opponent's court, even from a terrible set. The ball must be kept in play.

2. The hit should be to the opponent's disadvantage.

3. The ball should be killed (put down to gain a point or side-out). The kill is the most difficult shot to make consistently, and often an error will result if the kill is the attacker's only focus. To become a good spiker with consistent statistics, numbers 1 and 2 must be the primary focus, with kill attempts occurring only on the good sets. Success results from consistent play—without undue risk-taking on poor sets.

Your attackers must develop skills to hit every type of set. Beginners or intermediate players may need to poke or dink sets that are too low or too close. Advanced players, on the other hand, must acquire the ability to *attack* these sets. Sets that are back from the net and deeper than the hitter's normal range require high contact and lots of top spin. In advanced play these sets still should be skillfully attacked, rather than given as free plays to the opponents. This requires lots of practice time.

In training your attackers to become intermediate level players, have them develop two power shots, the line shot and the cross-court shot. However, it is equally important that they know when to use a power shot and when to dink or tip. The dink or tip is most effective on a good set, but the attacker must know what defense is being used by the other team before incorporating the tip. Obviously, just giving the ball directly to an opposing defensive player is not effective. The tip is best used in surprise, especially after the hitter has been spiking effectively and powerfully. In other words, it is best to dink after opponents have acquired respect for your spiker's power.

BLOCKING

Blocking is an advanced skill, one which becomes especially complicated and high risk when more than one player is blocking. In low skill levels, and especially with beginners, the best strategy is not to block unless the set is close. The degree of success in the skill of blocking is very low at any skill level.

The distance of the opponent's set from the net is a key for blockers. The farther away the ball is from the net, the less need there is to block. Unless the opposing spiker has two developed power shots, one properly positioned blocker is sufficient. A two-person block should only be used if the opponent's ability warrants it.

Advanced play presents your middle blocker with another strategic decision: when to commit to blocking center on a quick set (thereby giving the opposing setter an opportunity to set up a one-on-one situation — one blocker versus one spiker — in an outside position near the sideline). Coaching and statistical input are usually required for the middle blockers to be successful in making these decisions. However, your middle blocker should be aware of these two fundamental strategic considerations:
- *Honor the middle* when the opponent's primary spiker is attacking the middle.
- *Overblock the line* when the set is to an outside position and very close to the net.

Honoring the middle (guarding the middle closely) is necessary when the opponent's primary spiker is attacking the middle regularly with success. There are some further strategic considerations in this situation, however. A perceptive blocker can pick up certain cues and recognize when to honor the middle. Many setters only set the middle on the perfect pass. In addition, setters often develop observable habits, such as keeping their arms straight when setting the middle, or perhaps dropping their hands. The setter is sometimes out of range to set the middle attack, especially when the pass pulls the setter away from the net. With these cues in mind, your blocker will know much more reliably whether honoring the middle is required in each situation.

Overblocking the line should occur when the set is delivered by opponents to an outside position along and very close to the net. In this case, it is necessary to overblock the line to prevent the ball from being tipped, hit, or wiped off the outside blocker. Overblocking requires the outside blocker to position the inside hand on the ball.

SERVING

Service strategy depends on the ability of your athletes to perform the skill. Each of your players must have a reliable serve that measures up to the skill level of your competition. In addition to a *reliable* serve, their repertoire should also include a higher risk but *stronger* service attack. Generally, either the coach or an advanced player determines the positions to serve into the opponent's court or lineup. Still, every player makes a decision as to how to

serve aggressively upon rotating into the service corner. Ultimately, the player decides how much risk to take. Players should take the opportunity to be aggressive in the following circumstances:
- When seriously behind in score.
- When points are never made in a particular serving rotation.
- When the score is stuck in the middle of the game, especially in the middle game of the match.
- When your team's ability to side out is high.

Safe serving is more strategic in the following instances:
- When serving the first ball after winning the coin toss for service.
- After a time-out.
- After serving several points in a row.
- After a long rally.
- After the player in the preceding rotation has missed the serve.
- Any time after twelve points have been made in the game.
- When a strong front line rotation is at the net for your team.

RECEIVING THE SERVE

Receiving the serve is undoubtedly the most critical skill for establishing a team's success. Perfection in passing depends upon both the team's skill level and the effectiveness and power of the opponent's serve. These factors, listed in ascending order of difficulty, should be considered when receiving the serve:
1. Avoid being aced; try to at least touch the served ball.
2. Make the pass playable. Get it in the air somewhere.
3. Pass the ball between yourself and the setter.
4. Target the pass to the setter.

If your team cannot side out because of poor passing, change the receiving pattern. This alteration includes moving the pattern forward or back, flooding to one side, or covering an ineffective passer.

Any time passing is unsuccessful in a 6–2 offense, change immediately to a 4–2. The best passers should be in optimum position to receive the statistically highest percentage of serves (near the middle of the court). In tense situations, strong passers should extend their range and cover extra court area in addition to assuming the responsibility for getting the ball passed. In extreme situations, the best passers can take every serve.

If failure to side out is the result of a poor attack, the serve reception pattern should be varied to position the best attacker to spike—this position is left front. In beginning to intermediate play, the setter cannot be relied upon to perform a good set to any position but left front. This limitation requires patterns designed to allow the setter to set the best spiker in the left front position.

SUMMARY

Here is a summary of the points presented in this chapter:

Digging

- Learn to form defensive patterns.
- Get physically ready to play the ball before it is hit. Expect the hit.
- Try for every ball. Try for the ball with two arms.
- Defense must be trained. Catch and throw is a good method. If a player does not perform the trained duty, especially in forming defense (getting to court position after proper training), then substitute.

Setting

- Develop the ability to set to the left front; this is the most important target.
- Always deliver the ball well.
- Make a good set to a good hitter.
- Make a good set to a secondary hitter, but plan a shot for that hitter. That is, notice who the opponents are keying on. Get your secondary spikers into one-on-one situations, then set them for a line or angle hit.
- Never give a poor set to a secondary hitter. A bad set for a poor hitter may be a good, or at least acceptable, set for a good hitter. Secondary hitters require very good sets.
- Do not set a cold hitter or a hitter who has been unsuccessful at a critical time.
- Do not use trick or critical sets at the end of a game, especially at game point.
- When making points, continue to use the sets that are working. Change strategies in the game only when opponents stop your system.

Spiking

- Hit the ball in the court, even on terrible sets.
- Hit to the opponent's disadvantage.

Concerning kills:
- Skill must be developed to hit every type of set. That is, for close sets poke if necessary; for deep sets reach high and use top spin.
- Develop two power shots.
- If the dink is used, the hitter should know what defense the other team is in. The dink is most effective on a good set.

Blocking

- Practice each situational condition so that your players acquire trained responses.
- In low skill levels, do not block unless the set is close. Depth of set is important. The farther back the ball is from the net, the less need there is to block.
- Make sure an opponent deserves a two-man block.

Concerning blocking the middle:
- When the setter sets it regularly with success.
- When the main hitter is in the middle.
- When the setter has range to set the middle or shows a tendency to set it. That is, does the setter set middle only on perfect passes? Does the setter drop the arms or keep the arms straight, providing you with a cue?
- On close and wide sets, overblock to the outside to avoid being used (get the inside hand on the ball).

Serving

Serving can be either aggressive or safe, depending in part on the ability of the player. Thus, the key to tough serving is increasing your players' skill levels.

Use *aggressive serving* when:
- Your team is seriously behind in score.
- The player never makes points in the serving rotation. (The other team plays the serve like a free ball).
- The ability of your team to side out is high.
- When the score is stuck in a middle game.

Use *safe serving* when:
- Your team has just won the serve.
- After a time-out.
- After serving several points in a row.
- After a long rally.
- When the person in the rotation ahead of you missed the serve.
- Any time after twelve points.
- When you have a strong front line (hitters or blockers).

Receiving the Serve

- The pass must be playable. Avoid being aced, especially when no one even touches the ball.
- Pass between self and the net.
- Target the pass to the setter.
- If your team cannot side out and poor passing is the problem, change the pattern:

— Move up or back.
— Flood to one side.
— Cover the person being served.
— Any time you cannot get the pass in a 6–2, immediately change to a 4–2.
— Put the best passers in position to pass. Let the best passers take everything.
— If failure to side out results from poor hitting, change the serve reception pattern to get the best hitter in position to hit. This position is usually the left front. At the lower skill levels, you cannot count on the setter getting the ball anywhere but left front.

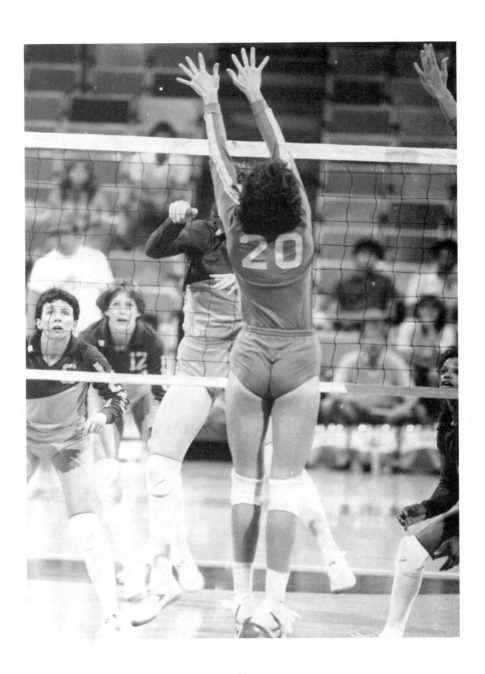

8

SYSTEMS OF PLAY

Ruth Nelson and Frances Compton

There are probably as many offensive systems in use today as there are coaches. Most coaches start out using one of the basic systems, but by the time it has been adapted to the specific abilities of their players, it has become a system unique to that program. Basically, your system is determined by how your setter penetrates — whether your setter(s) moves in to set from a front court or a back court position. This in turn is determined by your team's passing ability and the abilities of your setters.

While defensive systems are named with words and colors, offensive systems are named with numbers. Commonly used offensive systems include the 4–2, 5–1, and 6–2. The first number refers to the number of players who are designated hitters, and the second the number of setters. Sometimes the numbers add up to more than six because the setters are also hitters. In the 6–2 system, for example, the two setters each set while playing in the back court and hit after rotating to the front court.

The options and variations for each system are almost unlimited. Many factors will influence your selection of an offense. It is best to start with a basic plan and get more sophisticated as you and your players gain experience and knowledge.

OFFENSIVE PROGRESSION

College coaches have the distinct advantage of being able to recruit players to complement their preferred offensive systems. Coaches of younger players usually find it necessary to fit the system to the players. You may want to begin by using an offensive progression while evaluating the setting and hitting potential of your players.

Setting by Position

A simple way to begin is to designate a setter by rotational position. For example, have the center front set for a two-hitter attack, or have the right back player set for a three-hitter attack. Whoever rotates into the designated position (left, center, or right) becomes the setter. I call this a 4–0 when a front court setter is used and a 6–0 when a back court setter is used. (The zero means that there is no designated player who sets, only a designated setting position.) I believe that designating a setter by rotational position has a great deal of merit in terms of developing players' understanding of offensive concepts as well as aiding in their total skill development.

Front Court Setter Systems

Once you have identified your setters, you must consider whether or not you want to use a front court setter or a back court setter to run the offense. A front court setter allows for easier passing formations and generally less confusion among hitters, since there are only two. The target area for passing in a standard 4–2 is larger, so the passes do not have to be as accurate (Figures 8.1–8.5). Players pass to a position on the court rather than to the setter. Another advantage is that the setter is already positioned in the front court and generally has a shorter and straighter movement path to the ball.

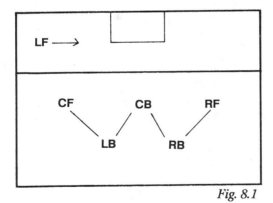

Fig. 8.1

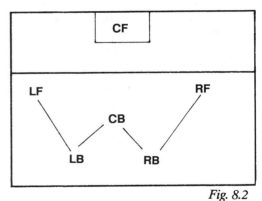

Fig. 8.2

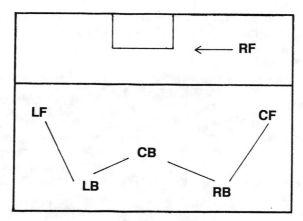

Fig. 8.3

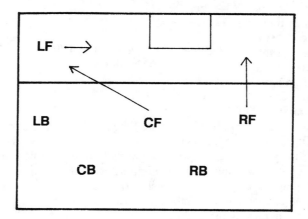

Fig. 8.4

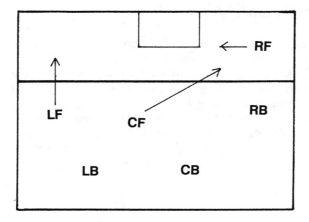

Fig. 8.5

In a front court setter system, hitting responsibilities are easy to define. All sets in front of the setter will be hit by the left front player, while all sets behind the setter will be hit by the right front player unless combination plays are used. A front court setter system can be made a great deal more sophisticated by using a "fake" hitter; this option will be discussed in a later section.

Fig. 8.6   *Front court fake setter moves in before service contact.*

The front court setter system may be less demanding on the passers and setters, but it places greater demands on the hitters. Strategically, the hitters must be smarter and more effective in a front court system because they are usually hitting against a two-player block. In a basic front court setter offense, there are fewer quick attacks or combinations, so the middle blocker has time to move to the outside to block. Thus, in addition to spiking the ball, the hitters must use tips (dinks), off-speed shots, and blockers' hands (wipe-offs). They must also use position hitting to find the holes on the court. Learning to exploit the blockers' weaknesses is also important. For example, hitters should learn to hit cross-court when the middle blocker is slow or late moving into position. Thus, if you have several smart and capable hitters and your players are average in passing and setting, a front court setter system may be just right for your team.

Back Court Setter Systems

In this system a player moves in from the back court to set so that three hitters instead of two can be in the front court. A back court setter system allows the coach to be more creative with the team's offense. This creativity tends to promote interest among the players as they become involved in the challenge of learning the system. As your players become more experienced, the excitement of making the offense more complex keeps players from becoming complacent. You really do not know the potential of your players until you create a challenging situation. Running a three-hitter attack with a back court setter sets the stage for future development — including plays, combinations, fakes, and back court attacks.

Passing determines the level at which a team can play. If you have a very good setter, you can work with average passing. If you have an excellent passing team, you can run a three-hitter attack with an average setter. If your opponents are comparable in skill, then set selection (choosing the hitter and the hitter position) will make the difference.

Remember that the efficiency of the pass is determined by the strength of your own servers. If your players serve tough to each other in practice, your team will be a much better passing team. Also remember that winning is not necessarily an indicator of offensive effectiveness. Winning shows that you scored points on serving and blocking as well. You cannot win on offense alone.

You may want to use a progression to move into a back court setter offense. You could begin by using a setter from the back court on free balls only. Your team should be able to pass free balls to the setter with accuracy. With good positioning of the setter, the hitter should be able to make proper approaches and the setter can execute

Fig. 8.7 Back court setter ready position.

the set as planned. On serve receive you may want to stay with a front court setter if your passing tends to be off target. By following this progression, your players will become familiar with the concepts of the 4–2 and 6–2 offenses. When passing breaks down, you then have more options.

Eventually you will progress to the point where you can run plays to capitalize on the hitting strengths of your own players and to confuse your opponent's defense. Having the option of moving a hitter to another position to enable him or her to hit the best shot is naturally advantageous. In order to have this option, your setter must learn to make good sets and good decisions. Set deception will come with experience.

The trend in passing is to pass the ball lower and faster. Using lower, faster passes facilitates better timing between the setter and hitter and allows the defense less time to position. However, the pass should always be high enough that the setter has the option of jump setting. Jump setting gets the ball to the hitter faster, makes the blocker commit, and reduces the chance of the setter setting the ball below the top of the net.

A fast attack is not limited to one set to the middle attacker. In using a fast attack, you are trying to hit the ball before the defense has time to position. The setter can set fast sets anywhere at the net. In order to use a fast attack, however, the setter must make precise sets.

In the back court setter system, passing and setting must be more exact. The hitter's job, aside from learning the patterns, is not as demanding as it is in a front court setter offense. In fact, the system is designed to create better situations for your hitters. Instead of going against a double block every time, your hitters should be one-on-one with their respective blockers. This offense can be very simple, or you can create your own options. You may be surprised at what your players can do. Offer them the challenge!

Fig. 8.8 Two-player front court coverage with fast attack.

BASIC OFFENSIVE SYSTEMS

The 4-2

The 4–2 is a front court setter offense with four hitters and two designated setters. There are two different ways to run the 4-2 offense. The standard 4-2 uses a center front setter with a left and right side attack. The right side 4–2 allows for greater use of the middle attack. These systems are explained below.

Standard 4–2. In the standard 4–2, the setter moves to the middle of the front court as soon as the ball is contacted on the serve. The setter has basically two options: set the left side attacker, or back set to the right side player (Figures 8.1–8.5). Play sets are not usually seen in the standard 4–2.

The advantages of this system are its simplicity, a larger passing target, easier setter movement, and less confusion among hitters. However, if your setter is small and you end up with a short block in the middle, your opponents may try to exploit this weakness. Also, as mentioned before, your hitters are usually hitting against a double block.

Right Side 4–2. In the right side 4–2, the front court setter moves to the right side of the court as soon as the ball is contacted on the serve. The setter can set the left side attacker or the middle attacker. The setter can position at the net (Figures 8.9, 8.10, and 8.11) or pretend to be a back court setter and line up behind the respective back court player (Figures 8.12, 8.13, and 8.14). For example, when playing the right front position, the setter lines up behind the right back player as the fake hitter. The setter must move into legal position before the ball is contacted on the serve. The setter usually steps in front of the back court player as the ball is tossed for the serve. Overlapping will be called if the setter fails to move into the correct position before service contact. It is important for the setter to jump set as many balls as possible so that the opposing blockers do not know if the setter is going to tip, hit, or jump set to the hitters.

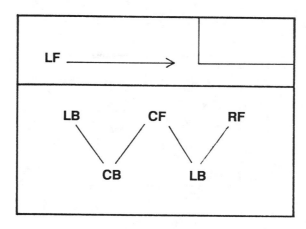

Fig. 8.9

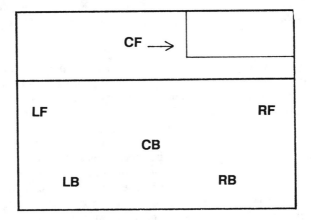

Fig. 8.10

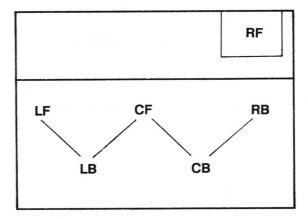

Fig. 8.11

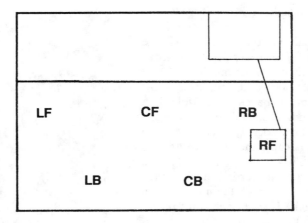

Fig. 8.12

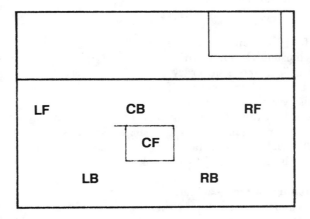

Fig. 8.13

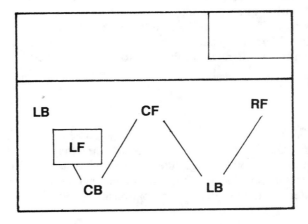

Fig. 8.14

The advantage of the right side 4–2 over the standard 4–2 is that you can have a middle attack and still maintain the benefit of simple setter movement. It is easier for the setter to set the middle attack area because it is not confined by the antennae, and, in addition, this lack of confinement makes the middle area difficult to defend. Your left side hitter can now hit against one blocker, or at least a late middle blocker, because the middle hitter has held the middle blocker. If your setter is small, you can have a taller player in the middle for blocking purposes against a team that runs a three-hitter attack. If your back court player is used successfully as a fake hitter, your center hitter should also find a one-on-one hitting situation.

There are a few disadvantages to this system. The passes must now be made to the right side, requiring a little more accuracy than passing to the middle of the court. If you choose to disguise your two-hitter attack as a three-hitter attack, have the setter line up in the back court. This technique makes the setter's movement path longer, requiring more quickness. There is also more opportunity to overlap. Thus, with the right side 4–2 you can overcome some of the disadvantages of the standard 4–2, but you will still have only two eligible hitters.

Fig. 8.15   Position of front court fake setter prior to ball toss on service.

Player Positioning for the 4–2. Start out with your two setters opposite each other in the lineup. If there is a significant difference in the abilities of your two setters, put your best setter in the center front and your second best setter as the center back. Your best hitter starts at the left front, with your second best hitter at the right back. If your second best hitter is not your number 1 or 2 server, then start a tough server at the right back. Place your third best hitter at the left back and your fourth best hitter at the right front. If your number 4 hitter is not a tough server, then use a substitute to serve after the first rotation (Figures 8.16, 8.17).

The 6–2

The 6–2 is a back court setter offense with a three-hitter attack. All six players are hitters, and two of these players are also designated to set when they are in the back court. Having a back court setter gives you a left, middle, and right side attack. In the 6–2 offense, the setter moves into setting position after the ball is contacted on the serve. The passes must be made to the setter just right of the center front position.

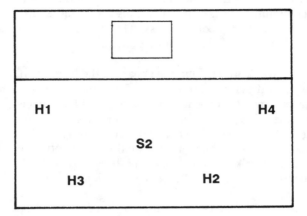

Fig. 8.16

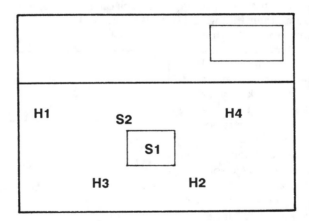

Fig. 8.17

The biggest advantage of this system is the potential for hitting options. It allows the coach and setter to create plays. Hitter specialization can make a tremendous difference in your offensive effectiveness, and the coach can capitalize on the unique hitting abilities of each player. Better communication is required because of the more intricate movement of hitters, and this tends to improve team cohesiveness. The blockers must look at three hitters instead of two, so you should get favorable hitting situations.

When running the 6–2 attack, four players are in the front court, and this can create confusion, especially on off plays and transitions. Your passers must be able to pass the ball to the setter with accuracy. A three-hitter attack requires more decision making by the setter, and with fast sets there is a greater chance of setter error. Therefore, you must devote more time to training the setters. The setter can no longer jump and hit or tip the ball over the net, because this would be a back court hitter violation. The setter must learn to set good sets from bad passes. Also, spiker coverage is generally weaker with a fast attack because players do not have time to get to their ideal coverage positions.

Player Positioning for the 6–2. Setters are usually placed opposite each other in the lineup. If they are not opposite, then one setter will set more rotations than the other setter. This situation could be used to your advantage. For example, you could have your better setter set at right front, right back, center back, and left back. As a result, your second setter will not have to set from the more difficult left back position.

Assuming that your setters are opposite each other in the lineup, their starting positions will still depend on their hitting abilities. It is vital to balance your attack by placing comparable hitters opposite one another. Thus you must first rank the skill levels of your hitters and setters. Usually your best setter starts in the right back if your second best setter is a strong hitter. If your second setter is not your number 1 or 2 hitter, as is often the case, then start your better setter at the center back, your second setter at the center front, and your best hitter at the left front. Place your number 2 hitter at the right back, your number 3 hitter at the left back, and your number 4 hitter at the right front (Figure 8.18).

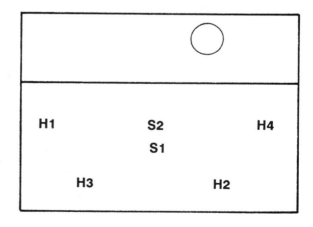

Fig. 8.18

The 5–1

The 5–1 is basically a combination of the 4–2 and 6–2 offenses. In this offense, there are five hitters and only one setter. When the setter is in the back court, a three-hitter attack is run (Figures 8.19, 8.20, and 8.21). When the setter is in the front court, the attack is run with

two hitters (Figures 8.1, 8.2, 8.3; 8.9, 8.10, 8.11). College teams usually use a middle attack (right side 4–2) when the setter is in the front court, but a standard 4–2 offense with the setter setting from the middle may also be used.

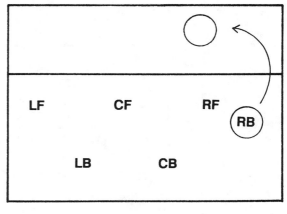

Fig. 8.19

Many of the advantages and disadvantages of this offense have been pointed out in the discussion of the 4–2 and 6–2, but there are some pros and cons that are unique to the 5–1 system. Relying on one setter will give that setter a far greater opportunity to develop setting skills in practice as well as in actual competition. The hitters adjust to the one setter, and there is less confusion as to who should set the ball on transition. Because of this greater experience, fewer setter errors should take place.

The problems occur when your setter is not mentally or physically prepared to play. Substituting for your 5–1 setter could mean a very difficult adjustment for your team. Also, most 5–1 setters are smaller than the majority of the hitters on the team. If the setter is not a strong hitter and blocker, your opponents will certainly use this weakness to their advantage.

At the international level, the 5–1 system is used by most of the top women's teams, including the USA's. These teams use the 5–1; training two setters to run such a highly sophisticated offense is far too difficult for them. Even with very talented setters of equal ability, it is very unlikely that two setters who must share setting duties on a fifty-fifty basis could develop the same capabilities as one setter who sets the whole system. Thus, if you have one setter whose ability is far greater than the others and who has the temperament and endurance to do the job, this system has the potential to be extremely effective.

Player Positioning For The 5–1. There are many trade-offs to consider when deciding on the most suitable lineup for your players. Here is one suggestion for positioning players for the 5–1 starting lineup: The setter usually begins at the right back if your team is serving (or the right front if your team is receiving), establishing a three-hitter attack for your first three rotations. If the setter starts at the right back, the hitters could be positioned as follows: the number 1 hitter at the left front, the number 2 hitter at the center back, the number 3 hitter

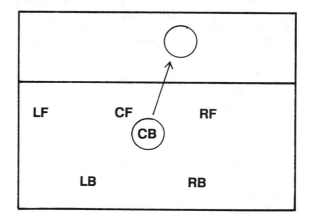

Fig. 8.20

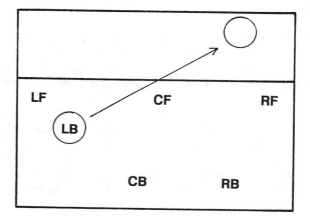

Fig. 8.21

at the center front, the number 4 hitter at the left back, and the number 5 hitter at the right front (Fig. 8.22).

OFFENSIVE VARIATIONS

You can have any combination of back court and front court setters and hitters. The challenge is to utilize the abilities of each player to the team's greatest advantage. You must experiment and try different combinations in order to arrive at the system that is best for your team in any given year.

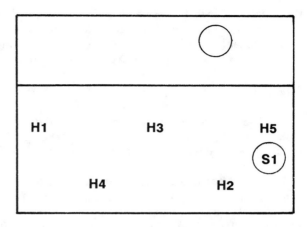

Fig. 8.22

The 6–3

One variation that I have found particularly effective is the 6–3. In this system all six players are hitters, and three players share back court setting duties. This system enables you to work your younger setters into the lineup to train along with your more experienced setters. Another big bonus is that your setters, who are usually your best all-around players, can now be used for passing and defense in the vulnerable left back position. You have more versatility in pass/receive formations. When passing breaks down with a back court setter, there is always a setter in the front court. You also have more options on transition when the setter cannot move in to set. Your lineup is more flexible because your two best setters do not have to be opposite one another (Figure 8.23).

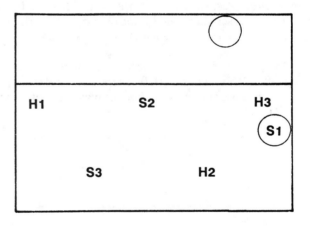

Fig. 8.23

The 6–3 is excellent for a moderately sophisticated offense. I used this system in 1974, 1975, and 1979 at the University of Houston when my team finished fourth, third, and fifth in the country. The system seemed to fit our personnel, and it provided an opportunity for my taller players (Flo Hyman and Rose Magers) to develop their all-around skills. The 6–2 would probably work better as your offense becomes more advanced, and eventually you may want to go to a 5–1 if you have a very capable setter.

The 3–3

The 3–3 system is essentially the same as the 6–3, except the setters set from the center front and the right front positions instead of the right back and the center back. The benefits of this system are the same as the benefits of the 6–3 (Figure 8.24).

Left Side Attack. In a left side attack, the setter runs the offense from a position left of the center front instead of from the right side of the court. The setter has the middle and right side attackers in front with the left side attack behind. This variation is designed to help the setter get in faster when playing the left back or the left front positions. It also allows a front court setter who is right-handed to attack easily. The main reason for running the left side attack is that it allows a faster attack on the left side against your opponent's right front blocker. The attack can be even faster if your center hitter is left-handed. The right front blocker is usually the setter or a weaker blocker because most teams attack fast on the right side of the court.

At LSU we ran a right side attack when the setter was at the right back (Figure 8.25) and a left side attack when the setter was at the left back (Figure 8.26). When the setter was at the center back, she moved to the right side if the ball was served cross-court and to the left side if it was served down the line (Figure 8.27). This movement was done because it is easier to pass the ball straight ahead than cross-court.

In order to run the left side attack, you must train your passers to pass left. There is nothing difficult about passing left except that players are programmed to pass right from an early age. If you are running a number of plays, the setter has the difficult task of reversing the set positions.

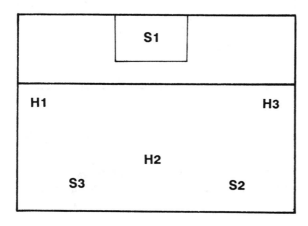

Fig. 8.24

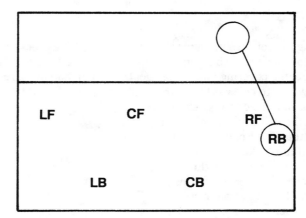

Fig. 8.25

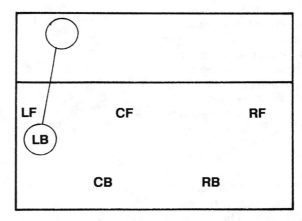

Fig. 8.26

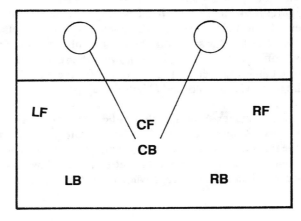

Fig. 8.27

SPIKER COVERAGE

Spiker coverage is not essential unless your team is getting blocked. In spiker coverage, players move into a position to back up the hitter in case the hit is blocked by the defense. If the ball is blocked, the covering players can get the ball up and prepare to attack again. The key to knowing where to cover is to watch the blockers' hands and the placement of the set.

If the set is off the net, the coverage should be tight because the ball could come down in front of the hitter. Close coverage is also necessary when the blockers are tall and are penetrating over the net. In this case the ball will probably be blocked down. If the blockers are blocking straight up but not over the net, then coverage should be deeper in the court.

As a general rule, the three players closest to the hitter take a low position near the 10-foot line, and the other two players balance the entire back court. The setter usually follows the set. The three closest players should not reach back to play balls. Instead, those balls should be played by the back court players. Spiker coverage for the standard 4–2 offense is shown in Figures 8.29 and 8.30.

Fig. 8.28 Close spiker when tall blockers are penetrating over the net.

This spiker coverage pattern is described as a 2–1–2. There are two players in fairly close, one slightly deeper, and two in the back court. On a left or right side block, the 1 slot is filled by the middle hitter (Figures 8.32 and 8.33) unless the hitter drives for a fast set. In this case, the setter fills the 1 position (Figures 8.34 and 8.35). When covering the center hitter, the coach may designate which player fills the 1 slot. I usually designate the left back player (Figures 8.36 and 8.37). When a front court setter sets from the right front to the left front, you may want to have the setter pull off of the net instead of following the set (Figure 8.38). If the setter follows the set and the ball is bumped up, then all of the front court players are bunched up on the side where the team was just blocked (Figure 8.39).

For a basic offense, spiker coverage should be complete. When fast plays are used, coverage becomes less defined because the players simply do not have time to position properly before the ball is hit. Many times the coverage will be the two players closest in and two in the back court. If the pass is poor, the setter will not have time to get into position. Players must learn to balance the coverage when the setter cannot move in.

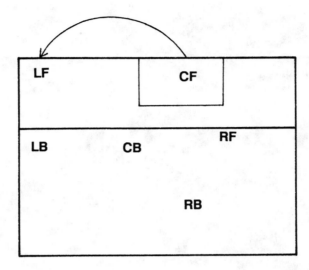

Fig. 8.29

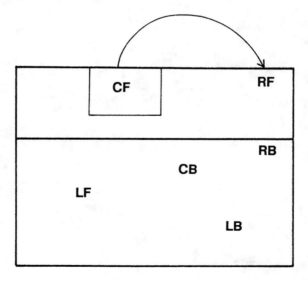

Fig. 8.30

Fig. 8.31   2–1–2 spiker coverage.

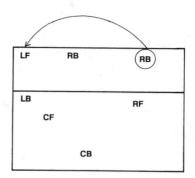

Fig. 8.32

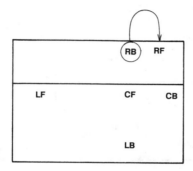

Fig. 8.33

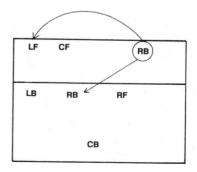

Fig. 8.34

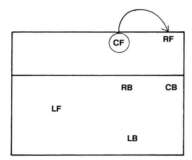

Fig. 8.35

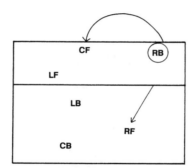

Fig. 8.36

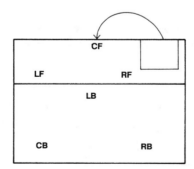

Fig. 8.37

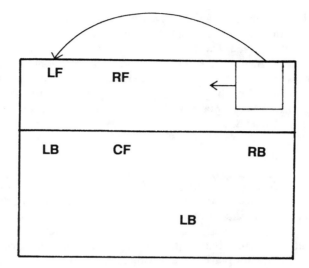

Fig. 8.38

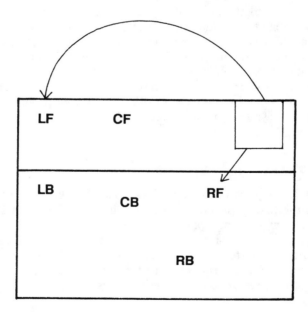

Fig. 8.39

MATCHING UP

Even after you have established an effective offensive lineup, you may find that in certain rotations your opponents are outscoring your team by a wide margin. Consequently, you must make adjustments. First, try switching blocking assignments or substituting for a weak blocker. Next, alter your own set selection. If these measures do not work, you may want to match up differently in the next game. You could rotate your lineup so as to match your best player against your opponent's best player. Another option is to match your best hitter against your opponent's weakest player or a short setter. You must do something! Matching up differently is worth a try.

Total Team Preparation

The importance of developing every player in order to achieve the concept of total team development cannot be stressed enough. All players must master all of the basic fundamentals. Very often tall players concentrate on hitting almost to the exclusion of passing and setting, while shorter players do exactly the opposite. Hitting effectiveness depends to a large degree on the quality of a team's ball control. Before you begin categorizing hitters and setters, make sure that all of your players are working hard at developing all of their skills.

Flexibility

Every system has its strengths and weaknesses. There is no set system that will work perfectly for your team without adaptations. Analyze the individual abilities of your players and design your system. Allow enough time for the system to succeed, but do not be afraid to make changes if it is not functioning properly. Players are generally more flexible and adaptable than you might first think. Remember also that with change you must expect some initial failures. Do not be discouraged. You and your team will gain a better understanding of how to achieve offense effectiveness as you work through your problems. The enthusiasm shown by your players as you experience success with your system will be worth your efforts.

SUMMARY

A coach should determine which system of play to use by taking into account a number of factors, including the team's passing ability, the setter's ability, and the way the setter penetrates. Each system has many options and variations available, and to select a system, it may help to designate a setter by rotational position. There are both front court setter systems and back court setter systems, and either a front court setter or a back court setter can be chosen to run the offense. A front court setter system is less demanding on the passers and setters, but it places greater demands on the hitters.

A team may utilize any combination of back court and front court setters and hitters. The coach should design the system by analyzing the abilities of the individual players, and then employing the combination that is best for the team.

Offensive systems are named with two numbers. The first number denotes the number of players who are designated hitters, and the second number denotes the number of setters. Basic offensive systems include the 4–2 and the 6–2. The 4–2 is a standard front court setter offensive system that includes the standard 4–2 and the right side 4–2. The 6–2 is a back court setter offensive system. The 5–1 system is a combination of the 4–2 and the 6–2 systems.

The 6–3 system is an offensive variation that can be particularly effective. In this system all six players are hitters, and three players share the back court setting duties. The 3–3 system is another variation similar to the 6–3 system except the setters set from the center front and right front positions.

The coach must make adjustments in the rotation if his or her team is being outscored. If the team is getting blocked, spiker coverage is necessary. A coach may also choose to switch blocking assignments, substitute for a weak blocker, alter the set selection, or match up players differently in the following game.

9

OFFENSIVE COMBINATIONS

Doug Beal

In 1965, most U.S. volleyball teams ran the 4–2 attack (four spikers, two setters). One setter and two spikers were at the net at all times, and most sets were high and wide. The most frequent variation was a quick set to the side or the middle. An attempt in 1966 to standardize the names of various sets yielded the following terminology (Figure 9.1):

- the four (or shoot) — a low set to the sideline
- the three — a medium set about halfway between the spiker and the setter
- the two — a set about two feet above net height right next to the setter
- the one (or quick, popularized by the Japanese) — a ball set right next to the setter so that the spiker can attack it on the way up rather than on the way down
- the zero (or regular) — the usual high, wide set.

Still in use today, this system has been complicated in two ways:

1. Some teams have redefined one or two signals — a three might be a quick ten feet away from the setter, or a five could be a soft lob back to the weak side.
2. Many more types of sets have been defined.

This chapter traces the evolution of the terminology associated with offensive systems as a way of introducing the offensive systems themselves. Then it explains in detail the general concepts, fundamental approaches, and offensive series used by the USA National Teams in order to show you in detail one fully developed approach to offensive combinations.

Today a three-spiker attack is popular — anyone at the net may attack the ball, and the setters are the people in the back court. This may be called a three-spiker attack, a multiple offense, or a 6–2. With so many combinations of setters, sets, and attackers, a more sophisticated system of naming sets became necessary. The attack positions along the net and the height of the set needed to be included. Several systems were tried, and in 1972 the Kenneth Allen team from Chicago (coached by Jim Coleman) worked out a variation of an earlier system of Val Keller's that worked in the following way (Figure 9.2):

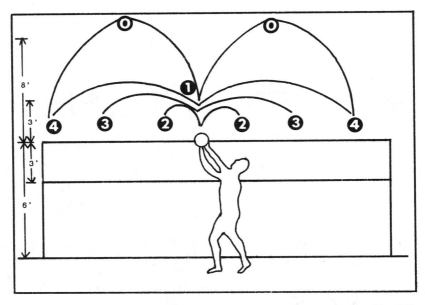

Fig. 9.1

ZONES OF THE NET AREA
(SETTING ZONES)

THE NET IS DIVIDED INTO A SYMMETRICAL SYSTEM OF ZONES
PASSING TARGET IS ZONE NO. 7

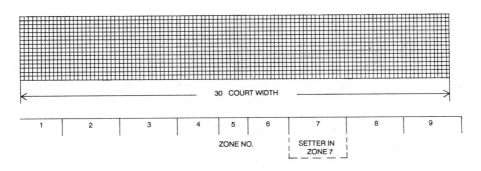

IN THIS SYSTEM THE HEIGHT OF THE SET IS DESIGNATED BY THE SECOND DIGIT; THE ZONE THAT
THE SET IS IN BY THE FIRST DIGIT.

Fig. 9.2

- The first of the two digits that name the set designates the attack position along the net, and the second the height of the set above the net.
- There are nine attack zones symmetrically distributed across the net, with zones one and nine extending outside the court.
- Sets are made to attack zones of designated width, and if the set is within the zone, it's acceptable.
- Regular sets are assumed to be higher than 2.4 m (8 ft.) above the net and are designated by a zero as the second digit.
- Special sets vary up to 2.4 m (8 ft.) above the net, and super-high sets are 4.6 to 6.1 m (15 to 20 ft.) above the net.

Thus a 52 is 61 cm (2 ft.) above the net and hittable in the center of the court (the 5 zone). A 30 is a regular height set (2.4 to 3 m or 8 to 10 ft.) hittable between 2.1 and 3.4 m (7 and 11 ft.) from the left sideline (the 3 zone). An 89 is a super-high set about 1.5 m from the right sideline (the 8 zone). The 9 designates super-high (4.6 to 6.1 m or 15 to 20 ft.). Thus, with the exception of zero, the lower the second digit, the lower and faster the set is.

As 1984 Olympic Gold Medal Coach, I modified the nine-zone system (Figure 9.3) by naming nine symmetrical positions with numbers 1 and 9 not outside the antennae (thus 6 becomes the most common position for the setter/target). Each slot is a meter wide. For the first time, attack corridors were designated (A, B, C, and D) for back row attackers. This is now the generally accepted method of terminology for U.S. offensive systems. It will be used throughout this chapter to explain offensive combinations.

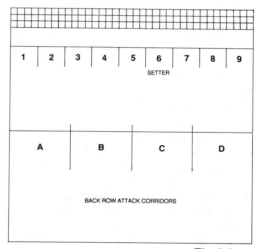

Fig. 9.3

GENERAL CONCEPTS

The idea behind the offense of the U.S. National Teams is to force the blockers to pinch in because of our attackers' inside moves. Then we can get the ball to the outside of the outside blockers, forcing them to reach away from the court to block the ball. We want to give our attack a cumulative effect by always initiating our offensive patterns the same way. Each attack approach requires very specific footwork and attack angle, but individual differences are allowable if the desired effect is obtained. All attackers run their patterns all of the time; continuous movement in the play set roles is essential to developing the cumulative effect we want.

The setter jump sets whenever possible; the offense and the passing are designed for jump sets. The setter's responsibility is to establish the same correct position every time. It is the attacker's responsibility to establish the correct position and timing relationship with the setter.

If possible, we threaten with all five attackers. Players must understand and be able to effectively execute both individual and team offensive tactics. We concentrate our attack on the deep corners off the quick sets and off many play set combinations.

We use specific one- or two-word communication. If this system is insufficient, we verbally call the play or set and rely on beating the defense with execution. The setter can audibly call off any play that is not developing properly; attackers then go to the next highest option. This strategy generally keeps the player in the same slot but raises the set or slows the play down. Some situations will signal automatic pattern adjustments. For example, when any pass crosses the midline to the left, the play set hitter options to a 94 (called by the setter or the hitter).

FUNDAMENTAL APPROACHES

This discussion assumes right-handed players; for a left-hander, reverse left and right side attack positions. (A left-handed middle attacker requires further modifications in the system.) All approaches off of service reception are basic four-step approaches (RL, RL) except that of the middle hitter, which will most often be three-step (LRL), and sometimes two-step (RL). The approach angles are straight lines as detailed in Figure 9.4.

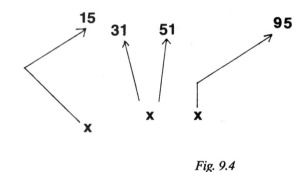

Fig. 9.4

The Left Side (Number 4 Attacker) Approach

Hitting high outside, the left front player in position 4 moves to about a 45 degree angle to the net and takes a full accelerating four-step approach (Figure 9.5). Hitting the 13 or 14, the left front moves more up to the line with a quicker, abbreviated approach. The player must start nearer the 10-foot line. The timing on the 13 has the setter touching the ball as the number 4 attacker is going into the last two (RL) steps of the approach.

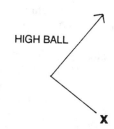

HIGH BALL

X

The Middle Attacker Approach

The middle attacker may line up in a variety of receive positions. But the approach and the result will always be the same. The keys to a successful middle attack are:

Fig. 9.5

- the hitter's ability to establish a consistent position and timing relationship with the setter.
- the hitter's being able to see the setter, blockers, and opponents' court.
- the hitter's being in an attack-available position every time.
- the hitter's developing range out of the middle.

The attacker never goes past the imaginary line created by the setter's feet and the net (Figure 9.6). The takeoff point is actually 50 cm (1 ft. 8 ins.) behind the line, and the ball is contacted at the line. The line for the 31 runs from the setter's left foot to the 3 slot.

Three steps (LRL) or two (RL) may be used. The two-step approach is usually used in fast transition. The second and third steps are often not as long and low as the basic approach, simply because there is not as much time, especially in transition. There is little opportunity for a strong heel-toe action, especially with the left foot (a third step). The feet hit almost flat footed. The arm swings (back and front)

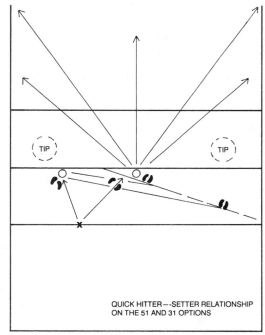

TIP

TIP

QUICK HITTER—-SETTER RELATIONSHIP ON THE 51 AND 31 OPTIONS

Fig. 9.6

are also abbreviated. A very upright swing, with little backswing, is preferred. Quickness of attack and range of attack are most critical.

The quick hitter must get the hitting arm up as quickly as possible to provide a target for the setter. The shoulders are at a 45 degree angle to the net, parallel with the imaginary line developed by the setter's feet. The ball is hit with a quick, short, upright arm swing, since the big windup is not possible or particularly desirable. Also, the attack is mostly based on wrist action, with little time for shoulder rotation. The setter, in certain situations, may lead back to the hitter's left shoulder to force a rotation to get by an over-playing block.

The approach begins essentially from the same spot on the left edge of slot 4 at the 10-foot line. If the serve goes over the hitter's left shoulder, the hitter pivots facing the ball, uses the left foot to plant back towards the receiver, uses a rocker step, and quickly goes left-right-left. If the ball goes over the hitter's right shoulder, the hitter pivots facing the ball, rocker steps off the right foot, and goes left-right-left. The middle attacker is able to go to the 31 or 51 from the same spot (Figures 9.7, 9.8, and 9.9).

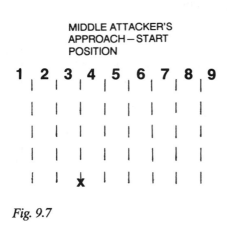

MIDDLE ATTACKER'S
APPROACH – START
POSITION

Fig. 9.7

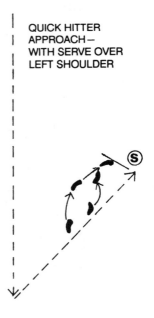

QUICK HITTER
APPROACH –
WITH SERVE OVER
LEFT SHOULDER

Fig. 9.8

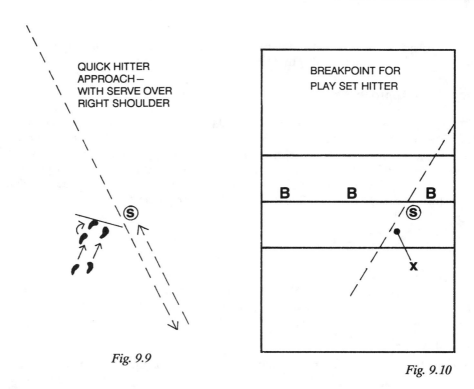

Fig. 9.9

Fig. 9.10

The Play Set Hitter (Position Number 2)

The play set hitter (number 2 position) initiates the break approximately 2.4 m (8 ft.) from a point on the net where the setter is in a direct line between the hitter and the opposing left side blocker (Figure 9.10). The play set hitter approaches each set on a straight line after either an appropriate fake or the break.

In terms of timing, the play set hitter makes a break just as the middle hitter is lifting off and the setter is contacting the ball. The left (or second) step of the four-step approach is planted approximately 2.4 m (8 ft.) deep, directly behind the setter, as the setter is contacting the ball.

For a wide X (33), the hitter (after the break) takes a long third (right) step, then plants the left foot in a position that puts the shoulders at a 45 degree angle to the net and allows the hitter to long jump to ball contact. For the regular X (43) the move is the same except slightly abbreviated. The tandem is hit in a position behind and between the setter and the middle hitter. The approach is right-left after the break, but shorter than the X plays. The fake X (73) is a pivot off the left foot break, then a right-left short drift to contact behind the setter. The flair-out (93) is the same pivot as the fake X (73) but uses a long right-left move with maximal long jump. The hitter floats to contact, catching up to the outside set. The ball is contacted outside the body line.

The X plays fade off the net so the ball is contacted 50 cm (1 ft. 8 ins.) behind the quick hitter. The flair-out is set parallel to the net or slightly toward the pin.

Deep Hitter Approaches

The back row attacker hits release sets or play sets that are 1.8 to 2.4 m (6 to 8 ft.) high. There is no need for faking in the approach because the front row play action is designed to screen back row movements. The approach is the basic four-step approach. The lift-off should be just behind the attack line, with the left foot the closest. The hitter long jumps to the set. Timing is based on the design of the play and height and depth of the set. The position of this set is approximately 2 m (6 ft. 6 ins.) back from the net.

OFFENSIVE SIGNALS

Offensive signals can be given three ways:
1. Each spiker audibly or visibly calls each specific set.
2. The coach predetermines a specific play to match each defense the opponent shows.
3. The setter calls the team patterns.

Generally, I believe the setter should determine the team patterns (much as a carefully trained quarterback calls his own plays). While it is probably a good idea to allow communication between the spiker and the setter (a modification of number 1), ultimately the setter should be able to determine specific weaknesses in the opposition, react to the situation, and call for an offensive pattern that takes advantage of the current offensive strengths and defensive weaknesses.

Just as a baseball, basketball, or football team has certain set patterns called by predetermined signals, so your volleyball team needs a series of patterns with specific signals. While the specific terminology of the nine-zone system described earlier in this chapter is useful during technical discussions (practices, time-outs), during competition you need a system that is more conducive to visible and audible communication. With one simple signal, the setter needs to be able to tell each of the three spikers his or her specific job on the current play. Thus, for example, Option 1 (signalled by using only the index finger) tells the left spiker to be ready for a regular (10), the center front spiker to hit a quick (71), and the right front to hit a back lob (93). By seeing that signal and recognizing that play, each spiker also knows his or her role in the overall team pattern.

Thus, there are three elements to the way an offensive combination is signalled:
1. A quick signal (hand or verbal) for quick communication during competition.
2. A two-digit number (or even number and letter) designation for accurate description and discussion.
3. The name of the team pattern or play

Thus, on the team level one play may be known as *insides* (or *left inside, right inside*); its sets may be designated as LF–52, MF–31, and RF–90 (92); and its signals may be thumbs up (left) or thumbs down (right). This may perhaps seem unwieldy, but in practice it works quite well. Tables 1 and 2 at the end of this chapter list the signals and sets used by the USA National Team. Each coach and team will, of course, have their own different signals and sets.

OFFENSIVE SERIES AND RATIONALES

A play series consists of a group of plays designed to create specific effects on an element of the opponent's defense. The following discussion includes descriptions of six offensive play series, with illustrations and the rationale for each. (The parts of each series are listed in Table 3 at the end of this chapter.) Until they pass a test on the pattern presently being worked on, your team should not attempt another progression. Beginning with a pass, the team should successfully execute the pattern in eighty out of one hundred attempts.

The 51 and 31 Series

The goal of the 51 and 31 series is to freeze the middle blocker and force the opponent's left side or number 4 blocker to reach outside the court. The timing is designed to create seams in the block and a piston effect on the opponent's block. Used effectively, with good serve-receive and continual quick-hitter pressure, the combinations within these series can create uncontrolled movement on the block and shake the block timing. Table 3 and Figures 9.11 and 9.12 give more details on this series.

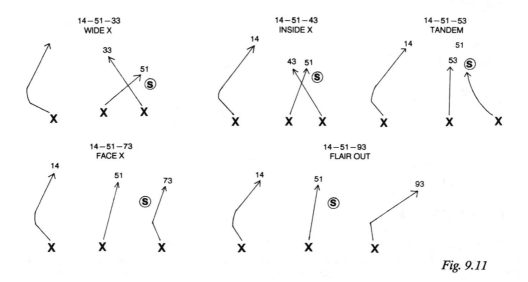

Fig. 9.11

151

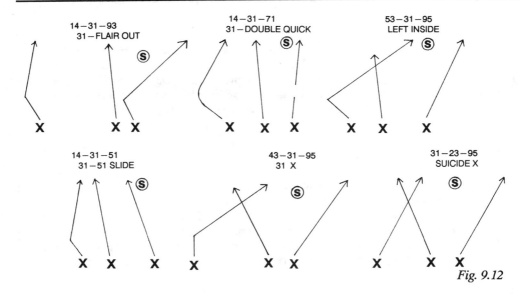

Fig. 9.12

The Reverse Series

The reverse series forces the opponents' block to their left, opening up our left side. This series can be thrown in between the 51 or 31 series after the opponent has made adjustments to the 51 or 31. Also, this series permits the team to change assignments for the hitters, allowing the flexibility either to change tempo or to put a particular hitter on a specific blocker (Figure 9.13).

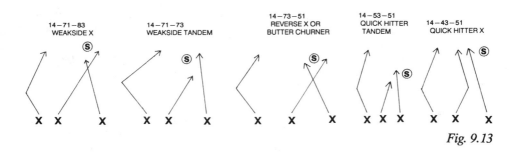

Fig. 9.13

The Isolation Series

The isolation series is used only occasionally and with discretion. It has three purposes: to change tempo, to isolate and nail one blocker, and in critical point-making situations after the opponent has made a long, methodical comeback and/or after there have been many side-outs (Figure 9.14).

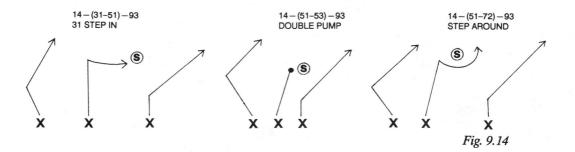

14 – (31–51) – 93
31 STEP IN

14 – (51–53) – 93
DOUBLE PUMP

14 – (51–72) – 93
STEP AROUND

Fig. 9.14

The Deep Hitting Series

The deep hitting series is used to maximize all the team's fire power, to change the angle and timing in the opponent's defense, and to add an option if the team is in a front row setter system (Figure 9.15).

The Spread Series

Once the other series have pinched the blockers inside, then the offense must get the ball to the outside of the blockers with low trajectory sets out to the pins. Blocking is most difficult when the blockers are forced to reach outside the court to block (Figure 9.16).

Innovations and Specific Sets

Four variations on the series described above are:
- Controlled deep corner hitting off quick sets and play sets: Most defenses are geared to play defense close in against the quick and play set attack. The corners are usually wide open.
- The fading X set (1 to 1.5 m or 3 ft. 3 ins. to 4 ft. 11 ins. off the net): The offense must add as many problems or variables to the opponents' blockers as possible. Timing a deeper set after gearing up for a tight set is difficult.
- Deep attack play sets: The use of the back row attackers has traditionally been with high release sets. The intention is to put maximum pressure on planning and timing the block by using long back row sets.
- The wide series: The offense gets the ball to the outside very rapidly, and then, slightly slower, to the middle as our safety valve.

SUMMARY

The names of various sets were standardized in 1966, but since then some of the sets have been redefined and new sets have been added. In 1972, a variation of the earlier stand-

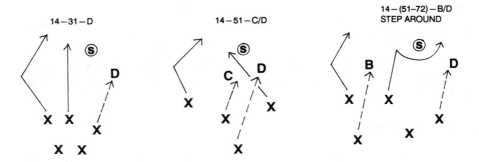

Fig. 9.15

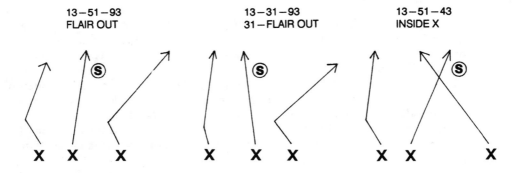

Fig. 9.16

ardization was composed. Each set is named with a two-digit number; the first number designates the attack position, and the second number designates the height of the set.

All approaches off of service reception are basic four-step approaches, and the middle hitter's approach is three-step or two-step. The various approaches include the left side approach, the middle attacker approach, the play set hitter approach, and the deep hitter approach.

Offensive signals can be given three ways: the spiker can call each set, the coach can predetermine the play, or the setter can call the team patterns. The best way may be for the setter to determine the team patterns, because he or she may be best able to choose the offensive pattern that takes advantage of the current offensive and defensive situation.

The team should have a series of patterns with specific signals, and the setter must be able to signal these visibly or audibly. There are three ways an offensive combination can be signalled: a hand or verbal signal during competition, a two-digit number, or the name of the team pattern or play.

A play series is a group of plays designed to create specific effects on an element of the opponent's defense. The team should be able to execute the pattern successfully 80 percent of the time. Six offensive play series are: the 51 and 31 series, the reverse series, the isolation series, the deep hitting series, and the spread series. Four variations on the series are: controlled deep corner hitting off quick sets and play sets, the fading X set, deep attack play sets, and the wide series.

Note: The first three paragraphs of this chapter are an adaptation of material first presented in "Recent Changes in the designation of Offensive Systems in Men's Volleyball" by Jim Coleman, in *International Volleyball Review*, Vol. XXIX (Jan.–Feb. 1973).

SET TERMINOLOGY		
HAND SIGNAL	**SET**	**DESCRIPTION/ZONE WHERE HIT**
Index finger	one set	Hitter is at peak of jump when the setter contacts the ball — the zone in relation to setter, 5–8.
	one and 1/2	Hitter takes off when the setter contacts the ball — the zone in relation to the setter, 5–8.
Index & middle fingers	two	Hitter is on the first step of a three-step approach when the setter contacts the ball — zone 5 & 6 — center of the net.
Wave of back of hand away from body.	31	Hitter takes off when the setter contacts the ball — zone 3.
Wave of back of hand with flash of two fingers.	32	Hitter on first step of three-step approach when the setter contacts the ball — zone 3.
Four fingers pointing down	Four (fast) 12	Hitter on first step of three-step approach when the setter contacts the ball — zone 1 (12).
Five fingers pointing down.	Five (fast) 92	Hitter on first step of three-step approach when the setter contacts the ball — zone 9 (92).
OTHER SETS		
Fist	regular	zone 1, 5–6, 9
Four fingers — pointing up	regular — four	zone 1 (14)
Four fingers — pointing down	regular — five	zone 9 (94)
Index & middle finger on fist of other hand.	high two	zone 5–6

On the above four sets, begin approach when the ball is halfway in its flight, at the peak of its arc.
"Once you start your approach, do not stop until you hit the ball." (ARM SWING: FORWARD – BACK – FORWARD)

Circle formed index finger & thumb (OK signal)	pump – one	Fake one set then hit a two (low).

Table 1 Quick communication signals.

PLAYS	**PLAY**	**SETS**	**SIGNAL**
1. Insides	a. Left inside b. Right inside	LF–52 MF–31 RF–90 (92)	Thumbs up Thumbs down
2. X or Fake X	a. X b. Fake X	LF–10 (14 or 12) MF–61 RF–52 LF–10 (14 or 12) MF–61 RF–82	Cross fingers Index & middle Wave of cards Index & middle fingers
3. Outsides	a. b.	LF–14 (10) MF–31 RF–82 (71–back) LF–14 (10) MF–31 RF–95 (92)	Pinky out Index finger & pinky out
4. Combine out- sides & insides	a. b.	LF–52 MF–31 RF–82 (81) LF–52 MF–31 RF–95 (92)	Thumb up & pinky out Thumb up, pinky & index out
5. Green/yellow back court switch (back court fakes)	Yellow Green	MF–90 LF–14 (12) RB–Fake 61 RF–82 (81) MF–10 LF–32 LB–Fake 61 RF–92	
6. Trick plays — back court fakes, pump ones			
7. Blocking serve plays			
8. Setter tipping (as back court player)			
9. 5–1 disguised as 6–2; setter tips or hits front court.			

Table 2 Team pattern signals.

SERIES	NUMBERED SETS	PLAY NUMBER	NICKNAME	COACH'S SIGNAL
51 SERIES				
Quick hitter has option of hitting 51 or 71 based on position of MB, except on play #4	14–51–33	1	Wide X	
	14–51–43	2	Inside X	
	14–51–53	3	Tandem	
	14–51–73	4	Fake X	
	14–51–93	5	Flair Out	
31 SERIES	14–31–93	1	31–Flair Out	Hook 'em Horns
	14–31–71	2	Double Quick	
	52–31–95	3	Left Inside	
	14–31–51	4	31–51 Slide	
	43–31–95	5	31 X	
	31–23–95	6	Suicide X	
REVERSE SERIES	14–83–71	1	Weakside X	
	14–73–71	2	WeaksideTandem	
	14–73–51	3	Reverse X: Butterchurner	
	14–53–51	4	Quick Hitter Tandem	
	14–43–51	5	Quick Hitter X	
ISOLATION SERIES	14–[31 51]–93	1	31 Step In	
	14–[51 53]–93	2	Double Pump	
	14–[51 72]–93	3	Step Around	
BACK ROW SERIES	14–31–D	1		
(Plays referred to here indicate the setter at the net). These can be run with 3 front row attackers.	14–51 Slide C/D	2		
	14–51 Step Around B/D	3		
	51–33X A/C/D	4		
	51–93 A/B/D	5		
	31–93 A/C/D	6		
SPREAD SERIES	13–51–93	1	Flair Out	
	13–31–93	2	31 Flair Out	
	13–51–93	3	Inside X	

Table 3 Offensive Series

10
SERVICE RECEPTION

Dave Shoji

Volleyball coaches change their serve reception formations for many different reasons. Hiding a weak passer and running a quick attack are two of the reasons we have seen variations of the standard W formation. The most important consideration in deciding what pattern to use for serve reception is your team's ability to cover the court efficiently. The next most important consideration is that the setters be able to get to the desired area quickly enough. If either of these considerations is not met by the service reception being used, the coach's offensive system cannot be implemented at all. Thus, the serve reception being used must satisfy these two requirements.

This chapter describes the basic service reception formation (the W) and its use with the 4–2 system, the 6–2 system (including the cup formation), and a number of special formations based on the 5–1 system.

THE W FORMATION

The W formation is the most versatile, reliable service reception formation for most teams, whether beginner or advanced. The W formation uses five passers to cover the court, regardless of front and back row considerations. The players are positioned as shown in Figure 10.1. Thus, the term W formation is used.

The formation should be placed on the court according to where the server stands. A general rule is that players 1 and 3 should stand on a direct line from the server to the corner of the court (Figure 10.2). Serves that fall in the shaded area are considered low percentage to attempt, so passers are concentrated between the two shaded areas. The rest of the formation requires even spacing between all players.

161

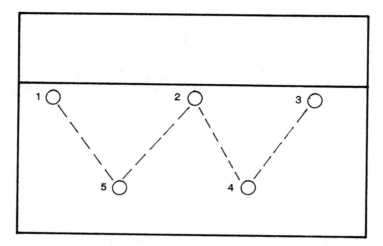

Fig. 10.1

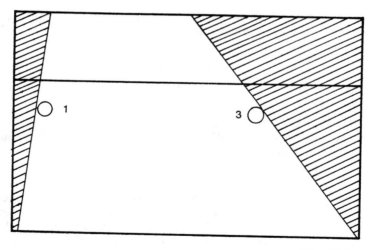

Fig . 10.2

The passing responsibilities in the W formation are shown in Figures 10.3, 10.4, 10.5, 10.6, and 10.7. Note that players 4 and 5 have much more area to cover than do players 1, 2, or 3. These players must be aware of this fact and be ready to cover this wide area.

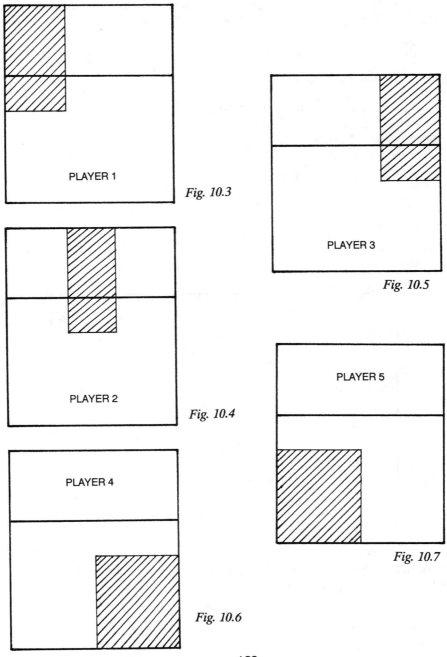

PLAYER 1

Fig. 10.3

PLAYER 3

Fig. 10.5

PLAYER 2

Fig. 10.4

PLAYER 5

Fig. 10.7

PLAYER 4

Fig. 10.6

The 4-2 System

The W formation can be utilized with a 4–2, 5–1, or 6–2 offensive system. In the 4–2 system, the setter may be placed at the net and the two remaining front court players lined up in positions 1, 2, or 3 (Figure 10.1). More specifically, when the setter is in the left front position, the hitters may be placed in the spread formation (Figure 10.8).

KEY TO DIAGRAMS 10.8–10.32

→ = DIRECTION OF PLAYER AFTER BALL IS SERVED.
LF = LEFT FRONT BLOCKER
MF = MIDDLE FRONT BLOCKER
RF = RIGHT FRONT BLOCKER
MB = MIDDLE BACK
LB   = LEFT BACK
RB   = RIGHT BACK
△ = BACK ROW PLAYER
○ = FRONT ROW PLAYER

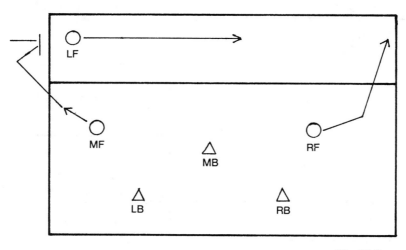

Fig. 10.8

The hitters may also be lined up in a shift formation, with spikers hitting the left front and the middle front as shown in Figure 10.9.

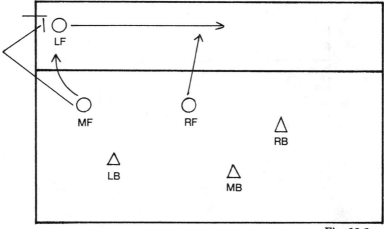

Fig. 10.9

A third option would be for the spikers to be shifted on the right side of the court, hitting from the middle front and the right front positions (Figure 10.10).

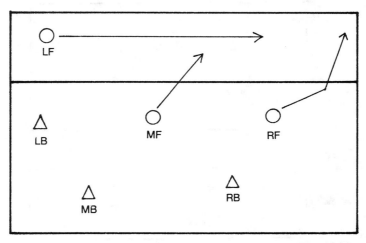

Fig. 10.10

When the setter is in the middle front, the same three options are available. The spikers are at the left and right front positions. (Figures 10.11, 10.12, and 10.13).

When the setter is in the right front, the same three options are available. The spikers then are at the left front and the middle front positions (Figures 10.14, 10.15, and 10.16).

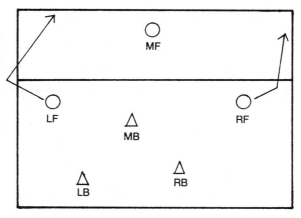

Fig. 10.11

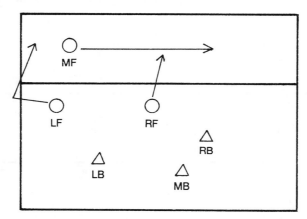

Fig. 10.12

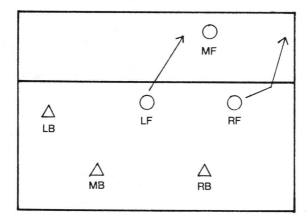

Fig. 10.13

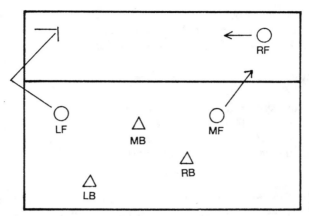

Fig. 10.14

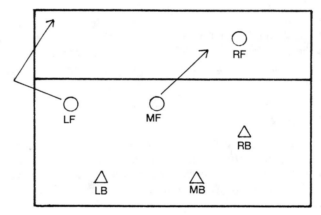

Fig. 10.15

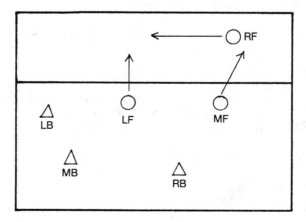

Fig. 10.16

The position of the setter before the ball is served may be varied to try to deceive the opposing team. The setter may appear to be a back row player, so that your team seems to have three attackers. Figures 10.17, 10.18, and 10.19 provide three examples of this.

The 6–2 System

In the 6–2 offensive system, a back row setter with three attackers is utilized, and the alignment is basically the same. The setter starts behind a front row player and moves to the net after the ball is served. The ideal position for the setter is between 2.4 and 3.7 m (8 and 12 ft.) from the right sideline. This position allows the setter to face the left and middle attackers (Figure 10.20).

When the setter is in the right back, he or she stands to the right and behind the right front player. When the ball is served, the setter runs to the designated (shaded) area (Figure 10.21). When the setter is in the middle back, he or she lines up on the right behind the middle front player (Figure 10.22).

A setter who is in the left back may line up two different ways. In Figure 10.23, the setter lines up to the left and behind the left front player. In Figure 10.24, the setter lines up to the right and behind the left front player. The setter cuts diagonally across the court to the desired area. In either case, this is the most difficult position from which the setter must reach the right front area.

The Cup Formation

The four-player or cup formation is also used with the 6-2 offensive system. The main reason for using the cup formation is that your middle (quick) hitter does not pass, which enables the hitter to hit a quick set easier. The middle front area is covered by the left and right front players. The back row players have the same responsibilities as they do in the W formation (Figure 10.25).

Left Front Responsibility/Right Front Responsibility

When the setter is in the right back, the quick hitter is at the net. After the ball is served, the quick hitter comes back off the net to approach for the quick hit as the setter runs to the right front area (Figure 10.26).

If your quick hitter is in the right front in this rotation, bring the right front player to the net with the setter and place the middle front player to the right side of the court. This allows the quick hitter to get to the middle of the court faster (Figure 10.27).

When the setter is in the middle back, both the setter and the middle front player come to the net. After the ball is served, the setter backs into position and the quick hitter gets off the net for the approach (Figure 10.28).

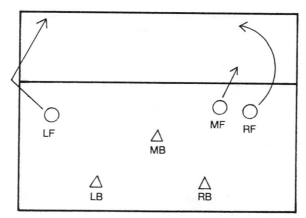

Fig. 10.17

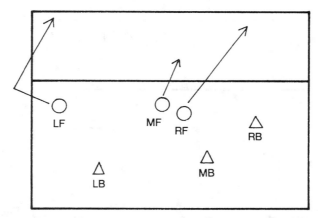

Fig. 10.18

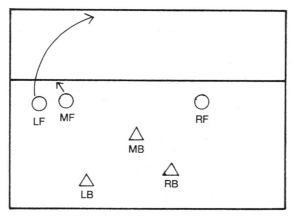

Fig. 10.19

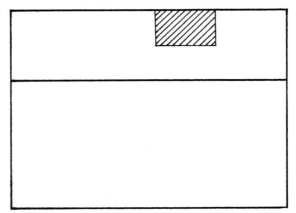

Fig. 10.20

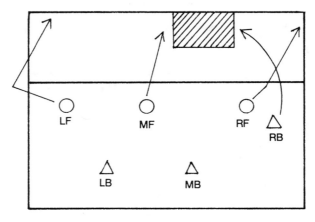

Fig. 10.21

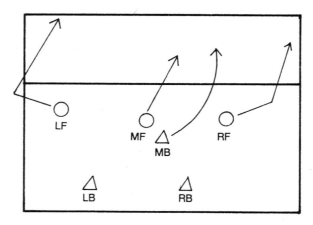

Fig. 10.22

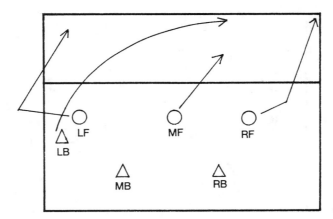

Fig. 10.23

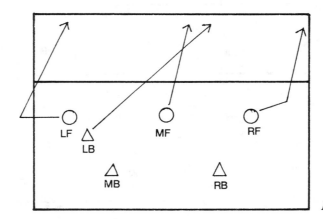

Fig. 10.24

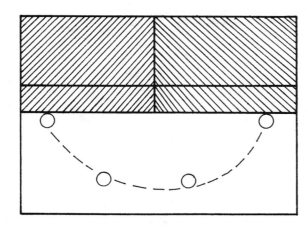

LEFT FRONT
RESPONSIBILITY

RIGHT FRONT
RESPONSIBILITY

Fig. 10.25

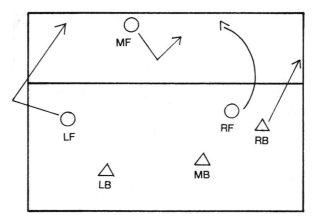

Fig. 10.26

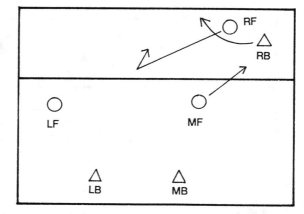

Fig. 10.27

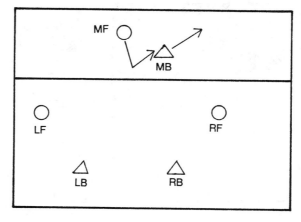

Fig. 10.28

Two other options may be used when the setter is in the middle back. Both options force the setter to stand in the middle of the court as if passing. Once the ball is in play, however, the setter must quickly run to the setting position. In Figure 10.29, the quick hitter is in the left front and the middle front hits outside on the left. In Figure 10.30, the quick hitter is in the right front and the middle front hits outside on the right.

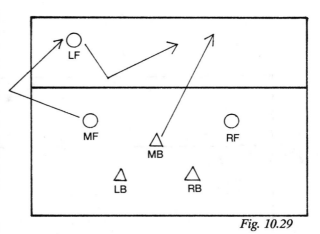

Fig. 10.29

When the setter is in the left back, he or she comes to the net with the left front player, but stands behind that player. The setter may move to the right so as to line up just to the left of the middle back. This allows the setter to be closer to the right front area. There are two options from this formation. Either the left front or the middle front player may hit the quick set, with the other hitting outside on the left. Figure 10.31 illustrates Option 1, and Figure 10.32 illustrates Option 2.

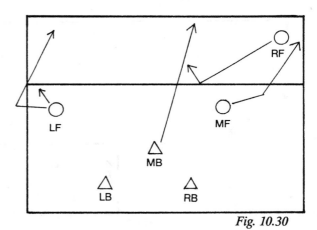

Fig. 10.30

Special Formations — The 5–1 System

Some teams on the international level have designed special formations to take advantage of great passers and/or hide weak passers. These patterns vary widely, and coaches should be very careful when utilizing these unorthodox methods. Other factors are often involved in formulating these service reception patterns, such as the role of back row attackers in a particular offense. Figures 10.33, 10.34, 10.35, 10.36, 10.37, and 10.38 show six formations that utilize a 5-1 offensive system with the same two players doing all the passing. Needless to say, these two players must be exceptionally quick and must also have great passing skills.

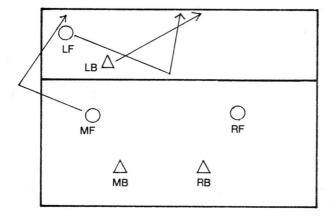

Fig. 10.31

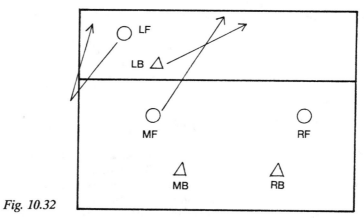

Fig. 10.32

KEY TO DIAGRAMS 10.33–10.44

● = SETTER
□ = MIDDLE BLOCKERS
△ = PLAYER OPPOSITE SETTER
○ = LEFT SIDE ATTACKERS

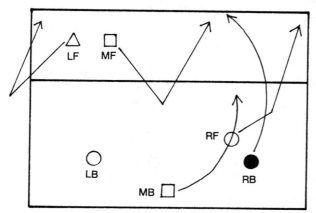

Fig. 10.33

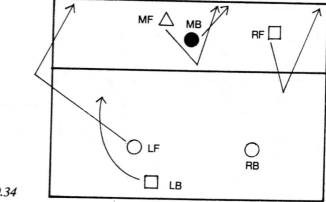

Fig. 10.34

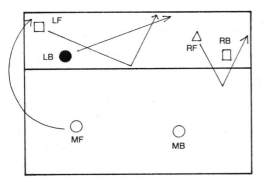

Fig. 10.35

Fig. 10.36

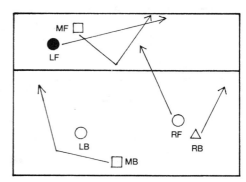

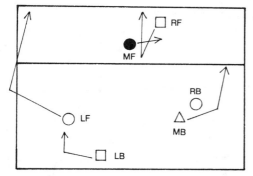

Fig. 10.37

Fig. 10.38

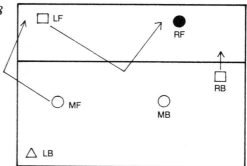

In the formation shown in Figure 10.33, LB and RF pass the entire court. MB moves to the right to hit a back row set. In the formation shown in Figure 10.34, LF and RB again pass the entire court.

In the next rotation, the same two passers are now in middle front and back as seen in Figure 10.35. Then RB moves to the right to hit the back row set, which is the third option, and RF may hit the play set or swing to the left (Figure 10.36).

In Figure 10.37, LB does not pass. MB swings to the right to hit the back row set. In Figure 10.38, RB may hit the back row set.

A team that wants to utilize three passers may line up in the manner shown in Figures 10.39, 10.40, 10.41, 10.42, 10.43, and 10.44. In this three-pass system, the middle blockers do not pass at all. The player opposite the setter and the outside attackers pass the entire court.

In the previous two systems (two-player and three-player receive formations), there is always a front court player involved in the passing. When this front court player moves deep to pass a serve, this player may not be able to be involved in the offense. Therefore, the team must have other hitting options. Usually teams will involve a back row attack, with the back court middle blocker hitting this set. The middle blocker must maneuver into position when the serve is in the air.

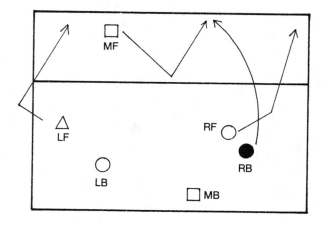

Fig. 10.39

177

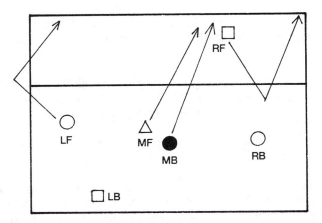

Fig. 10.40

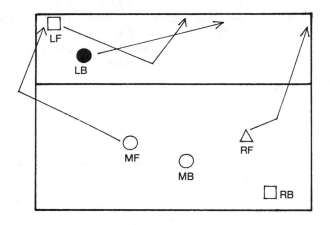

Fig. 10.41

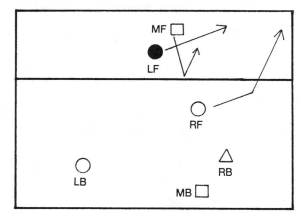

Fig. 10.42

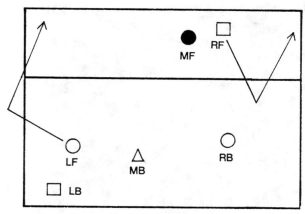

Fig. 10.43

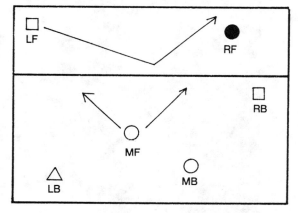

Fig. 10.44

SUMMARY

When trying to decide what pattern to use for serve reception, the most important consideration must be the ability of the team to cover the court efficiently. The second consideration should be whether or not the setter or setters can get to the desired area quickly enough. A coach can implement his or her offensive system when these two considerations have been met.

The basic serve reception formation is the W formation, and it can be used with the 4–2, the 6–2, and the 5–1 offensive systems. Coaches and players should know the positioning options available to them with each system.

11

NET DEFENSE: OPTION BLOCKING

Jim Coleman

The essential parts of this article were first published by the author in May, 1983. Its message is quite simple: "Play the percentages!" Its implications are quite complex: "Think while you are on the court!"

For the team desiring a fixed system for every blocking situation, this article has little to say but "good luck." For the team wishing to optimize the capabilities of its athletes, there is much to be gained for virtually any team at any level.

One of the reasons that the 1984 USA Men's Olympic Team was among the best in the world was that its members very successfully employed a rather complex system of option blocking, yet they were talented enough that standard blocking systems may have worked almost as well. Teams with less talented athletes have more to gain by choosing the correct blocking options.

THE BASIC PREMISE OF BLOCKING

In the 1974 World Championships for Men, I found that blocking was the best predictor of tournament rank. I also found that as a predictor of point spread, blocking was second only to attacking. Because of these statistical findings, it seems apparent that the teams with the best blocking will win the most games, matches, and tournaments.

There is an abundance of literature on blocking techniques. Coaches will launch into long discourses on the various techniques of blocking, but few pay attention to the tactical strategy of blocking. Blocking technique is generally considered to be the most difficult skill to learn, and as a result, many coaches believe that an outstanding blocker will play almost irrespective of other skills.

In recent years, there have been tremendous improvements in offensive strategy, while defensive improvement appears to be either in techniques or in the execution of predetermined patterns. Defensive patterns are routine and have altered little in the past fifteen years. In fact, defensive strategy may even have fallen backward during this era. Today defensive positions are often dictated by offensive considerations, whereas a decade ago defensive patterns were based upon defensive considerations. It is false economy to preempt good defense in the guise of offensive potential. Without defense, offensive considerations are a moot point. Thus, it is not wise to make defensive decisions based upon offensive considerations.

The Role of Probability

All volleyball strategies should be established on a probability basis. That is, all strategies should be designed so as to give the highest probability for total success of the team. Thus, great offensive potential is of little value if there is no defense. Likewise, great defensive potential is of little value if there is no potential for transition to an effective offense.

Interestingly enough, very little is known about the probabilities of success in volleyball. The majority of decisions are made on gut-level feelings rather than on hard data. As a matter of fact, almost no coaches, or even researchers, approach volleyball on a probability basis. The statistical studies reported by my co-workers and me (see bibliography at the end of the chapter) are the only exceptions to this. Yet players and coaches alike copy each other with some intuitive feelings that what is being copied is high probability volleyball.

Parallel Sports

For initial considerations, the basic tactical ideas in similar sports must be studied. Basketball and football are similar enough to volleyball that much can be learned from their strategies.

Zone Versus Man-to-man. In both basketball and football, defense takes one of two general forms: either zone or man-to-man. The same is true in volleyball. There are two implications to the zone/man-to-man idea. The original idea was that if the blocker did not stuff the ball (essentially man-to-man), the block should screen out an area of the court (zone). With predictable zones of the court screened out from hard attacks, the digging zones on the court are diminished in size and the probability of the ball being dug when hit into a digging zone is increased.

Today there is another possibility for the man-to-man defense: a blocker is designated to follow a specific spiker no matter where the attacker may move, making for perhaps a purer form of man-to-man defense. This parallel between sports can continue, for in the man-to-man concept, if my attacker does not get the ball, I then have the opportunity to become an assist blocker to help my teammates.

Mismatching Abilities. Basketball and football strategies call for producing mismatches of ability on offense and for matching abilities on defense. Thus, in basketball, the offensive team continues to run, pass, and screen until a player is entirely free to shoot or until a strong shooter is matched (mismatched) against a weak defender. On defense, strengths are matched against an opponent's offensive strengths and defensive weaknesses are hidden by matching them against an opponent's offensive weaknesses. These same considerations should be made in volleyball. However, volleyball is different from basketball and football in that players must play both net and back court, and the decision time to run a play is limited by the number of hits (three) per side.

In basketball defense, a weak defender is better than no defender; hence even a tiny guard attempts to harass the giant center who is shooting. However, in volleyball this is not a wise option, because a weak blocker tends to be worse than no blocker. A weak blocker often turns the mediocre spiker into an offensive superstar. The weak blocker is not only "used" by the spiker, but also disrupts the digger's ability to play effective defense. A good defensive option, which few coaches choose, is to not block.

Another consideration from football which we may apply is to stack the defense on each play against the most probable offensive option on that play. For instance, if a football team has to defend against third down and fifteen yards to go, the defense will drop off linemen and replace them with pass defenders. If there is a fourth down and six inches, the defense will load with defensive linemen and linebackers.

In volleyball there are not these substitution options, but there are options on the deployment of the defensive players. Each time a team serves, the serving team, now on defense, has the option of blocker deployment. Probability dictates that the best blockers should be deployed against the receiving team's most probable offensive option. If the serving team scores because the attacker is not successful, the probability that the same attacker will get the next set is diminished and blocking may need to be changed. With wise calculation of probabilities and a little luck, weak blockers often will never have to block on an entire trip across the net. At the same time, the defensive team will score points.

Defensive Deployment

Two other strategies can improve the probabilities of strong blockers blocking and weak blockers not blocking. The first is to make a good choice of serving targets. Effective serves to sidelines, or to selected front court receivers, can limit the receiver's offensive options. This strategy may increase the probability of strong blockers blocking and weak blockers avoiding the block. Second, blockers can fake movements to a given position and in this way confuse the opposing setters. Often setters are so engaged in keeping track of weak blockers that they become ineffective setters.

Not only do defensive teams have the option of blocker deployment, but they also may choose various defenses. In a given game or match, a specific defense or defensive modification may be chosen. Sophisticated teams have many options. For instance, a team may choose to vary defenses on each serve and may keep the defense hidden until it is too late for the offense to know what is happening. The USA Men's Team won the 1967 Pan Am Games and defeated the Soviets in the 1968 Olympic Games using a hidden defense system. The center back player kept an intermediate position until the ball was approaching the opponent's setter. At that moment, he moved into the predetermined red (6–up) or white (6–back) defensive position.

Today it is common for a team to run different defenses based upon specific hitters or on specific sides of the court. A team may run a standard defense against a power hitter hitting from the left side of the court, and, at the same time, may run a rotation defense against a different hitter who is hitting from the right side of the court. There are teams which always run standard against left side attacks and a rotation against right side attacks.

A wise coach frequently bases the starting team's rotational position on various offensive and/or defensive match-ups. Often high-jumping, slow blockers do not do well against combination plays, but will stop high regular sets quite well. On the other hand, shorter, quicker blockers do well against combinations, but are helpless against the high regular sets. Creating the appropriate match-ups may increase a team's probability for success.

The Assist Block

Not all blockers have equal blocking abilities, yet weak blockers are repeatedly given assignments which would challenge power blockers. This practice can be avoided. Many times weak blockers are assigned to block next to more skillful blockers. When this situation occurs, the good blocker should be given the freedom to position the block and to block in a one-on-one manner, with the weaker blocker assuming the role of the assist blocker.

The assist blocker performs two functions. First, the assist blocker fills the hole next to the principle blocker. This prevents the low, off-the-arm shots which sometimes plague good blockers. Second, the assist blocker soft blocks, which has two effects: 1) it forces the spiker to hit higher, and 2) it makes the ball easier to dig. By concentrating on soft blocking rather than on blocking kills, a player who is a weak principal blocker can avoid blocking errors and become a contributing assist blocker.

THE BOLD STRATEGY OF OPTION BLOCKING

The idea behind option blocking is that in order to gain defensive probabilities, the blockers will commit to, or overload on, a play, a player, or a position.

There are four separate but not completely independent components of option blocking. These are: 1) read versus committed blocking, 2) positional commitment, 3) positional overload, and 4) stack blocking.

Read Versus Committed Blocking

The quick middle sets (sets 51, 61, and 71) were conceived with several goals in mind. The first, obviously, was that they could score points. The second was that, since the spiker jumped before the ball was set, the blocker would also have to jump early (committed block) in order to stop the attack. If the blocker committed before the ball was set, the blocker, with feet in air, would have a difficult time moving to block balls set quickly to the outside. The immobilization of the center blocker is quite an effective technique against most teams. The third goal was to give the center blocker as many choices as possible, because the more choices the center blocker has to process, the slower is his or her reaction to the specific set being made.

Today bigger and smarter center blockers are taking another option to stop the middle and to be effective on other sets. They are not jumping with the quick attacker. Instead they are waiting for the ball to be set and attempting to read the setter-hitter combination. They are often conceding the high, quick, middle attacks, and are tiptoe blocking the more common lower, slower, or mis-timed plays. They are then free to move to combination plays or outside sets. Center blockers who are tall and have good perception of the entire offensive system of their opponents are doing very well with the read blocking maneuver.

Positional Commitment

In this form of option blocking, the blocking team commits a player to a specific potential quick set. The option blocking tactics used by the USA Men's Team in 1979 and 1980 were as follows: option four blocking, option three blocking, and option two blocking.

Option Four Blocking. The defensive left front blocker, position 4, is committed to jump with — to block — the opponent's quick middle attack (71 set). The reason for using this tactic is to defend against a probable X or crossing pattern. With the middle hitter stopped by the outside blocker, the middle blocker can concentrate on stopping the opponent's second attacker coming into the middle on the crossing pattern. If the play is run into offensive zones 8 or 9 (to the left of the committed blocker), the offense has won the tactical battle. At this point, the defense has two weak hopes. The committed blocker may be able to recover enough to make a blocking attempt. The best chance for the defense is for the zone 5 digger (down the line) to be prepared to dig the unblocked shot. For this reason, it is important that the diggers be knowledgeable about the blocking options being employed. If the zone 5 digger knows that unblocked digging is the first responsibility, the digger will have a chance to be successful. If there is no knowledge of the probability of this unblocked attack, the probability of digging success is quite low. In the commonly used defenses today, too often the outside blocker gets caught guessing on the inside block and the zone 5 digger is caught unaware of this extra responsibility. Thus, while processing other less likely possible shots, the zone 5 digger misses the major, unblocked one.

Option Three Blocking. The center blocker, position 3, is committed to jump with — to block — the offensive quick hit (sets 31 to 71). For many years, this has been the standard defense to stop middle attacks. The primary blocking will be one-on-one, and the defense will be vulnerable to crossing patterns. In order to defend against the crossing patterns, the outside blockers may pinch toward the center blocker. With this strategy, the threat of the crossing play has virtually assured offensive success to relatively quick outside sets (14s and 94s). This success has been made even more probable by the choice of outside blockers. Usually the bigger, better blockers are in the middle, committed to the "one" sets which take little mobility to stop, and the smaller and/or less mobile blockers on the outside are responsible for the quick, mobile actions which they are incapable of stopping.

Option Two Blocking. In option two blocking, the front right blocker (position 2) is committed to jump with — to block — the offense 31 set (many teams call the 31 a 3 set, a quick set about 3 m or 10 ft. from the left offensive sideline). The reason for using this defense is to stop a probable 31 set, to defend a left side X-play, or to defend the left inside plays. This option leaves the defensive right side (position 2) vulnerable to quick outside attacks (14 sets). Considerations here are similar to those discussed in the section on option four blocking.

Positional Overload. Positional overload deserves the greatest amount of consideration, for it is the boldest of the option blocking tactics, and it holds the most practical application for a team that is mismatched on defense. It is also the most easily applied by a less experienced team. Two concepts are important in positional overload:
1. Overload the blockers on the best or most probable hitter.
2. Invite the opponents' weak hitter to be set.

To approach this concept, consider the case in which one very weak blocker is at the net along with two relatively strong blockers, and they are facing an opponent who has three respectable hitters. Some coaches would choose to have all three blockers in blocking roles, but there is another alternative, and that is to use only the two good blockers and allow the other player to dig. If this third player cannot block, it is hoped that he or she is a good digger. Assign one blocker, commonly the blocker second in ability, to go man-on-man with the opposition's best outside hitter on the net. Have the other blocker assigned to block both other hitters, but cheating toward the better one (Figure 11.1).

With this blocking alignment, the weak blocker is now a digger, which is that player's preferred position. Now there is one certain blocker on the best hitter, and occasionally there will be two blockers on that hitter's high sets. There will always be a blocker on the number 2 hitter, and there will usually be a blocker on the number 3 hitter. Of course, the defense invites the setter to set the number 3 hitter, hence, a defensive victory. It is often found that the number 1 blocker is perceptive enough to pick up crossing patterns of the number 2 and

3 hitters. Many times the best blocker will have a greater probability of stopping the crossing patterns alone than two blockers would if one of those blockers is very weak.

The essence of positional overload is to continue this manner of thinking to cover the situations in which blocking assignments different from the routine ones should be considered. In the most common of these, two blockers are used to stop the more routine, but more devastating, power hitters, while one blocker defends against two less powerful hitters. The defensive alignment might be the one shown in Figure 11.2.

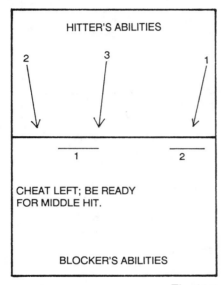

Fig. 11.1   Fig. 11.2

Defensive position 2 has been overloaded to stop the most probable hit. The weaker hitters are invited to attack the ball, while the most perceptive blocker is allowed to do what he or she does best, and that is to move to block the ball unhampered by surrounding blockers. It is strongly recommended that this option be considered any time the offensive team passes poorly. It is also probable that there are times when the blockers wish to disguise this overload until the offensive setter sets the ball.

The deployment of blockers will depend upon the individual blocking skills and the relative skill levels of the offensive players. If the number 1 hitter is so dominant as to get "all" the sets, then the defensive number one blocker should probably go with that hitter. When the number 3 blocker is not a strong principal blocker, the number 2 and 3 blockers should shift positions. In this situation, the number 2 blocker should be allowed to go one-on-one against the strong hitter, with the weaker blocker blocking in the middle, using an assist block to stop lower, cross-court shots (Figure 11.3). Similar strategies may be worked out with the best offensive hitters in other attacking positions.

Overload blocking should be considered if the offense is using a front court setter. Too many teams deploy weak blocking tactics only for the resulting offensive simplicity (Figure 11.4). Offensive transitions do not occur if the ball cannot be dug—this system invites defensive disasters.

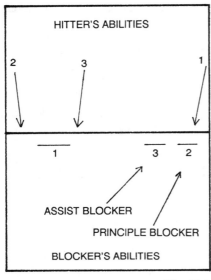

Fig. 11.3

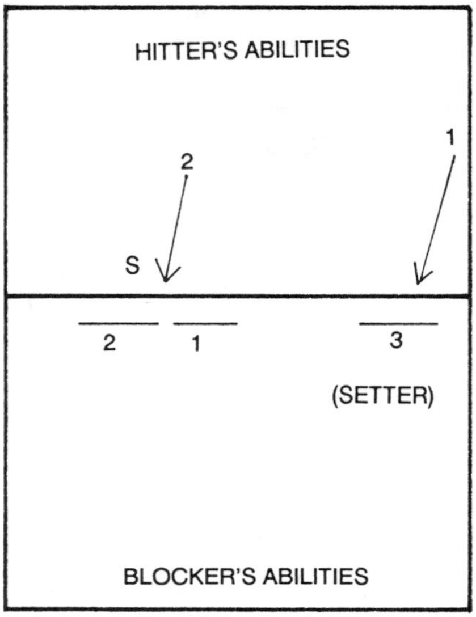

HITTER'S ABILITIES

2   1

S

2   1   3

(SETTER)

BLOCKER'S ABILITIES

Fig. 11.4

In this common defensive strategy, the best two blockers are enamored with the offensive number 2 hitter faking in the middle. Meanwhile, the offensive power hitter is having a field day against the setter, who is a weak blocker. The defensive considerations should be as shown in Figures 11.5, 11.6, or 11.7.

With the appropriate choice of these alignments, the offensive "outside cannon" will not have a free shot at killing the ball. But there will be some defensive challenge to this powerful hitting. With the deployment of the number 3 blocker (setter) either on the outside or in the middle, there are two advantages:

1. The offensive transition, which has a higher probability of happening now, can still take place.
2. If number 3 should be an assist blocker, the assist blocker may be better in the middle (Figures 11.5 and 11.7), for balls hit over number 3 will be more easily dug. If number 3 is on the outside, the probability of the weak blocker being "used" or "tooled" is great.

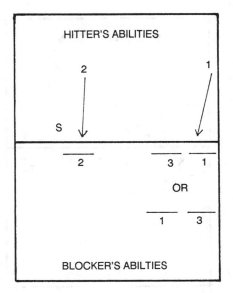

Fig. 11.5

KEY TO DIAGRAMS 11.6 & 11.7

N   = NORMAL OUTSIDE BLOCKER
C   = COMMITTED BLOCKER
S   = STACKED BLOCKER
Ⓢ   = OFFENSIVE SETTER
S   = STACKED BLOCKER FOLLOWS TO
      COMBINATION (POSITION 2) B.

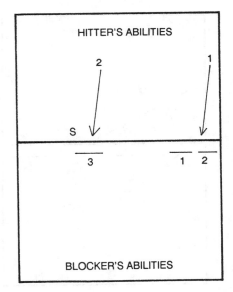

Fig. 11.6

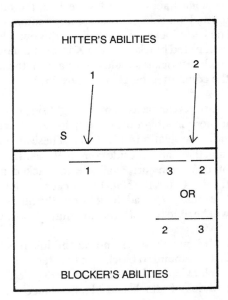

Fig. 11.7

Stack Blocking

The stack blocking system is commonly used against teams that use crossing patterns effectively. A blocking stack consists of one blocker positioned near the net in normal blocking position and a second blocker positioned slightly behind and to the side of the first blocker. The first, close blocker is normally committed to the fast attacker sets (sets 51, 71, and 81). The second, stacked blocker then follows the attacker hitting the combination set.

For instance, if an offensive team runs an X or a fake X play, the committed blocker will jump with the quick middle attack (set 71). The stacked blocker will follow the offensive position 2 (right side) hitter (Figure 11.8). If the fake X is run, the stacked blocker blocks on the outside. If the X is run, the stacked blocker becomes the middle blocker.

There are a great number of options with blocking stacks. If, in Figure 11.8, the fake X or normal outside sets are most common, the stacked blocker is stacked on the outside of the committed blocker. If the X is most common, the stacked blocker should then stack on the inside of the committed blocker (Figure 11.9).

Stacks can be used on the right side of the court if there is a high probability for an offensive left side combination and a 31 set. These are less common than the right side combinations. In addition, other options are available to stacked blocking teams. Often the stacked blocker will be perceptive enough to read the setter on the quick sets and will be able to assist the committed blockers.

It is not always the normal middle blocker who is the committed blocker in the stack. The choice of blocking positions should be decided by probabilities of attack and blocking success. So the usual middle blocker often will be the stacked blocker. If the best attacker is in position 4, the

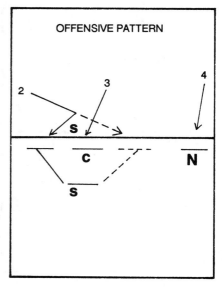

Fig. 11.8

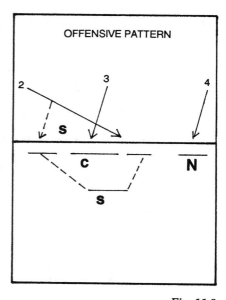

Fig. 11.9

normal middle blocker may be moved to the outside to go one-on-one with the best hitter, while the other blockers participate in the stack.

SUMMARY

Offensive tactics have occupied the minds of many coaches during the past decade. Because of this emphasis on offensive strategies, defensive tactics have remained stagnant. It is time for blocking strategies, and thus total defensive strategies, to be reevaluated. Tactics, not techniques, should be emphasized. Rapid improvement in blocking effectiveness can be achieved by enhancing blocking tactics. For higher probability defense, coaches should consider the possibilities of option blocking. Coaches should choose strategies based on the greatest probability of success. To improve the probability of strong blockers blocking and weak blockers not blocking, you can choose a serving target, or blockers can confuse opposing setters by faking movements. Various defenses may be chosen by defensive teams, and a team may choose a defense based upon specific hitters or on specific sides of the court. It may be a good idea to base the starting team's rotational position on various offensive or defensive match-ups.

Option blocking allows players to gain defensive probabilities. There are four components of option blocking: read versus committed blocking, positional commitment, positional overload, and stack blocking.

BIBLIOGRAPHY

Beal, Douglas (1984 USA Men's Olympic Coach). Personal communication.

Coleman, James E. "The Relationships Between Serving, Passing, Setting, Attacking and Winning in Men's Volleyball." Unpublished thesis, George Williams College, 1975.

Coleman, James E. "A Statistical Evaluation of Selected Volleyball Techniques at the 1974 World's Volleyball Championships." Unpublished dissertation, Brigham Young University, 1975.

Coleman, James E., and Terry Ford. "Option Blocking." *Journal of the National Volleyball Coaches Association* IV, no. 2 (May, 1983): 3–12.

Coleman, James E., William Neville, and Bea Gorton. "A Statistical System for Volleyball and Its Use in Chicago Women's Volleyball Association." *International Volleyball Review* 27 (1969): 72–73.

Coleman, James E., William Neville, and Greg Miller. "The Four Point Statistical System Used for Backcourt Defense." *International Volleyball Review,* 28 (1971): 38–39.

Miller, Greg. "Statistical Artifacts and Suggestions." *International Volleyball Review,* 29 (1972): 37–38.

12

FLOOR DEFENSE: BACK COURT DEFENSE

Terry Liskevych and Bill Neville

Offense captures an audience's immediate attention; defense wins matches and eventually wins championships. The best defense combines two factors: sound techniques (in blocking and individual defense) and teamwork (to take as much of the floor as possible away from the opposition). The best team defense reacts quickly and spontaneously to the requirements of any situation. This chapter presents the functional philosophy, technical principles, and formations of floor defense.

FUNCTIONAL PHILOSOPHY

There are three components to the philosophy of defense: the right attitude, an appreciation of tactical considerations (the role of the block and the placement of diggers), and effective communication.

Attitude

You must instill in your players the attitude that no ball will hit the floor at any time, that no ball is impossible to retrieve, and that every ball will be played with maximum effort every time. No value judgment on whether or not a ball is playable is ever made during play. The athletes simply play as hard as they can and make every effort on each sequence until it is terminated. We call this behavioral attitude *relentless pursuit*. Relentless pursuit means that each player believes "every ball comes to me" and "I will play every ball." This conditioning will heighten players' levels of concentration and physically prepare them to respond.

Before you will be able to condition your players to believe they will play every ball, you will first have to convince each player that, "While I am in my defensive area, I will position myself so that every ball will come to me." For example, if the opposing spiker was set to spike a ball from outside the antenna in their left front position, your left back player would position himself or herself in an advantageous area to dig the cross-court spike.

Controlled aggression is required to get in position on the court and to be physically prepared to dig. A volleyball player cannot play defense with reckless abandon. Such recklessness would be disruptive and would make the team's defense ineffective. Promote an attitude of highly aggressive behavior that is controlled enough to work in a coordinated team effort.

The key points concerning defensive attitudes are as follows:
- Think "relentless pursuit."
- Believe "every ball comes to me."
- Get into position!
- Play with controlled aggression.

In summary, defense is an attitude — a total commitment to the fact that every ball is playable until proven otherwise (until after a sincere, maximum effort fails).

All players respect other players who give their maximum effort all the time. Relentless pursuit on defense is undoubtedly the clearest evidence of this level of intensity. A team can win many points, games, and matches through continued defensive prowess.

Tactical Considerations

Tactical considerations include two components of team defense. The first component is the block, the first line of defense. The second component is placement of the diggers (to be discussed later).

Role of the Block. The first tactical decision is to determine the block's role. Will the block be deployed primarily to take away an area of the court, or will the purpose always be attack blocking? At a higher level of play, athletes can combine those two kinds of blocking based on specific situations. For example, a ball that is set tight should be attack blocked on the opponent's side of the net, even in a game or match when the primary tactic is to block cross-court areas.

Area blocking dictates where the opponents can hit: they can hit anywhere except where your players are blocking them. The back court defense fills in around the block. *Attack blocking* dictates that the opponents cannot hit the ball anywhere — the block is everywhere. This tactic is effective for good blocking teams who are reasonably sure they can stop the ball at the net, but deployment of the back court defense is more difficult. In either system, the floor defense must build around the block and what it is doing. But the blockers must recognize that they also have some back row responsibilities. The diggers should not feel required to dig the whole court.

Placement of Diggers. An important tactical consideration for floor defense is placing the best diggers in the areas that are most likely to be attacked in each specific situation. As in blocking or attacking, it should always be a goal to put your team's strengths in the most advantageous positions. In floor defense as well as in blocking, deploying your best diggers or blockers and making necessary adjustments will require switching. Switching as it relates to blocking is termed "option blocking," which was discussed by Jim Coleman in Chapter Eleven. This concept also applies to digging and team defense.

Switches can be called:
- During time-outs (initiated by the coach).
- Prior to the serve (by an experienced, responsible player).
- On a bad pass situation (such as a simple switch when a high ball to the opponents' number 4 hitter is the only logical option, and the middle back switches to the left back).

Switching the best diggers into the areas most likely to be attacked is very logical. As you look at each rotation, you must identify your best diggers and determine where they best perform their skills. You should adjust your defensive personnel based on the opponents' arsenal and how your opponents deploy in any given situation.

In advanced or experienced teams, a designated back row player can be given the responsibility of setting the defense. This individual must consider each player's ability to get into position. For example, the server who needs to get over to the left back may be limited in serving effectiveness or may simply be ineffective against the fast attack, or because of transition responsibility the setter may need to play right back.

Switching adds to the complexity of playing the game, and it is not necessary when there is no significant difference among the skill levels of your athletes (or in the skill levels of the opposing players). The return for making the switch must be justified.

Another individual tactical consideration requiring switching is if an off-side blocker cannot establish strong defensive position. Automatically that player should cover the tip. To establish court position, the back row defenders must key on the blocker's moves and adjust accordingly, balancing the court.

In the previous paragraphs we focused a good deal on individual tactics. We spoke of individuals switching positions for various reasons. This is also true of tactical adjustments in the team's defense. It is actually more common to see a complete team switch from a player-back to a rotational or player-up defense. These tactical adjustments are usually made because of the opponents' tendencies. The situations in which to make the switch are the same as previously mentioned. A common defensive tactical adjustment is to combine two different floor defenses to accomplish a desired coverage. A floor defense can be played with different blocking assignments or philosophies — whatever it takes to be effective in stopping the opposing team.

COMMUNICATION

There must be ongoing, clear communication during all defensive situations. Coupled with the communication must be the consistent adherence to the rules of defense. Furthermore, the same trigger word must be used.

There are three types of communication:
1. The communication of direction.
2. The communication of execution.
3. The communication of confirmation.

It is not always necessary to use the three types in every situation, but your players must be trained and prepared to use the communication necessary to complete a smooth play. Each type of communication uses different trigger words.

Communication of Direction

Trigger words include:
- *Switch* — the middle back on a high ball would change with either wing to present optimal digging.
- *Rotate* — a defensive captain call movement.
- *Tip* — alerts an adjustment.
- *Deep* — stay on perimeter.
- *White* or *Back* — which type of defense to use.

Communication of Execution

Trigger words include *mine, me,* or *ball* — an execution trigger word such as *mine* should be uttered every time by the player about to make contact.

Communication of Confirmation

Trigger words include *yours, okay, (Name)* — all confirm that the ball belongs to the other player.

Communication should be monosyllabic, concise, and clear. One of the most devastating blows to a team's tempo is losing a point or serving opportunity because of a failure to communicate.

TECHNICAL PRINCIPLES

Before we discuss the technical principles involved in playing defense, you should realize that the largest part of defense is played before the ball is attacked. If we look at the defensive sequence, it will become clearer:

1. Assume the base or starting position
2. Read the developing play
3. Adjust position
4. Move to the final court position
5. Take final body position
6. The ball is attacked
7. Reaction position is retrieved or pursued

As you can see, five steps in the defensive sequence occur before the ball is attacked.

When teaching defense, we usually break it down into the following steps:

1. **Starting or base position.** Any time a player hits the ball over the net to our opponents he or she should immediately get into a starting/base position. In all cases, the player should strive to be in a starting position before an opponent touches the ball.
2. **Read position.** This position is decided by the pass to the setter, the set direction, and the spiker's approach. The ideal is to be in the read position by the time of the hitter's foot plant at take-off. Sixty to seventy percent of the athlete's success in defense is related to this step in the sequence. This step determines the athlete's area of responsibility. The defensive posture the player assumes should allow both forward and lateral movement. This is achieved by positioning on the inside balls of the feet with a rounded back and arms bent in front of the body. This type of stance allows the player to lean into the attack. Caution must be taken not to rush in or move while the ball is being contacted.
3. **Adjust position.** This position is the spot from which the player initiates actual defensive play. The player focuses in on the spiker and fine tunes the area of responsibility to a primary zone of effectiveness. Like a computer, the athlete analyzes the last bits of information to set the exact stationary position. The digger computes the spiker's relationship to the ball and net and the relationship of all these factors to the block. This information is analyzed at computer speed, and the result is the adjusted position for the digger. This position must be assumed as the spiker begins to swing at the ball.
4. **Reaction position.** Your athlete actually plays the ball from the reaction position. The digger reacts from the adjusted position into the primary zone of effectiveness to play the ball. This movement is made immediately after the spiker hits the ball. During the reaction to the ball, the body should not contact the floor until after the digger has made a play on the ball. The arms should be between the ball and floor, coming up to meet the ball. The ball should be played in front and within the

midline of the body whenever possible, and the feet should be more than shoulder width apart at contact. There should be minimal arm swing except for directional control. The best control can be achieved by simply angling the platform to the target. If the athlete is completely off balance after contact, an emergency technique (i.e., collapse, dive, or roll) may be employed as a landing that will prevent injury.

5. **Emergency position.** The emergency position covers the secondary zone of effectiveness. It would be used, for example, when a ball touches off the block or is hit to an open area. The player's focus is primarily on the ball, and he or she moves as quickly as possible to make some kind of play on the ball to keep it off the floor. The more experienced players will also concern themselves with positioning during the play so the ball will rebound near a prescribed target or area. After the play on the ball, the athlete will be required to execute some method of landing (i.e., dive, roll, or slide).

The On Help Principle. The on help principle is an important but neglected principle in defense. "On help" means to play a position so that teammates are on the court side of you. For example, your cross-court defenders should play with their backs to the sideline or facing the opposite sideline. As you visualize this when the dig is made, the player is playing the ball toward the rest of the team, who will thus be in a position to better help play the ball. Another example would be a line digger playing with the foot on the line and in front of the inside foot so the rebound angle is "on help," or back toward the team and court.

The Pursuit and Relay Principle. The pursuit and relay responsibility principle is another important but neglected principle in defense. The block should be touching most attacked balls. Some will be terminal ricochets, but most will be deflected to the back row, where defensive pursuit is possible. The usual deflection that is pursuable goes deep out of the back of the court. Most often the middle back defender, by virtue of court position, will have first contact pursuit responsibility. The wing digger closest to the trajectory follows, prepared to make second contact. The rest of the team should automatically move toward the pursuit in preparation for the third contact. If the ball is deflected off the block out of bounds, the wing digger nearest the ball pursues, followed by the middle back. The absolute necessity is pursuit by everyone.

Additional Principles. Other principles of a technical nature that deserve to be mentioned are the following:
1. Always play the ball in front of you.
2. Lean into the attack but do not rush it.
3. Never move after the arm swing has started.
4. Play every ball with two hands.
5. All defenders must know their second contact responsibility.

The following checklist can be used by you or your athlete in evaluating your use and understanding of the philosophy and principles of defense:

USA Women's Volleyball
Philosophy and Principles of Defense Checklist

Objectives of Defense

[ ] To position yourself between the flight of the ball and the court.

[ ] To dig the ball to zone 7 (settle for nothing less than perfection) so that the setter has all options available.

[ ] Nothing will hit the floor at any time — relentless pusuit.

[ ] Always follow the ball with your eyes during every instance that it is in play.

[ ] Put yourself in a position so that the ball coming over the net can be played by you — "every ball is coming to me."

[ ] Do not hit the floor if you do not have to. Never be on the floor before your arms contact the ball. The floor and the ball can be contacted simultaneously.

[ ] Recognize that you are responsible for a defensive area, not just one precise spot.

[ ] Always attempt to play the ball with two arms.

[ ] Be aggressive, but under control — controlled aggression.

Defensive Positioning

Defensive positioning occurs prior to the attacker's contact with the ball. The most important aspect of defense is reading the play correctly. Positioning on the court is a series of adjustments that are always mental, and sometimes physical. Taken in stages, a player must anticipate:

1. Overpass.
2. Setter tip or spike on second hit.
3. Set direction.
4. Set position — zone, deep, on, quick.
5. Attacker approach — under (early), late.
6. Attacker tendencies — line, cross-court, deep, sharp, seam, off hands, straight down, offspeed, roll, top.
7. Over block — weak blocker, hole, position (block line, block cross-court, block both, give seam).
8. Use of antennae and court to your advantage.
9. Need for perimeter defense — It is easier and much more efficient to move toward the center of the court than away from the center of the court. This is opposed to the theory of centrality which dictates that everyone always congregates in the center of the court. Thus, wing players (positions 1 and 5, RB and LB) should use the sideline as their guide. In middle back defense (position 6, MB) the middle back should use the endline as the guide. Be sure to remember the area where most balls are hit in an international match (Figure 12.1).
10. The importance of parallel movement — There should be parallel movement between players who are digging in the back court (Figure

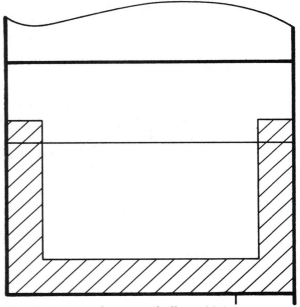

Fig. 12.1 Area where most balls are hit in an international match.

12.2). For example, the six players on defense must respond as a unit, even though there is separate coordination within the first line of defense (blockers) and the second line of defense (back row diggers).

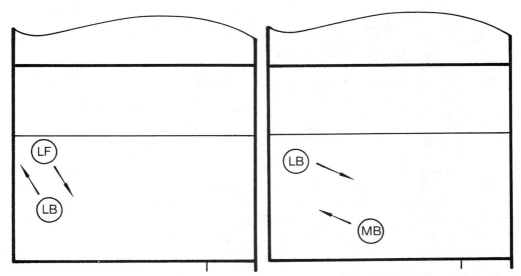

Fig. 12.2 Parallel movement.

Blocking. The block is the foundation of your defensive alignment. A back row adjustment will be made if:
1. You are blocking with one, two, and/or three players.
2. You attack block or area block.
3. You are blocking line or blocking cross-court.

Design your defense according to:
1. The strengths of your players.
2. The areas where your opponents are most apt to hit.
3. The weaknesses of your players.

Attitude. The most important aspect of defense at the international level is attitude. It is most difficult to teach, because it involves:
1. Hard work
2. Discipline
3. Concentration
4. Perseverance
5. Desire

Physical position. Before and at the time of the attacker's contact with the ball, the defender should:
1. Stand on the inside balls of the feet.
2. Be ready to move forward and laterally.
3. Lean into the attack, but should not rush it.

4. Stand with a bent back and bent knees.
5. Place the arms in front of the body.
6. Take a step before moving the arms.

At the time of the defensive player's contact with the ball (your contact):
1. Keep the arms between the ball and the floor and parallel to the floor.
2. The arms should come up to meet the ball, not go down with the ball.
3. Always play the ball in front of you.
4. If at all possible, keep the body's midline behind the ball.
5. Use minimal arm swing except for directional control. The forearms should be angled toward the target.
6. The feet should form a stable base at contact.
7. If the ball is not directly to you, lunge first. Dive and/or roll as a last resort.
8. If the ball is hit above your waist (knuckler), you must play it with a fist (overhand) or turn and take a step to play it.

DEFENSIVE FORMATIONS

Base or Starting Position

All defensive activity begins from the base or starting position, which is determined by the opponents' offensive abilities. The most common base position in collegiate play is the one you see in Figure 12.3. The distance from the net is very arbitrary and depends on the opponents' offense. If a team attacks quickly from the middle, the starting position for the back row diggers moves closer to the net.

The theory of centrality is an important factor in establishing a base position (Figure 12.4). The tendency is for everyone to congregate at the center of the court because everyone moves forward and never backs up. If forward movement, then, is the easiest movement to make, it should be the last movement that has to be made. In applying this concept to defend against the short, quick attack, the defense would start close in order to be in position ready to play the quick attack. The movement of the defensive players would have to be backward with a reaction forward, as opposed to starting back, moving forward, and then reacting backward.

In Figure 12.5, you can see another variation to the base position. This is usually used against a lower level opponent, one who has a tendency to play the second ball over the net.

Another consideration for establishing your base position would be the type of defense you are going to play. Figure 12.6 shows an example of a base position that might be used for a team that plays opponents who may pass the first ball in error over the net or attack with the second ball. It also is an easy base position to use if you intend to use a player-up defense. Therefore, a secondary consideration is the ease of transition from your starting position into your read position.

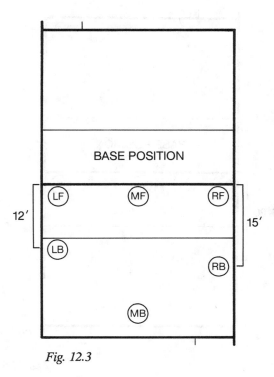

Fig. 12.3

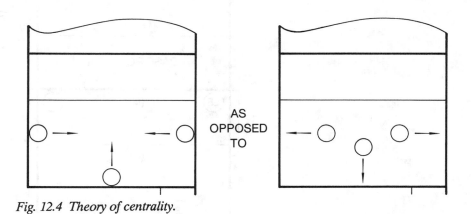

Fig. 12.4 Theory of centrality.

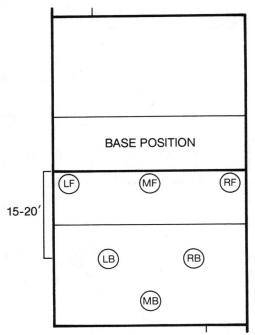

Fig. 12.5

Fig. 12.6

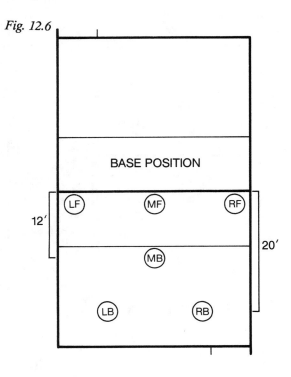

Player-back Defense (White or Standard)

The player-back defense is a perimeter defense that primarily covers the outer areas of the court, while the block covers the center of the court. All defenses are variations of this basic defense. In Figure 12.7, you will observe the zones of responsibility when an opponent is attacking from the left front or their number 4 position. The non-involved blocker retreats and straddles the 10-foot line, always facing the attack. The blocker should open to the court first and then slide away from the net. The middle back is always on the endline. The middle back makes primarily lateral movements, in order to cover from corner to corner. A common error occurs when the middle back begins to creep too close, because then a lateral and backward move must be made. A teaching technique that may help in training a middle back player is to put a piece of tape two feet from the endline, from sideline to sideline. This will emphasize the primary area of responsibility. The middle back player (number 6) positions in the seam of the block and reads and adjusts from there. If you look at Figure 12.7 and compare it to Figures 12.8 and 12.9, you will observe the difference in positioning based on the seam of the block.

In the player-back defense, the right and left backs cover the balls in the middle of the court. The cross-court diggers should play with their backs to the sideline. In Figure 12.7, the left back should position just off the inside hand of the block. When the middle blocker is involved, the player positions off this blocker's inside hand, back to the sideline, deep in this zone of responsibility. This player is the main cross-court digger. The right back player in Figure 12.7 covers against a line shot spike or dink. In Figure 12.8, with the attack from the opponent's right front, the right back player becomes the main cross-court digger.

If you are defending against a quick attack, like a 31 set, you should always try to have two blockers up. In Figure 12.10, the movement of the back court defense is shown in respect to this situation. The right back moves up to cover the tip while the middle back moves into the strong shot of the hitter, which is usually in line with the direction of the hitter's approach. This may change once you determine the particular tendencies of that hitter. Figures 12.11 and 12.12 show the defense formation for a quick set in the middle or behind the setter.

For a high set in the middle, the left front and right front blockers should move in and set up on the middle blocker, forming a three-player block as shown in Figure 12.13. This situation may also occur against a high set to the left or right sides. As shown in Figures 12.14 and 12.15, if the block is well formed, good and solid, the left and right back players will adjust to cover the tip. The middle back would position to be in line with the approach angle of the spiker.

The next group of diagrams (Figures 12.16, 12.17, and 12.18) shows the probable back-court alignment when only one blocker is able to jump to defend at the net.

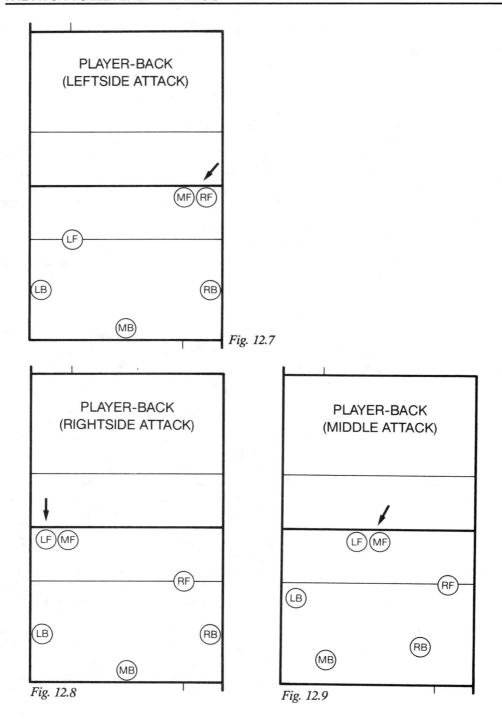

PLAYER-BACK
(LEFTSIDE ATTACK)

Fig. 12.7

PLAYER-BACK
(RIGHTSIDE ATTACK)

Fig. 12.8

PLAYER-BACK
(MIDDLE ATTACK)

Fig. 12.9

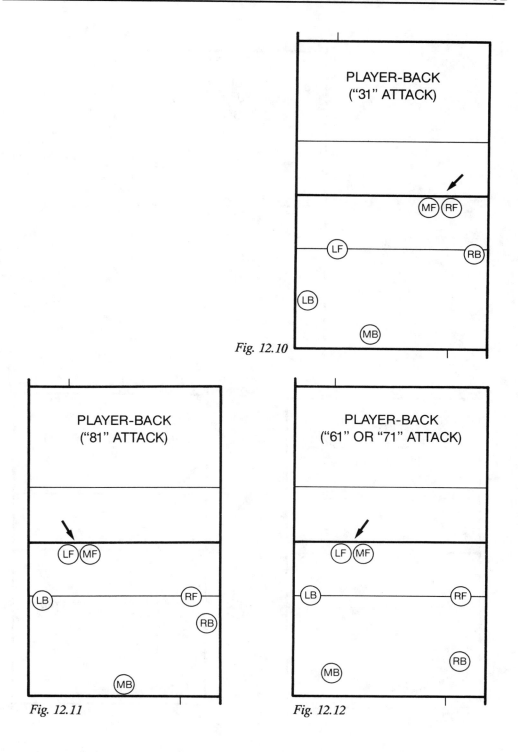

Fig. 12.10

Fig. 12.11

Fig. 12.12

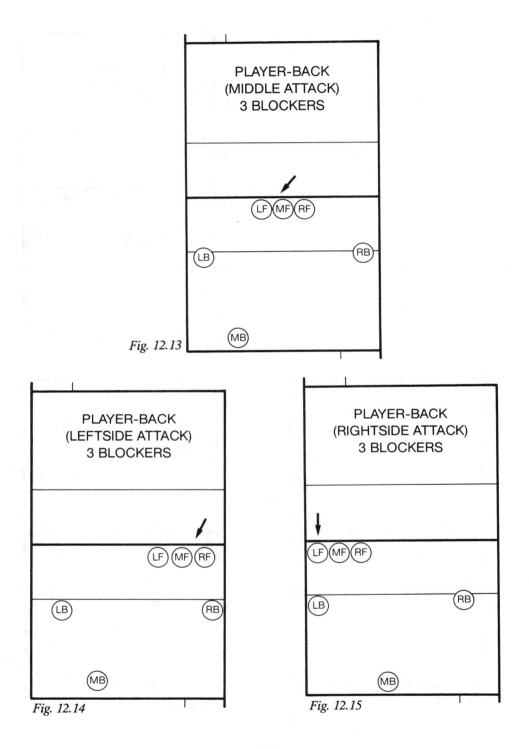

Fig. 12.13

PLAYER-BACK
(MIDDLE ATTACK)
3 BLOCKERS

Fig. 12.14

PLAYER-BACK
(LEFTSIDE ATTACK)
3 BLOCKERS

Fig. 12.15

PLAYER-BACK
(RIGHTSIDE ATTACK)
3 BLOCKERS

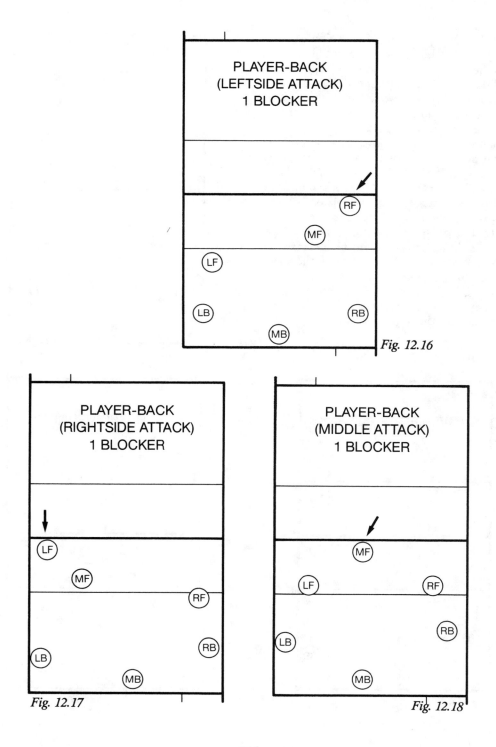

Fig. 12.16

PLAYER-BACK
(LEFTSIDE ATTACK)
1 BLOCKER

PLAYER-BACK
(RIGHTSIDE ATTACK)
1 BLOCKER

Fig. 12.17

PLAYER-BACK
(MIDDLE ATTACK)
1 BLOCKER

Fig. 12.18

The group of diagrams beginning with Figure 12.19 deals with the areas of responsibility, movement patterns, and tip responsibility. Figure 12.19 shows the areas of responsibility during a left side attack. The areas are outlined with dotted lines, showing the general area each player is to cover. Figure 12.20 shows movement patterns so that all movement is coordinated to avoid collisions. If a ball is hit to a seam, then both players go for the ball. One goes short or in front and the other goes long or behind. This is the concept of parallel movement. The last of these diagrams, Figure 12.21, shows tip responsibility in this defense. If the set is inside or the block takes the angle away, the left front player releases to cover the tip. If the block seals line or the set is on or beyond the antenna, the right back player releases for the tip.

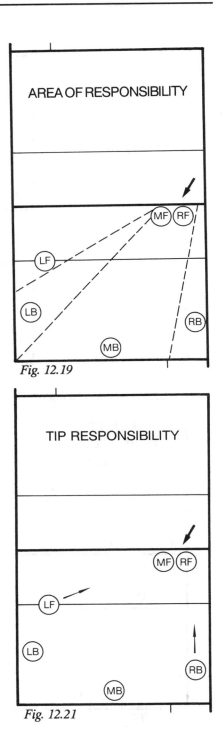

Fig. 12.19

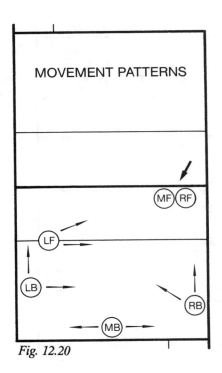

Fig. 12.20

Fig. 12.21

Player-up Defense (Red or Six-up)

The player-up defense primarily involves covering the center of the court and limiting the perimeter coverage to three players instead of four. This variation of the player-back defense positions a defender near the middle of the court behind the block. In Figure 12.22, you will observe positions when an opponent is attacking from the left front or the number 4 position. The non-involved blocker retreats just beyond the 10-foot line, back to the sideline. The blocker should open to the court first, and then slide away from the net, staying closer to the sideline than in the player-back defense. The left back now plays near the endline. This player should be playing the season in the block and be concerned mainly with balls over or off the block deep into the court. If you look at Figure 12.22 and compare it to Figure 12.23, you will observe the differences in the positioning of the left back and right back players based on the side of the court being attacked.

In this defense, the player-up covers balls in the middle of the court. The player-up should play behind the seam in the block at approximately 3.7 m (12 ft.) deep as shown in Figure 12.22. This player is primarily responsible for covering tips, roll shots, and touches of the block that fall short. In Figure 12.23, with the attack from the opponents' right front, this player assumes a position similar to that described above except closer to the other sideline.

In Figure 12.22, the right back player is the primary line digger. This player positions approximately 6.1 to 7.6 m (20 to 25 ft.) deep depending on the ability of the opposing spiker to hit the ball down. The line digger must also consider the formation of your team's block in establishing the correct position.

If you are defending against a strong middle attack, you should always try to have two blockers up. In Figure 12.24, the movement of the back court defense is shown in respect to this situation. The right back moves toward the baseline and covers the cut-back shot over the block. The left back player covers over the block cross-court or inside the left front blocker if the block leaves a lot of court. The left front assists the middle blocker while the right front moves in to cover the cut-back shot of the hitter. This may change once you determine particular tendencies of the hitter. Figures 12.25, 12.26, and 12.27 show the defense formation for quick attacks from the middle or behind the setter.

For a high set in the middle, the left front and right front blockers should move in and set up on the middle blocker, forming a three-player block as shown in Figure 12.28. This situation may also occur against a high set to the left or right side. As shown in Figures 12.29 and 12.30, if the block is well formed, good, and solid, the left middle back will adjust to still cover the tip. The right back and left back will play the perimeter of the court.

The next group of diagrams (Figures 12.31, 12.32, and 12.33) shows the probable back court assignments when only one blocker is able to jump to defend at the net.

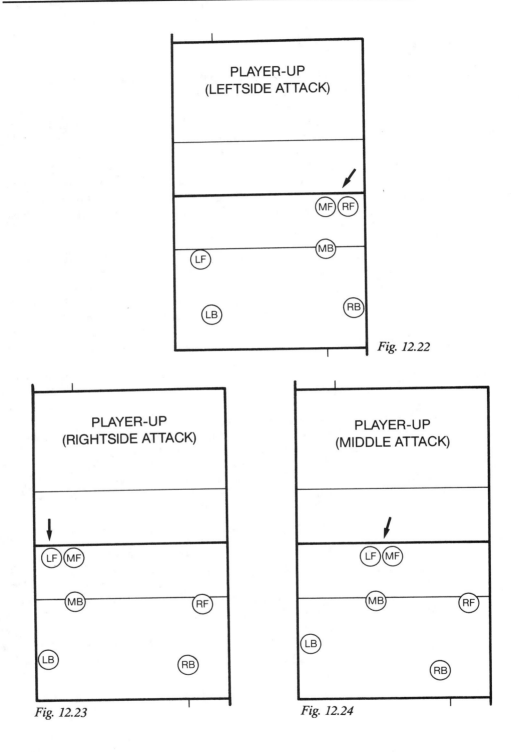

PLAYER-UP
(LEFTSIDE ATTACK)

Fig. 12.22

PLAYER-UP
(RIGHTSIDE ATTACK)

Fig. 12.23

PLAYER-UP
(MIDDLE ATTACK)

Fig. 12.24

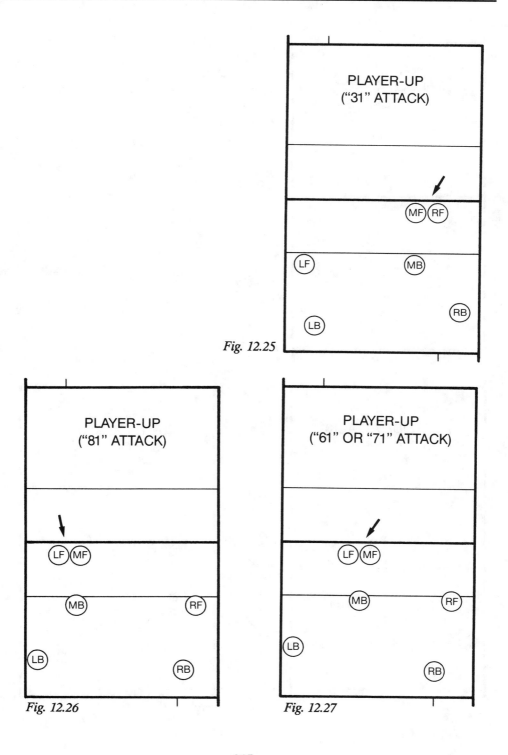

Fig. 12.25

Fig. 12.26

Fig. 12.27

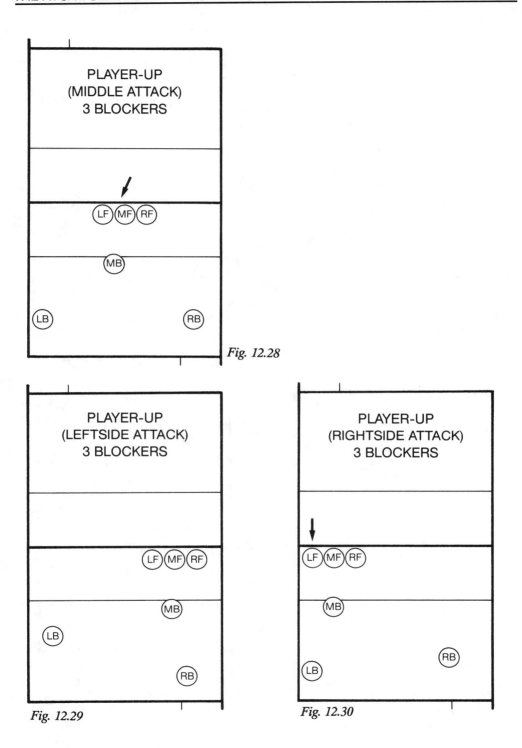

PLAYER-UP
(MIDDLE ATTACK)
3 BLOCKERS

LF MF RF

MB

LB   RB

Fig. 12.28

PLAYER-UP
(LEFTSIDE ATTACK)
3 BLOCKERS

LF MF RF

MB

LB

RB

Fig. 12.29

PLAYER-UP
(RIGHTSIDE ATTACK)
3 BLOCKERS

LF MF RF

MB

LB   RB

Fig. 12.30

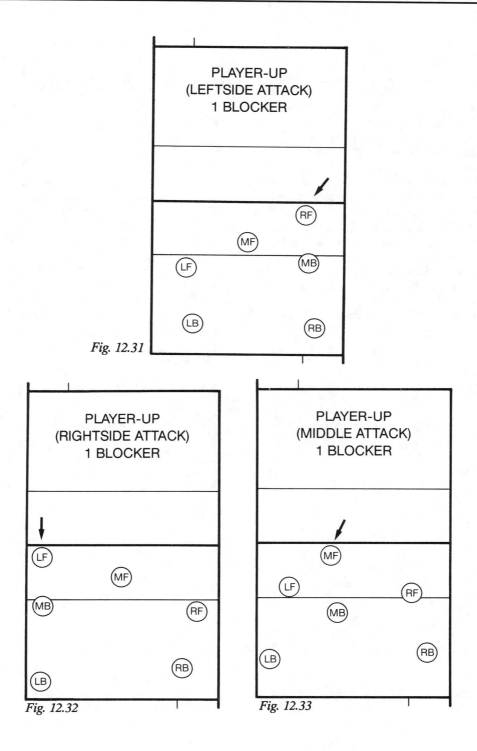

Fig. 12.31

Fig. 12.32

Fig. 12.33

The group of diagrams that begins with Figure 12.34 deals with the areas of responsibility, movement patterns, and tip responsibility. Figure 12.34 shows the area of responsibility during a left side attack. The areas are outlined with dashed lines showing the general area each player is to cover. Figure 12.35 shows movement patterns so all players' movements are coordinated to avoid collisions. If a ball is hit to a seam, then both players go for the ball: one goes short or in front and one goes long or behind. This is the concept of parallel movement. The last of these diagrams is Figure 12.36, showing tip responsibility in this defense. In the player-up defense, one person is always given this responsibility. In our diagrams we illustrated the middle back player.

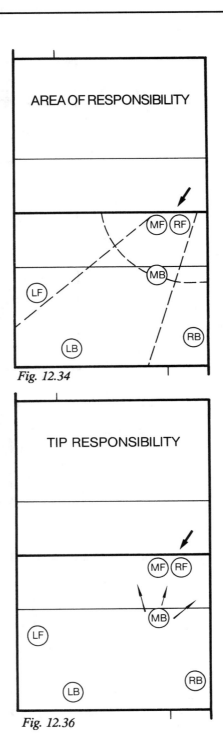

Fig. 12.34

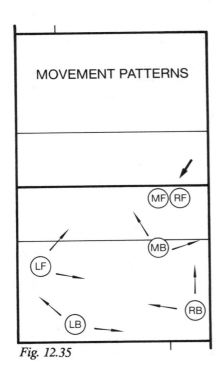

Fig. 12.35

Fig. 12.36

Rotational Defense

Strong Rotate. This defense is a movement defense primarily covering the corners of the court and the area immediately behind the block. This defense is a variation of the player-back defense.

In Figures 12.37 and 12.38, you will observe that the rotation is in the direction the ball was set. This is sometimes called the strong rotate since the defense is rotating toward the ball. The non-involved blocker retreats deep, positioning below the attack line facing the attack. The opposite wing player rotates deep to cover the cross-court corner. In Figure 12.37 it happens to be the left back player. The middle back player also rotates toward the ball to cover the deep line corner. Simultaneously the wing player on the line rotates up behind the block to cover a tip. In Figure 12.37 this would be the right back player. This rotation defense limits you to only three players covering the perimeter of the court but leaves one player available for tip coverage responsibility.

Figures 12.39 and 12.40 show attacks out of the middle; the rotation is based on which blocker assists the middle blocker. In Figure 12.39, the left front helps the middle blocker, forcing the rotation to the left. In Figure 12.40, the rotation is to the right since the right front assists on the block. In this situation the right back releases for tip coverage, forcing a rotation to the right.

In Figure 12.41, using a three-player block against a middle attack complicates this defense since either of the wing players can release to cover the tip, leaving two remaining deep players. These players can play the corners or most frequently attacked areas.

If you are defending against a quick attack, like a 31 set, the philosophy of trying to get two blockers up should still prevail. In Figure 12.42, the movement of the back court defense shows the rotation to the right, releasing the right back for tip coverage. The rotation will be limited since the play is so quick, making it more difficult to cover the corners. Figures 12.40 and 12.43 show the defense formation for a quick set in the middle or behind the setter.

In the case of high sets, it may be possible to have three blockers up. Figures 12.41, 12.44, and 12.45 show the formation following strong rotational principles. The rotation is always to the side from which the ball will be attacked. If the corners are your major coverage priority, you may be all right. As you can see in the diagrams, you are now short one back court defender; therefore, your priority is to block the ball.

The next group of diagrams (Figures 12.46, 12.47, and 12.48) shows the probable back-court alignment when only one blocker is able to jump to defend at the net.

Figures 12.49, 12.50, and 12.51 illustrate the areas of responsibility, movement patterns, and tip responsibility for the strong rotate defense.

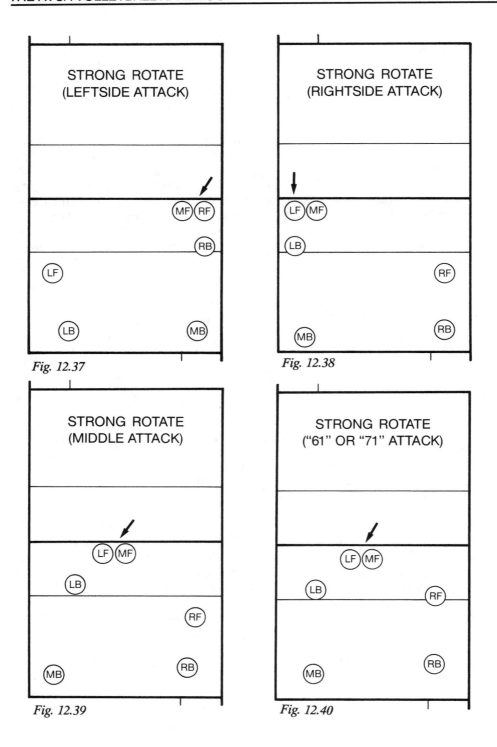

Fig. 12.37

Fig. 12.38

Fig. 12.39

Fig. 12.40

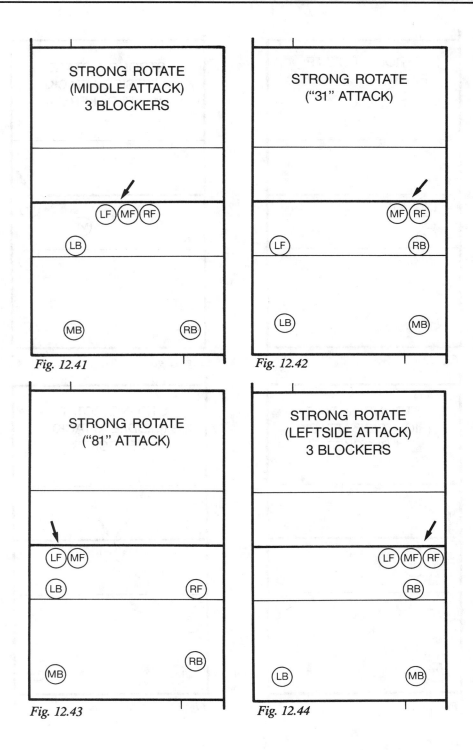

Fig. 12.41

Fig. 12.42

Fig. 12.43

Fig. 12.44

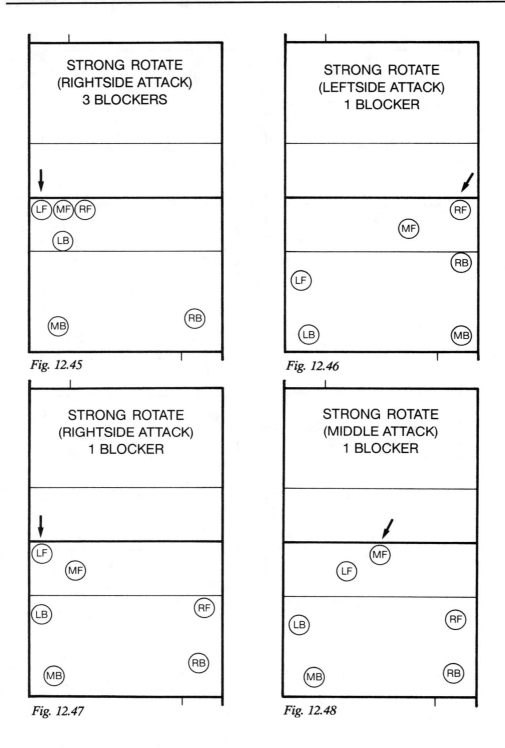

Fig. 12.45

Fig. 12.46

Fig. 12.47

Fig. 12.48

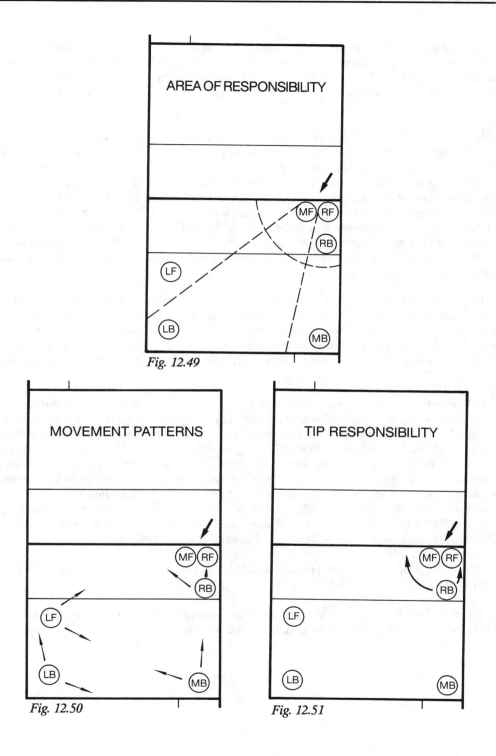

Fig. 12.49

Fig. 12.50

Fig. 12.51

Counter Rotate (Blue or Slice). The counter rotate defense is also a movement defense that primarily covers the corners of the court and the area immediately behind the block using the off-side or non-blocking front court player. The rotation in this defense is away from the side where the ball has been set. This defense is again another variation of the player-back defense.

In Figures 12.52 and 12.53, you will observe that the rotation is in the opposite direction the ball is set. Therefore, if the ball is set to the opponent's left front, the team rotates to the left. This is sometimes called a counter rotate since you rotate in the opposite direction from which the ball is set. The non-involved blocker rotates in behind the block, pushing the other players to rotate so the line digger will back up covering the deep line. The middle back will cover the deep cross-court corner. The wing player closest to the non-involved blocker rotates up to cover the power cross-court shot. In Figure 12.52 it happens to be the left back player. With the non-involved blocker (sometimes called the off-blocker) rotating to cover the tip, this counter rotation defense also limits you to only three players covering the perimeter of the court.

In Figures 12.54 and 12.55 showing an attack out of the middle, the rotation is based on which blocker assists the middle blocker. In these two diagrams, we illustrated the left front helping the middle blocker forcing the rotation to the right. Of course, the rotation would be to the left if the right front helped out in the block, which the left front, non-involved or off-blocker released to cover the tip. Figures 12.56 and 12.57 illustrate the 31 attack and the 81 attack.

In Figure 12.58, using a three-player block against a middle attack complicates this defense since all blockers are participating in the block. A rule of thumb to go by is the wing on the side of the usually non-involved blocker would then create the rotation by moving to cover the tip. In Figure 12.59 when the attack is coming from the opponents' left side, the last blocker to be involved would be the left front. Once the left front decides to block, the left back continues to rotate in to cover the tip. This positions the middle back and right back covering their respective corners. The attack to the opponents' right front as shown in Figure 12.60 causes a similar rotation to the right. In the case of a three-player block in the middle as shown in Figure 12.58, the rotation would most likely come from the right since the right front traditionally would be the last to be involved in helping out the middle.

The next group of diagrams (Figures 12.61, 12.62, and 12.63) shows the probable back court alignment when only one blocker is able to jump to defend at the net.

Figures 12.64, 12.65, and 12.66 again illustrate the areas of responsibility, movement patterns, and tip responsibility for the counter rotate defense.

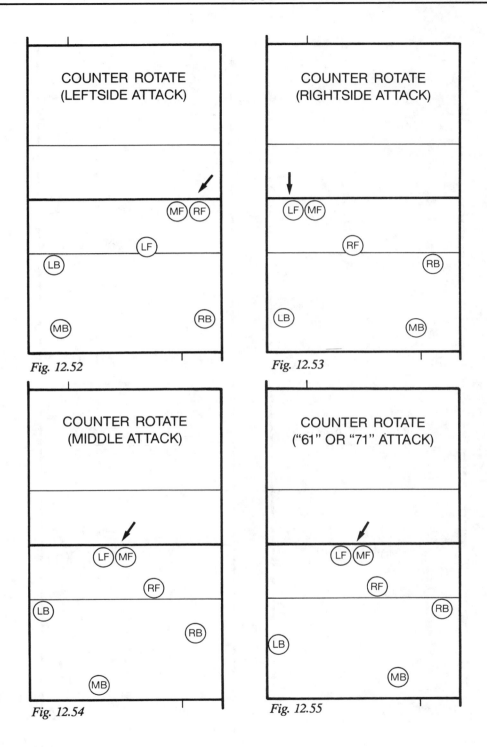

Fig. 12.52

Fig. 12.53

Fig. 12.54

Fig. 12.55

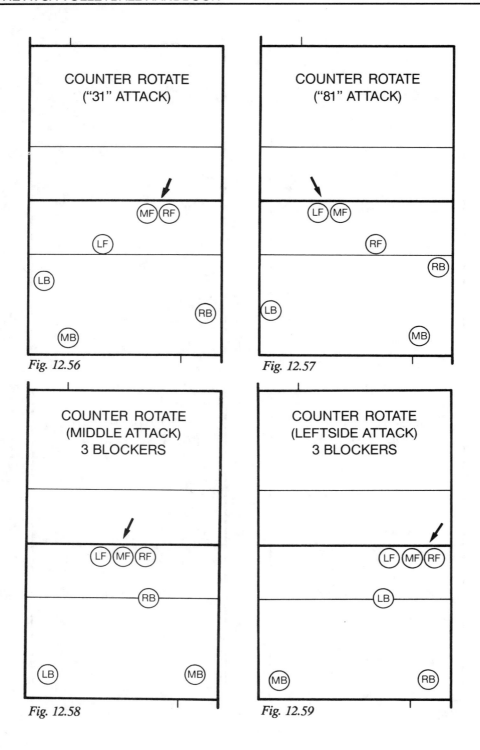

Fig. 12.56

Fig. 12.57

Fig. 12.58

Fig. 12.59

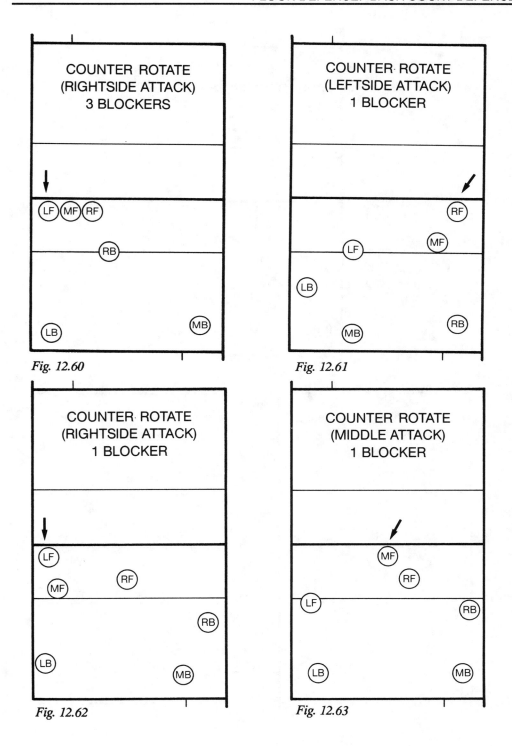

Fig. 12.60

Fig. 12.61

Fig. 12.62

Fig. 12.63

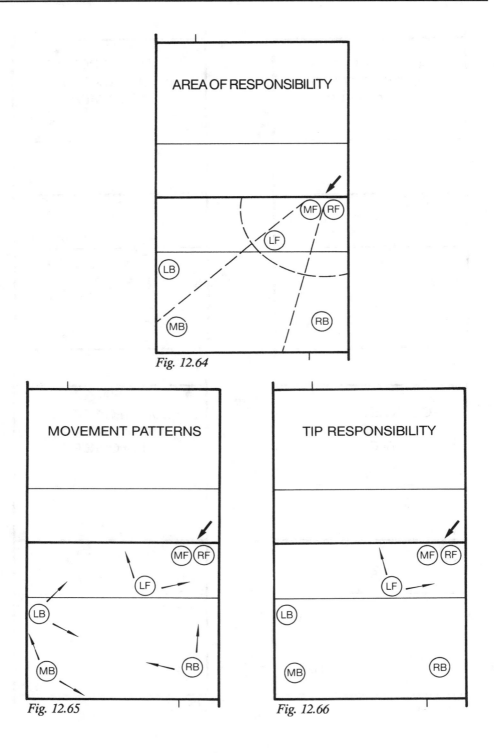

Fig. 12.64

Fig. 12.65

Fig. 12.66

SUMMARY

Defense is a significant part of volleyball that accomplishes two things. First, defense scores points. The average team should score three to five points per game off floor defense. Second, defense can change or solidify the momentum in the team's favor. A great dig or save can inspire a team, whereas lack of effort or missing easy defensive plays has the opposite effect.

The three components to defense are the right attitude, an understanding of tactics, and effective communication. Most defense is played before the ball is attacked, and in teaching defense, it is helpful to teach a seven-step defensive sequence. In addition, players should be familiar with the principles of defense including the on help principle, the pursuit and relay principle, and the principles used by the USA Women's Volleyball Team. Players must also know and practice the various defensive formations, especially the player-back defense, the player-up defense, and the rotational defense. It is important for players to remember the old adage, "Offense scores points, but defense wins games."

13

ELEMENTS OF TRANSITION

Andy Banachowski

Explaining the elements of transition in words on paper seems every bit as difficult as perfecting and performing them on the court. The difficulty begins with defining "transition" as it occurs on the volleyball court. The dictionary defines "transition" as a period of passing from one condition, activity, or place to another. It sounds simple. In basketball, transition is easily observed as the players move from one end of the court to the other. In volleyball, transition seems to be most frequently explained as going from defense (digging) to offense (spiking). But there are many other transitional aspects of volleyball that also need to be discussed. Every time the ball crosses the net, many transitions occur. For example, switching from offense to defense can be just as important a transition as the generally accepted notion of going from defense to offense. Additionally, because of the rotational alignment of our game, many minor transitions can occur that will enhance your team's positioning and performance.

Before I discuss these aspects of transition, I want to comment on the relative importance of the transition game. During the 1970s volleyball was a pass-set-hit game that resulted in points mainly when the passing broke down. It still is, because passing is still crucial to a team's success, but it was even more so then. Let me explain how that can be. Until the rules were changed in 1977, so that the blocker's contact no longer counts as one of the three allowable contacts, a team would have only two hits to return the opponent's attack, assuming that the block touched the ball. This restriction usually resulted in a free-ball pass over the net that gave the receiving team the opportunity to pass-set-hit again. Under these rules, transition was an even more vague concept. It was little understood, little practiced, and little perfected. With the rule change that eliminated the blocker's contact as the first hit, transition became easier to execute, and its importance became more apparent in determining the outcome of the game.

I still believe that serving and passing are the two most important factors in deciding the winner of a match, but if these two elements are equal, the next determining factor is who can play the better transition game. This concept is especially true for the women's game, because men's volleyball is such a power-oriented game. (The next important element for the men is the block since their game consists primarily of pass-set-hit-block, resulting in a quick point or side-out depending on which side of the net the ball hits the floor.) The women's game, although it is becoming more powerful, still consists of rallies that excite the fans with outstanding defensive plays and continual action. There is much more transition played on the women's court, thus it is more important in determining the winner.

The most important element of transition is ball control. Quickness, agility, and anticipation are additional skills that must be constantly employed. Finally, an understanding of the transition game and the formations used to run it are crucial to its success. There are two main types of transition: rotational transition and defense-to-offense transition.

Fig. 13.1   Ball control and teamwork are necessary to make successful transition plays. Here the MB digger (#21) gets in low and digs to the target area, where the setter awaits the ball.

ROTATIONAL TRANSITION

Rotational transitions are minor changes that can greatly enhance your individual and team performances if executed quickly and properly. These transitions allow you to position your team for its best attack or defense. But if performed slowly or poorly, these transitions will usually negate the advantage you are trying to obtain.

The serving team should make its switches immediately upon contact of the ball by the server. In the front court, the middle blocker should quickly move to the middle, maintaining a position closest to the net. The outside blockers should quickly run to their assigned blocking areas, crossing behind the middle blocker when necessary. In their rotational position, the players should establish a minimal distance (without forming a screen for the server) from one another to allow for an even quicker switch. In the back court, players should also make switches to their assigned defensive areas as designated by your coaching philosophy (specialization versus generalization) and defensive system. Caution should be exercised to avoid screening and overlap violations.

For the receiving team, usually only the designated setter will be making a rotational transition as the serve is contacted. The setter must move to the passing target area, while the other players concentrate on passing the served ball. After the ball is passed, rotational transition may begin to occur. Some teams like to make their back court switches while the ball is being set so that they have completed their switching before they position themselves for hitter coverage. Then they can quickly move to their assigned defensive position after the attack is completed. For instance, a left back player who normally plays middle back can move into the hitter coverage positioning of the middle back position and thus establish the switching before moving back to defense. This makes the transition from offense to defense smooth since the players are already in their normal, more practiced defensive positions.

Other teams prefer to wait until after hitter coverage to make back court switches, thereby emphasizing hitter coverage before transition to defense. This is a more sequential approach to the game and requires that each player be familiar with each coverage assignment.

In the front court, the attackers frequently cannot make any rotational switches until the attack has been completed. An exception would be to run a designated play with the hitters attacking from their defensive positions. For instance, a middle blocker who is in the right front area can be called upon to hit the X. This requires this player to move to the middle of the court to spike and it also positions the player for defense.

Once the attack has been completed (the ball crosses the net), front court players can make rotational or positional changes following the same guidelines as on defense. Depending on the caliber and tempo of play, however, I believe these switches are the most dangerous to make, because this is the time that the opponents are trying to "out-transition" you. That is, they are trying to dig-set-attack your attack while you are switching positions. For you to switch slowly or at inappropriate times increases their chances of success in transition.

This type of offense-to-defense transition in the front court should be utilized with certain guidelines in mind. The middle blocker must always get to the middle. Outside hitters should only switch if the dig is not controlled within the court boundaries. If the dig is not controlled, then you will have enough time to get to your desired position. If the dig is controlled, you will still have more success stopping their transition with the players in position, rather than with players getting caught in switches and/or being late for the play.

These elements of transitional play should be practiced any time scoring or side-out work is called for.

DEFENSE-TO-OFFENSE TRANSITION

To successfully run a transition game, in the sense of going from defense to offense, the key element is ball control. Whether a ball is dug from a spike or from a deflection off the block, the dig must be executed skillfully enough — with enough height and accuracy — to allow the players time to make the transition.

In a normal defensive alignment with the blockers "up" (blocking the spike) and the diggers positioned properly, your defense must come up with a dig that allows you to execute your transition offense. This dig must be high enough to allow the other players to position themselves for offense, and accurate enough (to the normal target area) to allow you to run an offensive attack. As the digger prepares to play the ball, the other players must anticipate the next action and ready themselves.

Fig. 13.2   A perfect dig allows the setter (#46) to set the middle (#37) a quick set, while the other players move in to cover the attack.

If you are using a back court setter, the setter must release from the back court defensive position and get into the front court to set the ball. When the setter sees that the ball is hit away from the back court position, he or she can release to a setting position. If the dig is not accurate, the setter can call for help from a teammate.

The front court players must ready themselves for an attack: as the blockers are landing, they must locate the ball and move off the net to get ready to make their normal approach for an attack. Their path off the net should take them to their usual starting position for an attack. In doing so, they should follow a pattern that will avoid a collision with the back court setter coming forward. The remaining front court player, who is already back off the net in a digging position, needs only to move into the normal starting attack position.

Fig. 13.3   While the ball is in flight to the setter, the MF player (#37) gets in position to attack.

All of these actions must be taken quickly because there is usually very little time for them, depending on the height of the dig. All the players must know their responsibilities — who is to dig, who is to set, and who is to attack — and be skilled enough to perform them. They must be able to anticipate the action which will take place and have the agility and strength to perform these physical skills quickly.

235

If you have a front court setter, as soon as the ball goes by the blockers, the setter must move to the target area for the dig, while the other front court players get off the net and prepare to attack. This is the pattern that you practice repeatedly from your normal defensive position to make your transition swift and smooth.

Another situation that you must also practice is called a free-ball situation, which occurs when the opponents cannot generate an attack and must bump (forearm pass) the ball over the net. The forearm pass is the key that can be used to trigger this formation for your team. Whenever you see the opponents begin to bump the ball over the net, all of your players should call out "free ball" and respond quickly by assuming their free-ball formation. This formation should be the same as your service-reception formation. The ball comes over the net relatively slowly. If your team recognizes the free ball quickly, there is plenty of time for each player to get into position. The front court players should back off the net to their normal receive positions, which will also allow them to attack. The setter, whether front court or back court, moves to the normal target area for the pass.

Since this free ball is usually an easy ball to pass, and each player should be in the attacking position, this is the best time to run one of your offensive plays to confuse your opponents. However, this is also a "must" time to score a point or side-out, and you should not do something so intricate that it will hinder your chances of scoring.

Another situation that may also occur is a down-ball situation. This is defined as a situation in which you feel your chances of digging the ball are better than your prospects of blocking the attack. It usually occurs when the opponents' set is not on target and the hitter can still swing at the ball, but not well enough to generate a potent attack. It can happen if the set is too deep in the court or too wide, or the hitter is too late approaching and does not jump, or the attack is so weak as not to warrant blocking. When this situation occurs, someone designated to recognize it calls out "down ball." Often the middle blocker is responsible for calling down balls since that player should be most skilled at recognizing when to block and when not to block. Or you could assign that responsibility to your most experienced player. All the players, however, should be practiced enough to anticipate when the down-ball situation is going to be called.

When a down ball is called, all players must respond quickly because the ball is usually still to be attacked. Often the "down" call is late or inaudible to the back court players. Many times they recognize it too late. Quickness is even more important in this transition, since your players must move to a new digging position in such a short time.

Some teams like to use the same formation as a free ball for a down ball since it means the players only have to learn one formation. If you are using a simple 4–2 offense, these formations can be easily accomplished, especially if the opponents' attack level is not too high. If you are using a 6–2 or a 5–1 offense and the setter is in the back court, you may have difficulties trying to use the same free-ball formation for a down-ball situation.

My theory is that if a down ball is called, the hitter must be in some kind of trouble and will probably try to hit a safe shot and keep the ball in play. To counter this situation, I want to put my best digger in the middle of the court to dig. This player is the primary digger and has the green light to dig whatever can be reached. The wing diggers (line diggers) should position themselves in their respective area of the court at least 1.5 m (5 ft.) in from the sideline and slightly behind the primary digger. From this position, they should read the hitter and adjust accordingly. This positioning allows for the best coverage of the court where the hitter is most likely to hit the ball. If the opposing hitter has known tendencies, the formation can be adjusted accordingly.

The front court players must also become active in the down-ball formation. There are different ways to accomplish this. The left front player should move off the net to a digging position. The other two front court players must also be active. One must get off the net to a digging position while the other should stay at the net, ready to get any ball just trickling over the net and to assume the role of setter once the ball is dug.

I used to keep the middle front player at the net and pull the right front player back, which made it very easy to get a balanced digging formation. This strategy works well if your middle front player is your setter, such as in a basic 4–2. However, our middle front player is an attacker, and I have found it much better to keep the right front player at the net (this is our normal position for the setter) while bringing the middle front player to the right side of the court to dig. This strategy enables us to have the same digging formation as previously described and gives us the most benefits for a quick transition. The middle of the court is open for our primary digger to dig as many balls as possible, our middle attacker is off the net ready to attack, and a setter (or designated setter) is at the net ready to set.

If your primary setter is in the back court and the hit is away from that position, the setter can release to the front court to assume the setting role. Coming into the front court, the setter yells "I'm in" and the right front player will relinquish position to back off the net and become an attacker.

If the back court setter digs the ball, or cannot release quickly enough, the right front player becomes the setter. This player must be a capable setter to run your offense or set a high set to an attacker. If the pass (dig) is close to the net, this player can attack the ball. This is an ideal position for a left-handed setter-attacker. If the pass is off the net, the right front player can call for help and a teammate can step in and set the ball.

DRILLS FOR TRANSITION

Perfecting the transition game requires a thorough understanding of each player's responsibilities and good communication among the players. It also requires a lot of practice of the skills and formations employed to be successful. Since ball control is essential, the most basic skill necessary is digging. The following pages describe fourteen digging drills:

Drill #1: Dig to target, any position/add setter.
Drill #2: Pass to target, free ball/add setter.
Drill #3: Dig three spots to target.
Drill #4: Half-court digging, stressing balance/communication.
Drill #5: Dig-set, two players/one releases to set.
Drill #6: Back court diggers, three in down-ball formation dig to target.
Drill #7: Dig-hit, dig to setter, ready to hit.
Drill #8: Back court-front court.
Drill #9: Block to hit, two players versus coach; hit to back court, setter releases to run transition.
Drill #10: Three versus three (can add two sets of three).
Drill #11: Team defense versus coach.
Drill #12: Six versus six, free ball, one hit.
Drill #13: Six versus six, down ball, one hit.
Drill #14: Six versus six, free ball/down ball, two hits.

Drill #1: Dig to Target

From a position above the net on the opposite side of the court, the coach can repetitively hit balls at a player who must dig the ball to a specific target area. The player should repeat a specified number of digs successfully to the target area, and then alternate with another player who plays the same defensive position. Other players shag stray balls. A setter, who must run down each dig and set it to a specified target, can be added to this drill (Figure 13.4).

Drill #2: Pass to Target

From the opposite court, the coach tosses balls across the net to two lines of waiting players. The player passes the ball (overhand or forearm passes) to a specified target. The player then shags the ball and returns it to the coach, and then returns to the opposite line to await another turn (Figure 13.5).

Drill #3: Dig Three Spots to Target

From a position above the net on the opposite side of the court, the coach hits a ball at a player (P1) who must dig the ball to a specific target area. The player (P1) then moves to another defensive position on the court, and the coach hits a second ball. Then the player (P1) moves to a third defensive position on the court to dig the third ball hit by the coach. The next player (P2) in line follows the same pattern. When all players have moved to the other side of the court, the drill continues with the direction of movement reversed. This allows players to work on moving to their right and left. The drill can be varied to require a

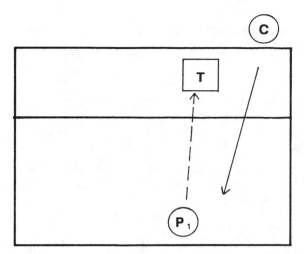

Fig. 13.4

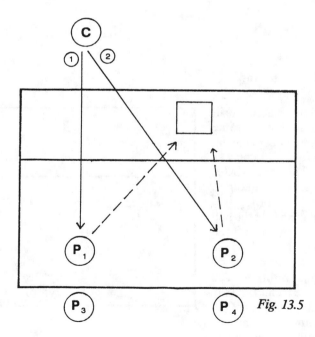

Fig. 13.5

successful dig to the target area before the player is allowed to move to the next digging position (Figure 13.6).

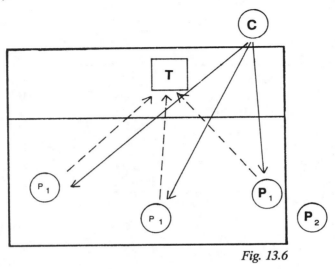

Fig. 13.6

Drill #4: Half Court Digging

This is a continuous action drill with the coach located on the same half court as the three diggers. The object is to keep the ball in play as long as possible. The coach spikes the ball at a player who will dig it, and then one of the other two players must step in and set the ball to the coach. The digger and the non-setting player should balance the court until the setting player returns to a digging position. The coach will continue to hit the ball. All diggers must be ready to set the ball, and communication among the players should be stressed to ease balancing and covering the court at all times (Figure 13.7).

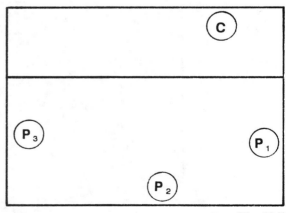

Fig. 13.7

Drill #5: Dig-set

The coach hits balls at two lines of players. The non-digging players must then set the ball to a specified target area. Two new diggers step onto the court to continue the action (Figure 13.8).

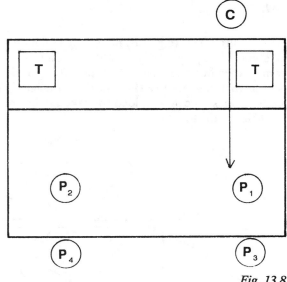

Fig. 13.8

Drill #6: Back Court Diggers

Back court players are positioned in the down-ball formation of the coach's choosing, and then the coach continuously hits balls at the diggers until they dig a specified number of balls to the target area, or until a set period of time, say two minutes, has elapsed. This will sharpen their digging skills and their teamwork (Figure 13.9).

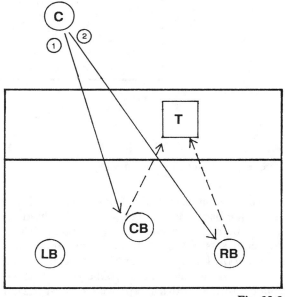

Fig. 13.9

Drill #7: Dig-hit

A front court digger (e.g., LF) must dig a ball hit by the coach from above the net on the opposite side. The player (P1) must dig the ball to a setter who will then set the ball. The digger must then become an attacker and get in position to hit the ball being set. This drill works best when a second (P2) or third (P3) digger is included and the players alternate. One or two blockers can be added to make the hitting more difficult and the drill more realistic (Figure 13.10).

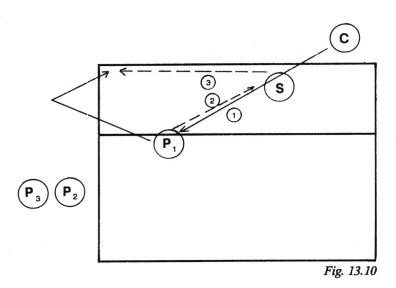

Fig. 13.10

Drill #8: Back Court-Front Court Dig

This drill is the same as drill #7, but with an additional player on the court. This additional player is the back court digger (e.g., LB) behind the front court digger (e.g., LF). Two balls are hit before the players change position. The first ball is hit to the left back digger, and the setter sets to the left front player. Immediately after the attack, the coach hits a second ball at the left front player, who must get into defensive position after the first attack. The ball must be dug and set back to the player who will attack for the second time. Players then rotate positions, with a new player moving to the left back and the left back player moving to the left front. One or two blockers can be added, and players should be encouraged to cover the hitter at all times (Figure 13.11).

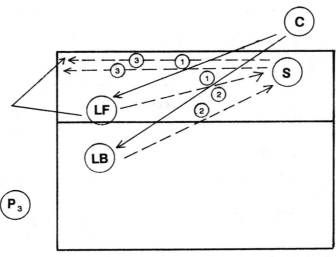

Fig. 13.11

Drill #9: Block to Hit

Two players take a blocking position versus a coach on the opposite side of the net. The coach will hit the ball over, around, or off the blockers to a back court digger. As the digger digs to the target area, a setter will come into the front court to set the ball to one of the blockers who has quickly moved off the net into an attacking position. The same blockers should stay in the drill until they have successfully completed a specified number of transition attacks (Figures 13.12 and 13.13).

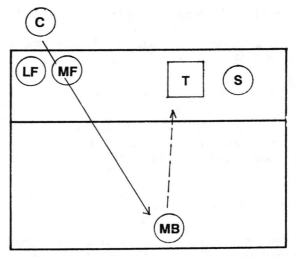

Fig. 13.12

243

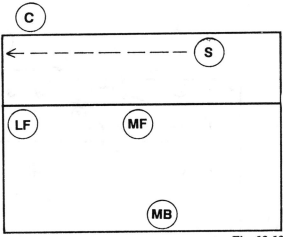

Fig. 13.13

Drill #10: Three Versus Three

Three players are positioned on each side of the net, and their objective is to successfully and successively dig-set-hit the ball back and forth across the net. With beginning players, ball control should be stressed with the goal being to keep the ball in play as long as possible. Whenever an error is made, a new ball is introduced at that point to correct the error, and play continues. Multiple variations can be introduced to alter the drill. These include making all attacks from behind the 10-foot line or adding another set of three players on each side who exchange positions with the set of three on the court whenever the ball crosses the net (Figure 13.14).

Drill #11: Team Defense Versus Coach

The coach attacks balls against a team of players. This allows proper positioning on each play and gives the coach the opportunity to repeat exact situations. The players must play good defense and convert the transition to attack successfully. This is a very controlled drill and allows for excellent teaching. Players should be rotated frequently (Figure 13.15).

Drill #12: Six Versus Six, Free Ball

Two complete teams are on the court. One team is allowed only one hit to get the ball across the net the first time. The coach tossing the ball should make the toss so that the team will have to bump the ball across the net, thus assuring a free-ball situation. This allows the other team to practice free-ball situations continuously. They should run the free ball plays you have designed, and the ball should be played out with each team having three hits (Figure 13.16).

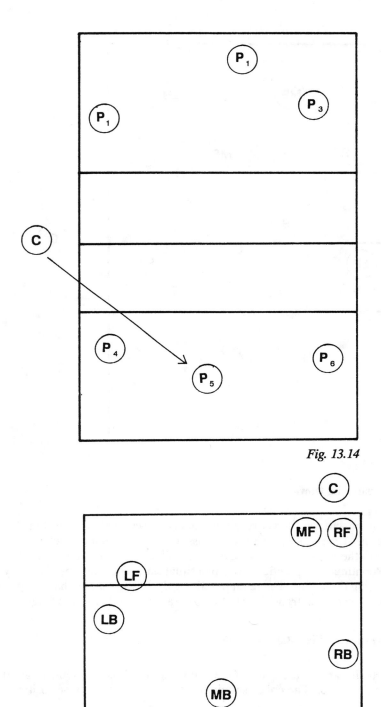

Fig. 13.14

Fig. 13.15

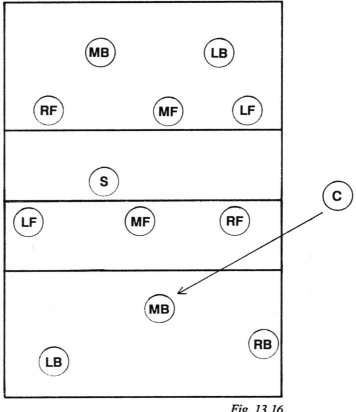

Fig. 13.16

Drill #13: Six Versus Six, Down Ball

Two complete teams are on the court. One team is allowed only one hit to get the ball across the net the first time. The coach should toss the ball so that an attack can be made, but deep enough off the net so that the blockers will call a down-ball situation. This allows the other team to continuously practice down-ball situations. The ball should be played out with each team having three hits. The team practicing down balls should have to perform a specified number of successful transitions before they are allowed to rotate (Figure 13.17).

Drill #14: Six Versus Six, Free Ball/Down Ball

Two complete teams are on the court. One team is allowed only two hits to get the ball across the net the first time. The coach should toss the ball in a variety of positions so the different situations will be set up. This will force the defending team to distinguish regular defense, down-ball or free-ball situations, and react accordingly. The ball should be played out with each team having three hits (Figure 13.18).

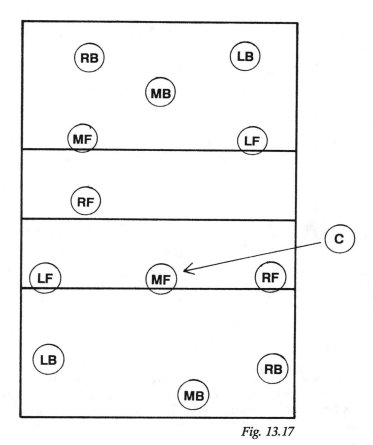

Fig. 13.17

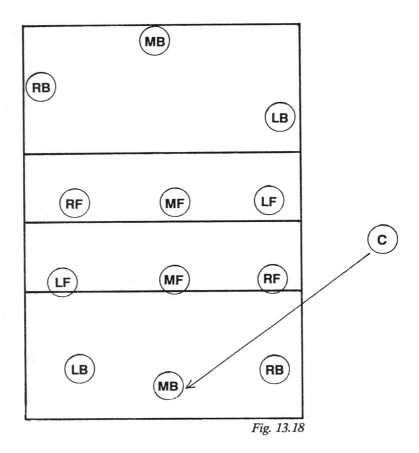

Fig. 13.18

SUMMARY

Transition is a very important element of volleyball, probably the most important element after serving and passing. There are two main types of transition: rotational transition, which includes minor changes; and defense-to-offense transition. The main transition in volleyball would be going from defense to offense, but many minor transitions occur in every game.

Important components of transition are ball control and transitional formations. Transition plays must be made quickly, and players must be familiar with various possible situations that may occur, such free-ball or down-ball situations.

Each player must have a thorough understanding of his or her responsibilities, and must be able to communicate effectively with the other players on the team. Players must practice drills emphasizing skills, formations, and ball control.

14

ADMINISTRATION OF A VOLLEYBALL PROGRAM

Stephanie Schleuder

Anyone who has coached knows that the time spent in the gymnasium is only a small part of a coach's job. At the collegiate level, a head coach's job description reads like a job description for the chairman of the board of a major corporation. The head coach's job involves a myriad of responsibilities, including staff supervision, public relations, budget management, program planning, recruiting, and coaching. Ultimately, the success of any collegiate sport program can be directly related to efficient management.

This chapter presents an organized, practical approach to the administration of a collegiate volleyball program. Organizing a program in the configuration of a corporate structure can prove to be a valuable method of maximizing one's efforts as head coach.

PHILOSOPHY AND GOALS

Before beginning to plan the development of a volleyball program, a coach must have a clear understanding of where and how the athletic program fits into the hierarchical structure of the institution. Lines of authority and communication should be well established (Chart 1).

The philosophies of the university, formed by the board of trustees and the chief executive officer, are reflected in written statements depicting the institution's missions and policies. These philosophies shape all programs within the institution. Responsibility for developing an athletic program which embodies the philosophies of the institution lies with the athletic director. The athletic director sets goals for specific sport programs and selects coaches who are responsible for meeting those goals. By consulting with the athletic director, the head

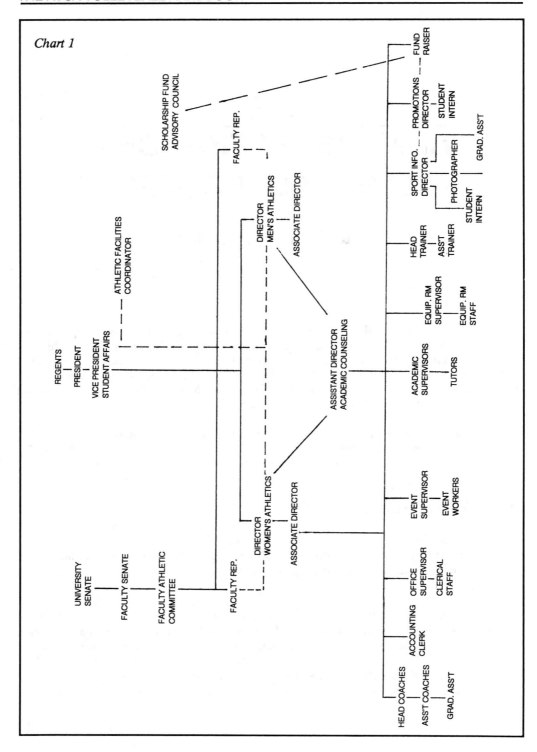

Chart 1

coach in turn designs and implements strategies for operating the program within the parameters set by the athletic director and the institution.

Since the athletic director is the coach's direct link with the administration of the institution, and the director will make all decisions about the sport programs, it is essential that good communication exists between the athletic director and the coach. Probably the most vital component in creating a successful sport program is the compatibility of the coach's philosophies and goals with those of the athletic director. If disharmony exists here, the coach can do one of two things. The coach can modify philosophies and goals so that they are compatible with the athletic director's, or the coach can develop a comprehensive plan to "sell" the athletic director a new package. Regardless of the approach, it is important that the two individuals come to an understanding. There should be a detailed outline of the program goals and needs, and there should be a clear understanding of the strategies which will be used to accomplish the goals.

Any coach who presents an organized plan for the development of his or her program will increase the chances for gaining the support of the athletic director. Below is a sample of a presentation that is designed to outline a coach's goals and needs for developing a volleyball program. Obviously, this outline should be written to reflect the individual goals and needs of a specific program, and the coach who prepares it should also be prepared to defend each request. Comparisons with other successful programs can be most helpful in defending requests. In any areas where problems exist, it is essential for the coach to gather supporting data which will illustrate the necessity of the requests being made.

Outline for Volleyball Program Development

I. Performance Goals
   A. Year one: Qualify for the conference championship—have a winning record.
   B. Year two: Qualify for the conference championship while improving on the previous season's record.
   C. Year three: Qualify for NCAA championship play-offs by finishing first or second in the conference — be nationally ranked.
   D. Long-range: Be consistently competitive nationally; make an appearance in the Final Four.

II. Program Goals
   A. Gain national recognition — developed through consistent performance at highly competitive levels; evidenced by national rankings.
   B. Generate revenue — substantially increase attendance at home events.
   C. Develop support groups — start a booster club and identify local target groups for promotions.
   D. Improve public relations — through clinics, demonstrations, and public speaking engagements — make the public more aware of the program.

    E. Develop respect—the volleyball program should be synonymous with quality—stress proper conduct of coaches and players, performance in matches, and efficient organization of the entire program.

    F. Establish professional recognition—the coaching staff must be active in professional organizations and must serve in positions of leadership.

III. Program Needs
    A. Coaching staff
        1. Full-time assistant
        2. Graduate assistant
    B. Improvement in services of the support staff
        1. Academic advising—tutors, study halls
        2. Athletic trainer—travels with team
        3. Secretarial—additional staff necessary
        4. Sports information—travels with team
    C. Full allotment of scholarships
    D. Increased travel budget—specific outline
    E. Increased recruiting budget—specific outline
    F. Promotions and publicity
        1. Expanded media guide and brochure
        2. Event promotions
            a. Recruit a band, cheerleaders, and mascot.
            b. Target high school groups.
            c. Target university students.
            d. Target specific community groups.
            e. Create gimmicks to draw spectators.
        3. Media coverage
            a. Print media
               i. Need pre-game coverage.
               ii. Need game reports and coverage.
              iii. Need human interest stories.
            b. Electronic media
               i. Secure radio broadcast contract.
               ii. Secure live or tape-delayed television coverage.
              iii. Provide radio and television with public service announcements for their own use.
    G. Facilities—availability at prime-time
        1. For practice during season
        2. For competitive events
        3. For off-season practice
    H. Equipment needs

Once the philosophy and goals of the program have been established and an evaluation of the program needs has been made, the coach should begin organizing the program with the resources available. Much can be accomplished with little money, a lot of delegation, and a good master plan.

STAFF ORGANIZATION

Selecting a staff of well-qualified individuals who can work together toward common goals is clearly one of the most important tasks for the head coach. The head coach must determine the individual qualities which will complement and contrast with the coach's own. Regardless of the situation, the following would represent desirable qualities for any coaching staff member:

- Loyalty
- Creativity
- Integrity
- Honesty
- Enthusiasm
- Good communication skills
- Ability to motivate individuals
- Good knowledge of sport
- Self-motivation and the ability to work hard
- Goal orientation

All members of the coaching staff should have job descriptions outlining their duties and responsibilities. The head coach is responsible for supervising and evaluating the work of each staff member. Following are sample job descriptions for an assistant coach, a graduate assistant, and a team manager. These are written in general terms. As a head coach develops a program, the job descriptions should become very specific in nature. Usually, the more clearly responsibilities are outlined, the more productive the staff will become.

Assistant Coach Job Description

Pre-season

1. Coordinate distribution of practice clothes, equipment, shoes, and uniforms with the equipment room staff.
2. Organize physical testing materials for the first days of practice.
3. Coordinate the weight lifting program with trainers or the weight coach.
4. Organize travel plans:
   - Confirm motel reservations.
   - Secure game contracts.
   - Arrange for plane tickets and vans/buses.
   - Obtain maps and directions, when necessary.

       – Confirm practice facilities for road trips.
       – Prepare rooming lists for motels.
5.   Coordinate the completion of all paperwork needed by the department for each player (i.e., sports information profiles, NCAA eligibility forms, medical releases).
6.   Review the graduate assistant's and manager's job descriptions with each of them.

Practice

1.   Assist in all phases of practice planning.
2.   Conduct warm-up, conditioning, and cool-down phases of practice.
3.   Talk with trainers before each practice to check on the status of injured players.
4.   Supervise the graduate assistant and the manager to make sure they are fulfilling their responsibilities.
5.   Schedule individual practice sessions for players with specific weaknesses.
6.   Schedule videotape review sessions with players as needed.

Matches

1.   Gather players for the pre-game meeting.
2.   Conduct and/or supervise the warm-up.
3.   Perform designated pre-game duties assigned by the head coach (i.e., scout opposing hitters, turn in lineup).
4.   Perform designated duties during the match as assigned by the head coach (i.e., suggest offensive strategy to fit the opponents' defensive changes).
5.   Supervise the cool-down and gather the team for the post-game meeting.
6.   Call in the match scores when necessary.
7.   Meet with the head coach for match analysis and evaluation.
8.   Supervise the graduate assistant and the manager in their responsibilities.

Recruiting

1.   Prepare a recruiting budget and a master list of recruits.
2.   Organize the recruiting files.
3.   Organize contact sheets for each recruit and keep them up-to-date.
4.   Organize a master schedule for:
       – Talent assessment—watching recruits in games and practices.
       – Home visits.
       – Campus visits.
5.   Maintain contact with recruits throughout the year by:
       – Phone contacts.
       – Correspondence.
       – Mailing weekly press releases and news clippings.
6.   Request videotapes and solicit recommendations from high school coaches.
7.   Schedule, organize, and conduct all campus visits.

8. Keep the head coach constantly apprised of all recruiting developments.
9. Assist in making final decisions regarding scholarship offers.

Scouting

1. Prepare a master schedule of opponents' matches.
2. Prepare a scouting budget.
3. In consultation with the head coach, delegate scouting duties to staff members.
4. In consultation with the head coach, prepare scouting reports on all opponents.
5. In consultation with the head coach, evaluate and update all scouting reports after competition.

Post-season

1. Organize an off-season conditioning and weight-training program in consultation with the trainers and weight coaches.
2. Gather off-season (USVBA) tournament information and complete team registration.
3. Seek funding or sponsorship for the off-season if necessary.
4. Make travel arrangements for off-season competition.
5. Work with the head coach in setting up a competitive schedule for the following year.
6. Assist in preparing the budget for the following year.

Booster Club

1. Coordinate all club meetings with the head coach and the club president.
2. Coordinate the distribution of club membership materials.
3. Supervise the ordering and sale of club merchandise.
4. Meet with the departmental director of promotions to coordinate club promotional ideas with departmental promotion.

Facilities and Equipment

1. Meet with the facilities manager to coordinate schedules for all practices and matches.
2. Meet with the maintenance staff to arrange needs for practices and games (i.e., net setup, locker rooms, microphones).
3. Schedule facilities when opponents desire practice time.
4. Schedule practices at opponents' facilities.
5. Coordinate arrangements with the equipment room staff for home and away matches (i.e., laundering of uniforms).
6. Each spring, conduct a complete inventory of equipment and uniforms.

General

1. Assist in all phases of program planning.
2. Communicate and post office hours.
3. Be present at all staff meetings.
4. Be present at all player and coach conferences.
5. Attend all departmental social functions.
6. Assist in everyday office work, such as telephone calls and correspondence.
7. Attend as many athletic events as possible — support the entire athletic department.
8. Act and dress in a professional manner when representing the university.
9. When in public, support the head coach at all times.

Graduate Assistant Job Description

Pre-season

1. Record and compile all physical testing materials and results (i.e., vertical jump, weight).
2. Help plan all scouting and recruiting schedules.
3. Review the managers' job descriptions so that their responsibilities are clear.

Practice

1. Assist in conducting drills and other assigned duties.
2. Help the manager set up the gym for practice.
3. Assist during individual practice sessions when needed.
4. Help put equipment away after practice.

Matches

1. Help with warm-up.
2. Set up videotape equipment when necessary.
3. Instruct the ball shaggers in the three-ball rotational system.
4. Assist with statistics as necessary.
5. Perform other game duties as instructed by the head coach.
6. Meet with the coaching staff following a competition to evaluate the match.

Recruiting and Scouting

1. Assist in evaluating high school prospects.
2. Complete a written evaluation after watching each prospect.
3. Help scout opponents when necessary.
4. Help with on-campus recruiting visits when necessary.

Booster Club

1. Write and distribute a monthly newsletter to members.
2. Organize post-game receptions for all home matches.
3. Attend and take minutes at all club meetings.
4. Act as the liason between the club officers and the athletic department.
5. Assist in all areas of club operation.

General

1. Schedule weekly office hours with the head coach.
2. Help plan practices.
3. Conduct individual workout sessions when necessary.
4. Act and dress in a professional manner when representing the university.
5. Perform other duties as directed by the head coach.
6. When in public, support the head coach at all times.

Manager Job Description

Practices

1. Prepare the gym for practice by checking with the head coach to find out what is needed.
2. Check all equipment and balls for proper maintenance.
3. Assist with practice as directed by the coaches.
4. Store all equipment at the end of practice.

Home Games

1. Check with the coach for any special preparations.
2. Make a checklist of all the equipment required for the match, and make sure everything on the list is available.
3. Set up the videotaping equipment.

Away Matches

1. Make a checklist for the equipment needed on the road. Be responsible for this equipment while traveling.
2. Prepare and bring a bag with extra uniforms, socks, and knee pads.
3. Laundry and uniforms: Collect uniforms after each match for laundering.
4. Help pack and unpack the vehicle(s) used for travel.

Pre-match Duties
1. Set up the videotaping equipment.
2. Verify players' uniform numbers for the lineup sheets.
3. Greet the opposing team and see if they have any special needs.
4. Assist with team warm-up drills when necessary.
5. Secure and store all balls after the warm-up.

Duties During Matches

1. Keep statistics as designated.
2. Keep running totals of the substitutions and time-outs used.
3. Between games, compute designated statistical game totals for the coach's use.

Post-match Duties

1. Secure and store all balls and equipment, including video equipment.
2. Give the visiting coach a copy of the official score sheet.
3. Check the locker rooms to make sure that nothing was left and that the towels and uniforms are put away.

Statistics

1. Compile all statistics after matches and give them to the head coach.
2. Obtain a copy of the official box score from the sports information staff following all matches. If the team is on the road, also ask for a copy of the official score sheet.
3. Compile season total statistics and give them to the coach and the sports information director every Monday during the season.
4. Replenish the supply of stat forms when necessary.

SUPPORT STAFF

The support staff members are critical to the efficient everyday operation of the athletic department. In most cases, members of the support staff operate in cooperation with the head coach—they are not people who report to the head coach. Because of this, the coach must learn to function with these peers in a professional atmosphere. Understanding the primary duties of each member of the support staff is an essential prerequisite to working with each one.

The Sports Information Director

The sports information director is responsible for the direction, development, and implementation of all sports information released from the athletic department. This person serves as the spokesperson for the department by releasing pertinent information about the programs. Typical duties of the sports information director include:

- Writing, editing, and distributing news releases to newspapers, magazines, radio and television stations, and press services.
- Preparing information brochures.
- Keeping statistics, records, and other news material valuable to the media.
- Gathering personal information on team members and distributing it to the media.
- Arranging press box services, including lineups and statistics, for home and visiting teams.
- Maintaining pictorial and information files.
- Supervising the taking of athletic pictures to be used for publicity purposes.
- Supervising the writing and editing of all programs sold at home games.
- Supervising statistical crews at all home events and preparing box score forms for distribution at the end of each event.
- Communicating with the coach via weekly meetings during the season, post-game interviews, and other meetings as necessary.

Fig. 14.1 A program will grow and become successful if everyone involved works as a team.

The Director of Promotions

The director of promotions is responsible for the direction, development, and implementation of all special events and promotional activities for the department. The purpose of this position is to direct events (other than sports events) which will bring attention and/or funds to the department, and to promote athletic events so that attendance will increase. Some typical duties would include:

- Cooperating with the fund-raiser and sports information director in all event promotions.
- Negotiating radio and television contracts for athletic events.
- Representing the department in speaking appearances before civic clubs, alumni groups, booster clubs, and other organizations. Arranging such engagements for coaches.

- Organizing a promotional program for each sport season. Begin with identifying target groups and determining methods for reaching these groups.
- Securing outside funding for promotional programs and sponsorship of sporting events.
- Organizing special events that will raise money for the scholarship fund.
- Communicating with the coach via monthly pre-season meetings for planning season activities, and specially arranged meetings as necessary.

The Facilities Coordinator

The facilities coordinator is responsible for scheduling and maintaining all athletic facilities. All practices, special events, and home events are cleared through this person, who then is responsible for coordinating individual sports schedules so that conflicts do not exist. The coordinator also schedules necessary maintenance such as floor cleaning, painting, refurbishing, locker room cleaning, and all other related tasks. Communication between the coach and the facilities coordinator includes quarterly meetings to coordinate facility needs, memorandums for notification of upcoming situations, and emergency meetings as needed.

The Event Supervisor

The event supervisor is responsible for hiring and training all staff to work at events and maintaining security at all events. The event supervisor works in conjunction with the facilities coordinator in preparing the competitive site for competition (i.e., setting up nets, taping the floor, and assigning locker rooms). Some specific duties include:

- Hiring and training ticket takers.
- Hiring and training scorekeepers, clock operators, and a public address announcer.
- Ordering and supervising setup of the public address system and the scoreboard.
- Contracting all officials and linesmen for home events.
- Securing and training ball shaggers.
- Opening the building prior to the game and securing the facilities following the event.
- Hiring or retaining security people to work during the event.
- Communicating with the coach in a pre-season meeting to coordinate needs for home events, and in other scheduled meetings as necessary.

The Accounting Clerk

The accounting clerk is responsible for preparing payroll and personnel forms, maintaining accounting records, and handling cash. The accounting clerk is also in charge of advance checks for travel and purchase orders. In general, the person in this position deals with all budget items in the department. Communication with the coach is through budget requests, travel vouchers, requisitions, and monthly written budget status reports.

The Office Supervisor

The office supervisor is responsible for organizing and supervising all office workers including the secretaries, receptionist, and student workers. It is the supervisor's duty to make sure that the office runs efficiently and professionally. General office work performed by a coach's secretary would include these duties:

- Answering the telephone, taking messages, and making appointments.
- Performing routine typing, copying, and collating.
- Picking up and distributing mail.
- Maintaining files with correspondence and master lists for labels.
- Operating office machines.
- Ordering new supplies and keeping the office supply inventory.
- Running campus errands when necessary.
- Maintaining an accurate list of recruits and mailing weekly press releases.
- Assisting in making travel arrangements, including motel and plane reservations.
- Communicating with the coach via written work request slips and daily conversations and discussion of needs.

PROGRAM PLANNING

Once the coach has a thorough understanding of the workings of the athletic department, the process of planning the volleyball program becomes a more feasible task. Obviously, the interrelationships and intradependencies of the athletic department staff make careful planning an absolute necessity. Chart 2 maps out a yearly scheme for planning a collegiate volleyball program. It details the tasks that need attention and the time of year when each should be handled. Clearly, the head coach cannot attend to every item listed on this chart, but he or she must serve as the administrator of the volleyball program. The head coach must delegate responsibilities to the staff, work cooperatively with the support staff, and supervise the daily operations of the program.

Seasonal Conditioning

In order to elicit the best possible performance from athletes, it is essential that they be provided with a well-planned program for conditioning. The purpose of this program is to bring the athlete to a level of peak physical performance at the appropriate time of the year. Volleyball demands high levels of muscular endurance, cardiovascular endurance, strength, flexibility, speed, and agility. Conditioning programs, then, must be designed to develop these qualities.

TASK	SUMMER (June–July)	PRE-SEASON (August)	COMPETITIVE SEASON (September–December)	OFF-SEASON (January–May)
1. SEASONAL CONDITIONING	- general cardiovascular conditioning - weight training (strength) - speed, flexibility, agility, and endurance work	- specialized conditioning: agility, muscular endurance, flexibility - weight training	- general - strength maintenance - technical training - tactical training	- heavy weight training (strength) - jump training (plyometrics)
2. PRACTICE	- no organized team practice	- physical exams - physical testing - two-a-day practices until first week of competition - 2–4 hours per session	- Mon.-Fri. except on match days - 2–4 hours - videotape review session	- individual sessions - team practice, 1–5 days per week
3. SCHEDULING	- print schedule for distribution in fall	- distribute schedules	- get verbal agreements for next year's schedule	- confirm schedule for following year - send contracts - schedule USVBA competition
4. COMPETITION	- summer beach tourneys	- intrasquads	- competitive schedule - evaluate scouting and game plans	- register team for USVBA - USVBA competition (four player development)
5. RECRUITING	- initial contacts (phone, mail, and personal) - talent assessment at summer competition	- home visits - correspondence and phone contacts - plan schedule for talent assessment	- home visits - campus visits - talent assessment—watch matches - correspondence and phone	- correspondence and phone - campus visits for seniors - initial contacts for juniors (phone/mail) - signing of prospects
6. BUDGET	- redo budget based on finalized allocation	- submit team travel advance requests - submit scouting travel advance request - submit recruiting travel advace request	- turn in expense vouchers from trips - update budget status	- submit budget proposal for coming year
7. ELIGIBILITY	- compute team and individual grade point averages - verify eligibility	- verify individual eligibility - submit team roster for conference and national governing body - athletes register for classes	- arrange tutors and study halls as necessary - update roster for championship competition	- compute grade point averages for athletes - verify eligibility of incoming freshmen

Chart 2

TASK	SUMMER (June-July)	PRE-SEASON (August)	COMPETITIVE SEASON (September-December)	OFF-SEASON (January-May)
8. TEAM TRAVEL	- make motel reservations - reserve vehicles for travel - make plane reservations	- confirm all reservations - send rooming list to motels - submit season itinerary to athletic director	- carry game contracts to events - confirm practice times and facilities - gather receipts and submit upon return to campus	- confirm off-season travel plans
9. VOLLEYBALL STAFF MEETINGS	- meet as necessary - train new staff members - motivate staff for coming year	- daily meetings to plan and evaluate practices	- daily meetings to plan and evaluate practices - pre- and post-game meetings - weekly recruiting update meetings	- regular practice planning meeting - weekly recruiting updates - hire new staff as necessary
10. SCOUTING		- complete scouting schedule for season	- prepare scouting reports for team use - review videotapes	- file scouting reports for future reference
11. EVENT MANAGEMENT	- contract officials, linesmen, scorers, timers, PA announcer, court manager - coordinate schedules and facility needs for year	- train scorers, linesmen timers - organize event workers - retain security personnel - secure ball shaggers	- conduct and supervise events	- evaluate event management
12. INVENTORY/ EQUIPMENT ORDERS		- distribute practice clothes, shoes, and uniforms to players - assign lockers	- handle emergency needs	- take inventory - order shoes, uniforms, etc. - collect uniforms, non-perishables
13. PUBLICITY/ SPORTS INFORMATION	- gather information for media guide - plan design and layout of media guide - preliminary plans for video highlight tape	- prepare promotional plan for individual players - distribute media guide - organize and conduct pre-season press conferences - take action and head shots	- prepare and distribute weekly updates of statistics and results - produce promotional tape - nominate players for honors	- mail season summary - publicize signing of recruits - update All-Time records
14. PROGRAM PROMOTIONS	- identify target groups for promotion plans - arrange public speaking engagements to talk about team - conduct demo and exhibitions	- arrange for bands, cheerleaders, etc. - arrange public service announcements for local media	- implement promotional plan - continually work with media	- evaluate past season's promotional plan - develop comprehensive promotional plan for coming year - arrange demos and exhibitions

Chart 2 ,
continued

TASK	SUMMER (June-July)	PRE-SEASON (August)	COMPETITIVE SEASON (September-December)	OFF-SEASON (January-May)
15. AWARDS BANQUET			- set date and site for awards banquet - plan program needs and speaker	- select player honors and awards from past season - conduct banquet
16. BOOSTER CLUB	- appoint or elect officers - order perks to be given or sold to membesr	- conduct membership drive - plan events surrounding games - work with promotions director for special events	- conduct receptions and special events - mail monthly newsletter (throughout the year)	- plan and conduct post-season fund raising
17. CLINICS AND CAMPS	- conduct camps or clinics - evaluate success of event	- secure site, date, and facilities for summer camp	- write and print camp brochure	- distribute brochure - hire staff - register campers - plan program and order equipment
18. EVALUATIONS	- complete year-end report - evaluate success of program for past year	- evaluate players — individual performance skills	- evaluate team performance - conduct player conferences	- evaluate staff performance - evaluate recruiting - evaluate support staff
19. PROFESSIONAL INVOLVEMENT	- attend clinics and workshops	- keep up-to-date on rule changes, trends, innovative ideas - join professional organizations - be active in conference activities	- attend national championships and national coaches' conventions - run for offices in national association	- volunteer services for professional groups - attend workshops and clinics

Chart 2,
continued

Fig. 14.2
Well-conditioned athletes are able to perform difficult skills with little fear of injury.

The most logical time to stress strength development at the collegiate level seems to be during the off-season conditioning program. Weight-lifting programs should be designed to develop power and strength. Plyometric training (jump training) should also be incorporated into the off-season program.

The summer conditioning program should be designed to continue with strength-related conditioning. The summer period should also include programs designed to develop speed, flexibility, agility, and general cardiovascular endurance. Circuit training and sprint training are commonly used to develop these qualities. In addition, acrobatic training is necessary for developing agility, flexibility, and speed. Since the athlete usually works alone during the summer, these programs must be designed for individual work.

Pre-season conditioning should incorporate as many volleyball-type activities as possible. These specialized conditioning activities should stress further development of strength, flexibility, agility, and muscular endurance. Most often, the coach designs intense, demanding practices that lend themselves to the development of these qualities.

During the competitive season, athletes are primarily involved in technical and tactical training. Conditioning during this portion of the season is aimed at maintaining existing levels of fitness. As post-season tournament competition approaches, there is a gradual tapering off of physical work. The goal of this tapering is to enhance the body's ability to reach peak physical performance.

Practice

Much like seasonal conditioning, the practice schedule varies with the time of year. Pre-season practices should be longer and should stress individual skill repetition and heavy physical work. During pre-season practices, team play is limited and emphasis is placed upon individual performances. Moving into the competitive season phase of practice, the emphasis switches from individual performance to team-oriented drills that are designed to bring the team together as a unit. In the competitive season, repetitive drills are still used, but game situations become the central focus. The off-season provides opportunities for players to change techniques and improve fundamental skills. Although team play is limited during the off-season, it is important to provide some opportunities for play. Competition can serve as the athletes' reward for hard work.

Scheduling

At the collegiate level, scheduling is being done earlier and earlier each year. In most cases, conference offices put together master schedules several years in advance. When the conference schedule is complete, the coach may add non-conference matches or tournaments to the schedule. Some considerations in scheduling non-conference matches should be:

- Working within the budget.
- Adhering to institutional academic policies for days of class to be missed.
- Adhering to national governing body rules for the total number of allowable matches.
- Scheduling competition that challenges athletes (i.e., top twenty schools).
- Scheduling matches that allow travel to different parts of the country.

(The last two points are important when a team is being considered for berths in post-season tournaments.)

When the schedule is completed, contracts should be sent to each school. Form 1 shows the information found in a typical contract. (*Note:* Forms 1–12 appear at the end of this chapter.)

Competition

Playing the competitive schedule is the culmination of a year-long process of preparation. Once this period arrives, the coach should be well enough organized in all other aspects of the program that the principal focus of attention can be preparing the team for each match. Competition outside the primary season (USVBA, intrasquads, etc.) should be subordinate to the regular season schedule. It should be clear to the athletes that the primary season is the most important competition during the year.

Recruiting

In all likelihood, the ability of a coach to identify and recruit talented athletes to the program has a high correlation with the success of the program. Although many factors have significant influence on the coach's success, rarely can a coach take average athletes and transform them into a team capable of competing with the best in the country. Briefly outlined below is the recruiting process:

I. Identifying prospective recruits in their junior years.
   A. Subscribing to scouting services.
   B. Attending junior tournaments.
   C. Contacting state high school coaches for recommendations.

II. Initiating contacts during the summer before senior year and into early fall.
   A. Initiating correspondence.
   B. Initiating telephone contacts.
   C. Making initial home visits.

III. Making assessments of talent during the summer and fall of senior year.
   A. Attending Junior Olympic tournaments.
   B. Watching prospective recruits in high school matches — more than once if possible.

IV. Executing the final stages of recruitment in the fall and winter of senior year.
   A. Continuing correspondence.
   B. Continuing telephone contacts.
   C. Scheduling a visit to the athlete's school.
   D. Making additional home visits.
   E. Scheduling a campus visit for each athlete.
   F. Continuing to watch athletes compete whenever possible.
   G. Offering scholarships and signing athletes.

Assessing the talent and potential of an athlete is obviously an important task for the coach. Form 2, designed by Doug Beal, USA National Men's Coach, may be used for recording the potential of possible athletes.

Home visits are important in the recruiting process because they give the coach an opportunity to bring the program to the athlete and the athlete's family. Home visit appointments should be made at least two weeks in advance and should be scheduled at the convenience of the athlete and the athlete's family. In most cases, the visits should occur after the dinner hour and should be no more than two hours in duration. The primary objective of the initial home visit is to inform the athlete and his or her family about your program and to answer specific questions about the program. A typical home visit covers the following topics:

- Academics — bring specific academic information about the athlete's academic interests.
- University community — describe the university setting.
- Coach's philosophy — be ready to articulate your philosophy of coaching, both to the recruit and to his/her parents.
- University's commitment to the program — describe the type of support.
- Volleyball program specifics, including:
  - Budget
  - Scholarships
  - Items provided to athletes, such as shoes.

- Schedule and conference organization.
- Type and mode of travel.
- Facilities — practice and competitive.
- Staff — number and quality of coaches.
- Booster club
- Player promotions, such as highlight films.
- Dormitory facilities
- Program goals
- Description of returning players as it will relate to the prospect's status/position on the team.
- Coach's expectations for athletes in the program.
- Question and answer session.

The campus visit is a significant factor in the athlete's final decision. Whether the athlete selects your institution may well be determined by the perceptions of the program during one forty-eight-hour period. It is therefore advisable for the coach to plan the athlete's visit carefully. Form 3 outlines the type of information the athlete should receive prior to the visit. The student host should also receive a copy so that arrangements can be made for the recruit to be in the right place at the right time. Forms 4 and 5 illustrate other types of information-gathering tools that are helpful to the coach during the recruiting process.

Budget

Budget proposals are an annual ritual. Each spring, word comes down from the athletic director to prepare a proposal for the following year. The strategies for preparing these proposals vary depending on the financial environment at each institution. One strategy is to prepare a budget with built-in surpluses so that when it is cut, there will still be sufficient funds. Another strategy is to prepare a request which contains the bare minimum necessary for conducting the program. Whatever plan is used, be prepared to justify your requests. Once the actual budget is allocated, it is usually necessary to reassess the projected expenditures to insure that you operate within the budget. Primary budget items should include:

- Salaries
- Supplies
- Equipment
- Team travel
- Coaches' travel — scouting, clinics, meetings
- Recruiting
- Officials
- Telephone
- Game filming, videotape
- Player promotions, team promotions
- Memberships, subscriptions
- Scholarships
- Publications, media guide

Forms 6, 7, 8, 9, and 10 are examples of forms which can be used in making travel arrangements, requesting funds for travel, and returning unused travel funds.

Scouting

Scouting your opponents can provide your team members with valuable information for an upcoming match. However, the scouting report is most valuable to the coach. A good scouting report helps in structuring practices that allow your team to be more prepared to face the competition. With information from the scouting report, the coach may wish to make lineup changes, defensive adjustments, offensive changes, changes in serving strategy, or any number of other alterations. The key to providing team members with scouting reports is to know how much information to share. Sometimes the athletes can be so concerned with the opponents' tendencies that they fail to concentrate on their own play.

Scouting can become a very complex process of gathering data on opposing teams. A coach must decide what the relative value of detailed information will be to the team. Forms 11 and 12 are examples of very basic scouting information that can be gathered. Coaches who are unable to scout opponents may find it helpful to make notes about the opponents after the match. By attaching the box score to the following list of notes, the coach can at least be more prepared to meet the same team in the future. These items may be important notes to keep on your opponents:
- Offense employed
- Offensive tendencies and most successful play sets
- Defense, defensive adjustments
- Starting rotation
- Substitution patterns
- Serve receive formations
- Poor passers
- Best servers and type of serve
- Best blockers and blocking strategy
- Outstanding hitters and tendencies
- Ability of setter(s)
- General evaluation of match
- Mental toughness — do they fall apart — who is the key player

Event Management

The coach should delegate all the responsibilities of the event management to other members of the coaching staff or to the support staff. The coach will want to carefully supervise this process, since the image of the entire program is reflected by the manner in which the competitive events are run.

Inventory/Equipment Orders

The support staff in the equipment room should be charged with the responsibility of taking inventory and advising the coach about the condition of equipment and supplies. With this information, the coach should place necessary orders each spring. In most cases, institutions require that supply equipment orders be placed out on bid. To insure that you receive exactly what is desired, be sure to list all specifications and brand names.

Publicity/Sports Information

The sports information director has primary responsibility for publicity and sports information. The coach should serve as a consultant in preparing highlight tapes, media guides, and other informational materials regarding the team.

Program Promotions

The coach again serves as a consultant in promoting the volleyball program. In order to promote the program, it will be necessary for the coach to conduct demonstrations and exhibitions, work with the media, and be actively involved in public speaking. Advice from marketing experts is useful in developing a comprehensive promotional plan.

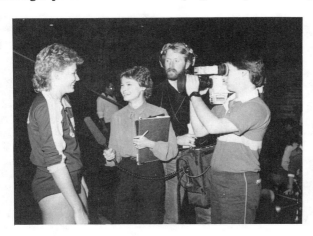

Fig. 14.3

Media exposure is an essential ingredient for a program's successful promotion.

Awards Banquet

Most athletic departments sponsor an annual banquet for all sports. However, these affairs rarely provide adequate time for a coach to recognize individual team members as he or she would like. For this reason, a separate volleyball banquet is a desirable event, and it can be as informal as a picnic or as formal as a banquet. The coach should determine the types of awards that will be presented to the players.

Booster Club

A booster club can do a great deal to enhance the image of your program. Such a club provides a base of support for your team. Set some goals for the booster club, such as increasing attendance at games, increasing public awareness of the program, and providing supplemental funds for special volleyball projects. Enthusiastic leadership for the booster club is essential.

Clinics and Camps

The coach should become involved in conducting clinics and camps. Clinics are usually directed at educating other coaches, whereas camps usually teach skills to athletes. Both camps and clinics offer the coach an opportunity to showcase the program. Summer camps can also provide opportunities to develop young athletes who may help your program in the future.

Evaluations

All areas of a program must be constantly evaluated if improvements are to be made. Evaluations conducted orally with staff and players are valuable for the participants, but these conversations should be accompanied by written evaluations. A year-end report should include an evaluation of every phase of the program.

Fig. 14.4

The ultimate success of a program is reflected in the team's performance on game day.

Professional Involvement

If the sport of volleyball is to grow, it is imperative for coaches to join and become actively involved in their national associations. Professional associations such as the American Volleyball Coaches Association were founded for the express purpose of promoting volleyball. The coach should also attend as many clinics as possible to keep abreast of current trends.

SUMMARY

A volleyball program should have well-defined goals and philosophy, which should be compatible with those of the university. The responsibilities involved in the administration of a collegiate volleyball program are great, but the magnitude of the job can be lessened if a systematic approach is taken. A well-organized volleyball program should accomplish three things. First, it should provide the athletes with every possible opportunity to succeed. Second, it should be a positive reflection of the university's philosophy. Finally, it should reflect the pride and professionalism of the coach.

CONTRACT

This agreement, made and entered into on the _____ day of _____,
19 ____, by and between the Athletic Associaiton of [college/university] _____
_____ and the athletic authorities of _____,
_____ their duly authorized agents, is in accordance with the following conditions:

- Sport:_____
- Place:_____
- Date of Event:_____
- Time of Event:_____
- Practice/Warm-up Time:_____
- Agreement on Officials:_____
- Special Agreements Concerning the Scheduled Event:
    - Locker Room:_____
    - Uniforms:_____
    - Equipment (training room, supplies, etc.):_____
    - Competitive Rules:_____
    - Financial (entry fees, guarantees, etc.):_____
    - Other:_____

Official Representative of Visiting Team	Official Representative of [COLLEGE/UNIVERSITY]
Coach_____	Coach_____
Telephone (_____)_____	Telephone (_____)_____
Address_____	Address_____
_____	_____
Director of [Men's/Women's] Athletics	Director of [Men's/Women's] Athletics
_____	_____
Signature	Signature
Univ. Phone (_____)_____	Telephone (_____)_____
Home Phone (_____)_____	

Please sign and return white & yellow copies to:

Distribution:
White copy: Home Athletic Director
Yellow copy: Home Coach
Pink copy: Visiting Athletic Director
Gold copy: Visiting Coach

[College/University]
[Men's/Women's] Athletic Department
_____
_____

Form 1 Sample contract used for regular season matches.

PLAYER EVALUATION REPORT

PLAYER_____ RH_____ LH_____ HT_____ WT_____
Position_____Vertical Jumping Ability_____(standing jump/two-step approach)
Year in school_____ACT_____SAT_____ _____ Class rank_____ GPA_____
Honors (League, State, National)_____
_____

USVBA Experience: Years_____ Club Name_____ Club Coach_____
_____

RATING CODE: 5 – Superior, 4 – Excellent, 3 – Good, 2 – Fair
[Circle one in each category]

SPIKING   5   4   3   2
What angle does player usually hit?_____
Can player hit the line?_____
Is he/she bothered by a 2–3 man block?_____
Does he/she spike deep sets as well as close?_____
Can he/she hit fast playsets?_____

SERVING   5   4   3   2
Type of serve player uses: Overhead Floater____ Overhead Spin Serve_____ Japanese Floater_____
Does he/she usually serve to the same spot and same depth?_____
Can player serve to the six positions on the court?_____
Is he/she an aggressive server?_____

SETTING   5   4   3   2   (Only for setters)
Is player able to set combination plays?_____
Can he/she effectively set fast to the sides?_____
Can player short set the middle?_____
Can he/she set the ball effectively with an underhand pass?_____
Can he/she set very high sets accurately?_____
Are sets close to sideline or in toward middle?_____
Does player always set direction he/she faces?_____
Does he/she tip-off overhead set?_____ How?_____
Can player jump set?_____

BLOCKING   5   4   3   2
Is player a good outside or center blocker?_____
Does player have good quickness?_____
Does he/she penetrate over the net?_____
Can player jump with: elbows_____hands above top of net_____?
Is he/she an aggressive blocker?_____

PASSING   5   4   3   2
Does player always have good lateral range in receiving zone?_____
Is he/she equally proficient in hard, soft, spin, and float serve receptions?_____
Can player pass consistently to target area?_____

Form 2 Player evaluation report for prospective athletes.

– 2 –

SPIKE DEFENSE   5   4   3   2
Does player handle hard spikes well?_____
How fast does player react to dinks?_____
Does he/she dive and roll with ease?_____
How efficiently does player get a ball hit away from him/her?_____

ATTITUDE   5   4   3   2
Is player a competitor?_____
Is he/she a pressure player?_____
Is player coachable?_____
Is he/she motivated?_____

OVERALL EVALUATION

(Circle one number in rating code that best describes him/her as a total volleyball player.)

5 – SUPERIOR

This player can execute offensive and defensive skills with a high degree of consistency. Player is able to analyze or anticipate opponents. Excels under pressure.

4 – EXCELLENT

Player may not excel in all areas of the game, but is outstanding in one facet of the sport. For example, outstanding on offense but is back-courted.

3 – GOOD

Average skills, not outstanding. Steady player, but does not excel in one particular phase of the game.

4 – FAIR

He/she may lack playing experience, but has potential to become a good player.

This player is capable of playing:
DIVISION I_____   DIVISION II_____   DIVISION III_____   J. C._____

University or College preference_____
Area of study_____

Remarks_____
_____
_____
_____
_____
_____

Date_____

Player evaluation report (Form 2), continued

```
┌──────────────────────────────────────────────────────────┐
│              (  CAMPUS VISIT ITINERARY  )                  │
│                                                            │
│  NAME _____    │
│                                                            │
│  HOST/HOSTESS _____    │
│                                                            │
│  ARRIVAL – DATE/TIME _____     │
│                                                            │
│        –  Airline _____                  │
│        –  Flight Number _____                        │
│                                                            │
│  HOUSING ACCOMMODATIONS _____     │
│                                                            │
│                                                            │
│  MEETINGS/ENTERTAINMENT                                    │
│                                                            │
│  ACADEMIC ADVISOR _____     │
│                                                            │
│  HEAD COACH _____     │
│                                                            │
│  CAMPUS TOUR _____     │
│                                                            │
│  PHOTO SESSION _____     │
│                                                            │
│  TRAINERS _____     │
│                                                            │
│  ENTERTAINMENT _____     │
│                                                            │
│  OTHER ACTIVITIES _____     │
│                                                            │
│                 _____      │
│                                                            │
│                 _____      │
│                                                            │
│                                                            │
│  DEPARTURE – DATE/TIME _____     │
│                                                            │
│        –  Airline _____                  │
│        –  Flight Number _____                │
└──────────────────────────────────────────────────────────┘
```

Form 3 Campus visit itinerary. Should be mailed to the prospective athlete before his or her visit.

VOLLEYBALL ATHLETIC GRANT APPLICATION

Date_____

Name_____ Date of birth_____
Age_____ Height_____ Weight_____ High school graduation yr_____

Home address_____
City_____ State_____ Zip code_____
Home phone_____ Social security number_____

High school_____ School phone_____
School address_____
Coach's name_____

High school class rank_____ Total number of students in class_____
Grade point average_____ ACT test score_____
                                SAT test scores_____ _____
What college, if any, have you attended?_____
JC graduated_____

Father's name_____ Father's occupation_____
Mother's name_____ Mother's occupation_____

What extracurricular activities, other than sports, have you participated in during high school? List
any special honors or awards. _____
_____
_____

What career or profession might you like to pursue? What will be your college major?_____
_____
_____

VOLLEYBALL INFORMATION

Years of participation_____ Favorite or best position_____
Standing vertical jump_____ Running approach jump_____ Reach_____

List any summer camps you have attended_____
_____
Individual honors_____
Team record and accomplishments_____
_____

[Please attach any individual or team statistics that are available.]

*Form 4   Athletic grant application, which should be completed by the prospective athlete
and returned to the head coach.*

———— VOLLEYBALL RECRUITING CONTACTS ————

NAME _____

HIGH SCHOOL _____

HOMETOWN _____

HEIGHT _____   POSITION _____

PROFILE _____
_____
_____

PERSONAL CONTACTS

	Date	Made by	Where	Comments
1.				
2.				
3.				
4.				
5.				
6.				

PHONE CONTACTS OR CAMPUS VISITS

Date	Made by	Comments

Form 5   Recruiting contact sheet. Most institutions are required to keep accurate records of the number of personal contacts made with recruits. This form is also helpful in keeping a recruiting history for each athlete.

TRAVEL ARRANGEMENTS

COACH_____ SPORT_____

DATE OF TRIP_____ DESTINATION_____

....

HOTEL/MOTEL

Hotel accommodations needed?_____ In what city?_____

Dates needed_____ Number of Singles_____ Doubles_____ Quads_____ Other_____

....

CARS/VANS/WAGONS

# Needed:	Destination	Pickup date/time	Return date/time
Cars ____			
Vans ____			
Wagons ____			

....

BUS

Destination_____

Departure date & time_____

Shuttle needed?_____ Approximate departure time, return trip_____

....

FLIGHT INFORMATION

Destination_____ # of reservations_____

When you must be at destination_____

Earliest possible time of return_____

[List names in traveling party]

....

MEALS

of persons_____ # of days_____ $ per day per person_____

Total_____

....

RENTAL CARS

Type and # needed_____

....

ENTRY FEE

Entry fee required?_____ Amount_____ Payable to_____

[Please note any special requirements on back of form.]

Form 6 Team travel arrangement form. Should be completed and turned in well in advance of actual travel.

STAFF/RECRUITING TRAVEL INFORMATION

Coach_____ **Team**_____

Date of trip_____ Destination_____
Hotel/motel_____
Address_____
Telephone_____

Reservation confirmation number_____

....

ROOMS

Type	Price	Dates reserved
Single_____	_____	_____
Double_____	_____	_____

....

TRANSPORTATION

Rent-a-car information_____
_____
Instructions_____
Gasoline expense_____

....

MEALS, etc.

Meals for_____days

Tickets for events (program, parking, etc.)_____

Recruiting of_____
Other purpose_____

TOTAL ADVANCE:_____

Form 7   Staff travel information. Should be completed at least two weeks prior to departure.

TEAM TRAVEL ROSTER

TEAM_____

TRIP TO/FROM_____

DATE_____

ROSTER

1. _____   14. _____
2. _____   15. _____
3. _____   16. _____
4. _____   17. _____
5. _____   18. _____
6. _____   19. _____
7. _____   20. _____
8. _____   21. _____
9. _____   22. _____
10. _____
11. _____
12. _____
13. _____

Manager _____   Trainer _____

Coaches _____

_____

_____

Form 8   Team travel roster, which lists all members of traveling party. Submit prior to departure.

TRAVEL EXPENSE VOUCHER

Name_____   Requisition No._____

Sport_____   Check No._____

Destination_____   Amount of Advance_____

Purpose of Trip_____   Budget No._____

Dates_____

This form should be turned in as soon as possible.. Please list "to" and "from" when turning in receipts from taxi expenses. Upon return, please remit the amount you did not spend, if any, in the form of a personal check payable to_____.

Date	Description of Misc.	Car Rental	Hotel	Misc.	B	Meals L	D	TOTALS
Totals								

NOTES:

Amount of advance   _____

Total amount spent   _____

Amount due University _____

Amount due you   _____

Form 9 Travel expense voucher, to be completed after return to campus. It is a detailed listing of expenditures, with receipts attached.

TEAM ITINERARY

DATE	DEPART (CITY)	ARRIVE (CITY)	MATCH/DATE/TIME	MOTEL	MODE OF TRANSPORTATION

Form 10 Team itinerary.

VOLLEYBALL STATISTICS
Scouting Chart

TEAM SCOUTING_____ vs. _____ Date:_____

serve reception formation
— starting lineup

rotation 2 formation
subs:

rotation 3 formation
subs:

rotation 4 formation
subs:

rotation 5 formation
subs:

rotation 6 formation
subs:

DEFENSIVE COVERAGE

Offense_____ Best blocker_____ Best hitter_____

Best passer_____ Weakest passer_____ Left-handed hitters_____

Best server (type)_____ Setters_____ Center hitter_____

Strong side hitters_____ Weak side hitters_____ Defense_____

Form 11 Scouting chart for gathering basic information on opponents' team play.

VOLLEYBALL STATISTICS
Shot Chart

Match_____vs._____ won by_____

Date_____ Site_____ Scores_____

player #_____ team____   player #_____ team_____   player #_____ team____
NOTES:

player #_____ team_____   player #____ team_____   player #_____ team_____
NOTES:

KEY

——— line of spike (no kill)   ⇒ spike blocker – deflection

• tip   ⇒ spike blocked – stuff

—• spike and point/side-out, kill   ~ off-speed spike

• tip and point/side-out

Chart each hit by originating the line for each hit at the approximate place the set was made in relation to the net. If the hit goes out of bounds, extend the line over (past) the sidelines.

Form 12 Shot chart for recording the hitting tendencies of individual opposing players.

15
PHYSICAL FACTORS

Ian Pyka

The factors involved in the training of an athlete can be categorized under two main headings: physical and psychological. Both are extremely important for total development of the athlete, but at least 75 percent of volleyball training comes under the heading of physical factors.

The basis of all training is the physical element. If a thoroughbred is not trained properly, the best jockey in the world will find it hard to win a race with that horse. The same principle applies to volleyball players. No matter how psyched up team members become, they will find it hard to win if their opponents are better prepared physically. This chapter presents the ingredients necessary for a good physical training program for volleyball.

PLANNING A TRAINING PROGRAM

Three factors must be remembered when setting up any physical training program. The first is *feasibility*. The program must be feasible financially, that is, there must be enough money for facilities and equipment, or for their purchase. You must also consider the time factor. It may not be feasible to plan on training four hours a day because of school, work, or even traveling time to the training location.

The program must also be *attainable*. Each individual training program must include an attainable goal in the same manner that each individual athlete must set his or her own performance goals for competition. It is not realistic to set up the same program for a high school team as for the Olympic team. For the less mature high school team, the Olympic training program might cause fatigue and possible physical injury, and might cause players to lose all interest in playing volleyball.

The third and most important factor is *specificity*. The training program must be specific not only to the sport but also to the individual. For example, you would not train a distance runner the same way you would train a sprinter. Why should a sprinter want to run distance all the time when his or her event is a sprint? In the same respect, you would not have a volleyball player train by shooting basketballs, because the arm movement in shooting is not the same as it is in spiking. Yet you may want this player to stuff or dunk basketballs in the hoop while standing almost directly underneath the basket. For the capable individuals who can do this, the movement of the jump and flexion of the wrists closely simulate the position of the block at the net. To maintain specificity, exercises or drills whose movements closely resemble those of the sport itself are very beneficial to the program and make for a more rapid improvement of skills.

As in any good recipe, the nature of the ingredients is important, but using the proper amounts of these ingredients is what makes or breaks the recipe. Anyone can put together a program for volleyball, but the successful coach sits down and plans a program with all the right ingredients in the proper amounts. Many coaches go into their seasons with very little planned. These coaches will encounter many problems during the season, such as player weaknesses, injuries resulting from weakness, and a plateau of progress not only at present, but carrying into the future. The successful coach, on the other hand, plans far in advance. How far? Some plan as far as a year in advance. This is very realistic, and it works.

Periodization

The idea behind planning the training program far in advance is called *periodization*. Understanding periodization and applying it to a volleyball training program can transform a mediocre team into a good one, and a good team into a great one. Periodization simply means dividing up a large block of time into smaller blocks; each smaller block (or period) of time contains different types of training routines. These routines would not vary widely, but just enough to change the pace a bit. The variations could be in the form of intensity, duration, frequency, or even type of exercise performed. Let me first define these terms and later give you examples.

Intensity is simply how hard someone works. It can apply to one exercise alone, or it can be adapted to the entire training day or period. For example, on a given day the team may work at 90 percent of its maximum capacity in the weight room. Two other days during the week they work at 70 and 80 percent of their maximum lifts. So, they have put in one light workout (70 percent), one medium workout (80 percent), and one heavy workout (90 percent). The average intensity of the weight workouts for that week would be 80 percent. The monthly workout intensities can be calculated in the same way.

Duration refers to individual workouts and is the amount of time it takes to complete the exercise or workout. The length of time the athlete works out can be very important during different parts of the cycle. For example, during the competitive season, the duration of the workouts should be markedly reduced, whereas during pre-season the workouts would be longer.

Frequency is the number of workouts put in during the day or week. As you will see, it is very important to vary the frequency of workouts once your competitive season begins. Using weight workouts as an example again, a coach might plan two workouts per week during the competitive season, and three workouts per week during the pre-season.

The **types** of drills or exercises performed do not vary as much as the intensity, duration, or frequency do. Every now and then, however, it is good practice to throw in something new or delete something relatively unimportant to keep the athletes from getting stale and losing interest.

The ultimate goal of periodization is for your team to achieve a maximal peak, whether it be at the end of a one-year or a four-year program. Application of the peaking system guards against one of the most prevalent sport diseases in our country today, and that is overtraining. In the following explanation of periodization (or peaking), you will see how overtraining can be prevented.

A Sample Training Cycle

Now let me try to paint a picture for you, incorporating all the training factors just discussed. Generally, all peaking cycles should be composed of an off-season period, a pre-season period, and a competitive period; Figure 15.1 shows a one-year cycle. At the beginning of your team's peaking cycle, in the off-season well before the season begins, conditioning should be the main emphasis. This will lay the groundwork for your entire season. During this period, workouts should be of low intensity and moderate-to-high duration and frequency. Most of the exercises should be tailored to build up the aerobic system. Endurance-type work is called for here, along with any drills which outline the volleyball skills and still meet the aerobic requirement.

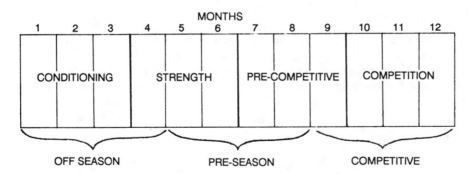

Fig. 15.1

Because the intensity will be low, duration and frequency of training must be increased in order to produce a training effect. So, during the conditioning phase, workouts should be planned so that the work itself is less than maximum (around 70 percent), the duration of the workouts is long enough to get a training effect, and the frequency of workouts is between three and six days per week (three days per week has been shown to be the minimum frequency needed to get a training effect). A large volume of exercises should be implemented during this time. The types of exercises or drills to be performed in the conditioning phase will be discussed in the final section of this chapter.

The *pre-season period* training should consist of strength-type activities. During this period, the body is already conditioned for heavier workouts. The intensity increases here to at least 80 or 85 percent, and the duration and frequency decrease slightly to allow the body ample recovery time. The volume of exercises also decreases, and emphasis is placed on using just the right exercise to guarantee the workout's specificity. Endurance or aerobic work is minimized here in order to establish anaerobic power, which deals with more intense bouts of exercise over shorter periods of time.

The *competitive period* is usually split into two components, minor and major. Although they are very similar in makeup, the former is just a buildup for the latter. The main difference is in the intensity of the physical training. Physical training in the major competitive period has the lowest intensity of the entire cycle, and it is during this time that the body undergoes its greatest replenishment of energy stores through rest. Exercises emphasize speed and quickness, with a decrease in intensity, duration, and frequency of workouts. Fine-tuning adjustments, either mental or physical, are also made here. A minor peak should occur after the minor competitive period, but the ultimate in performance should occur at the end of the major competitive period.

Often a twelve-month macro-cycle (Figure 15.1) is not feasible. In this case, I recommend condensing this macro-cycle into a shorter six-month cycle (Figure 15.2). In this cycle, the first two months would be conditioning; the second two months would be the strength phase; month five would be the minor competitive period; and month six would be the major competitive period.

The last alternative would be a four-month mini-cycle (Figure 15.3). This is still an effective cycle for advanced athletes who have already gone through one or more cycles prior to this one. It is less effective for first timers because of the limited time for developing conditioning and strength. Many times, the body cannot adapt as quickly to the shorter cycle and the athlete enters the next period without getting the full benefits of the previous period.

Planning for Periodization

How does one start to plan this periodization? The best way to arrange the program is not from start to finish, but from finish to start. Let me explain. The main reason for using a peaking cycle is to reach a physical and mental peak for a given competition. Therefore, the first step in planning is to select the major competition. Once this is achieved, the program is planned backwards from that point. For example, Figure 15.4 illustrates the planning for a peak for the Nationals in late June.

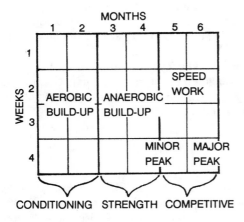

Fig. 15.2

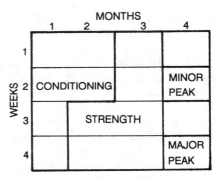

SIX WEEKS CONDITIONING
SIX WEEKS STRENGTH
FOUR WEEKS COMPETITION

Fig. 15.3

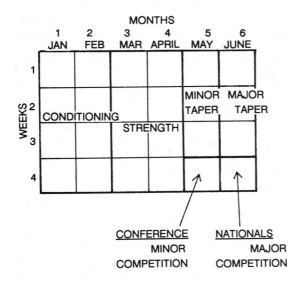

Fig. 15.4

Remember that the major peak should be planned according to the ability of your team. If the team has no realistic chance of competing in the Nationals, then the conference or perhaps a local tournament should be the major peak. No matter where the peak is to occur, the periods preceding it must be properly planned in advance to prepare for the peak.

You now have a general idea of how to set up a peaking cycle, so let us look at some of the methods used in this cycle to condition and strengthen the athlete for competition. The methods include providing basic nutrition, weight training, flexibility training, plyometrics, electro-muscle stimulation, and resistance training in the pool.

PROVIDING BASIC NUTRITION

Nutrition may be described as the relationship of foods to the health of the human body. Proper nutrition means receiving adequate foods and supplements in order to obtain the required nutrients for optimal health. Without the right combination of exercise and nutrition, optimal health and well-being cannot be maintained. For proper nutrition, all the essential nutrients (including carbohydrates, fats, protein, vitamins, minerals, and water) must be supplied and utilized in adequate balance.

The primary sources of energy used by the body are carbohydrates, fats, and protein. The typical diet probably takes in 50 percent carbohydrates, 35 percent fats, and 15 percent protein. The potential of food to be used as fuel is expressed in calories. The term "calories" is used to quantify the amount of chemical energy that may be released as heat when food is metabolized. Fat yields approximately nine calories per gram, whereas carbohydrates and protein yield about four calories per gram each. The higher the caloric yield, the higher the energy value of the food.

Carbohydrates

Carbohydrates are the chief source of energy for muscular exertion and for all body functions. Carbohydrates can immediately supply available calories for energy by producing heat in the body when carbon in the system unites with the oxygen in the bloodstream.

The main carbohydrates in foods are sugars, starches, and cellulose. The easiest sugars to digest are the simple sugars, those which can be found in fruits and honey. Table sugar is much harder to digest but is still less complex than starches. All starches must be broken down to simple sugars (glucose) for digestion. All carbohydrates must be converted to glucose before they can be used. Glucose, or "blood sugar," is used as fuel by tissues of the brain, muscles, and nervous system. A small part of this glucose is converted to fat, and it too is stored throughout the body as an energy reserve. Weight loss occurs when fat reserves are reconverted to glucose and burned as body fuel.

Fats

Fats are the most concentrated source of energy in our diet. In addition to their high energy contribution, fats surround, hold in place, and protect organs such as the kidneys, heart, and liver. A layer of fat insulates the body from abrupt environmental temperature changes and is responsible for preserving body heat. Fats also prolong the process of digestion by slowing down the hydrochloric acid secretions in the stomach, which gives the long-lasting feeling of fullness after the consumption of a fatty meal.

Protein

The most plentiful substance in the human body is water, followed by protein. Protein is vitally important in the maintenance of good health as well as in the growth and development of all body tissue. It is responsible for the building of muscles, blood, skin, hair, nails, and internal organs such as the heart and brain. Protein is needed for the formation of hormones, regulation of the body's water balance, and the formation of enzymes and antibodies. In addition, it is important in the process of blood clotting.

Studies have shown that adult protein needs do not increase significantly during physical activity. In fact, one gram of protein per kilogram of body weight is sufficient as a daily requirement. Excess protein intake cannot be stored. After the nitrogen molecules have been stripped off the excess protein, the remaining carbon skeleton is converted to either glucose or fat. The excess nitrogen is excreted in the urine.

Most meats and dairy products are complete protein foods, which means they contain all the essential amino acids. Most vegetables and fruits are incomplete proteins and must be balanced with complete proteins in the diet. Other sources of proteins include fish, poultry, soybean products, eggs, milk, milk products, and whole grains.

Vitamins and Minerals

Certain vitamin needs increase with physical activity. For example, some B vitamins serve as co-factors (the active portions of the enzyme) on enzymes involved in carbohydrate metabolism. However, increased physical activity is usually accompanied by an increased caloric intake to meet the energy demand. The vitamin needs in this case can be met with a sound diet. I do suggest, if you want your team members to cut calories and maintain or increase exercise, that you consider their taking a daily vitamin supplement.

If your team already takes vitamin supplements, make sure that they stay near the RDA listed on the product. Also remember that excessive doses of water-soluble vitamins, like B and C, will be excreted in the urine. The fat-soluble vitamins like A and D, on the other hand, accumulate. In extreme cases, overdosing can lead to headache, nausea, diarrhea, or even decalcification of the bones (the latter is associated with vitamin A).

The increased need for minerals which arises with exercise can also be met with an increase in the normal diet. All females and young males have the potential for low iron levels. This should be offset by the addition of a daily iron supplement. Desiccated liver is also an excellent supplement for an iron-poor diet.

Other Dietary Factors

In today's athletics, the travel schedule is a major part of any program. Coaches and athletes alike find it difficult to maintain an adequate, balanced diet when on the road. Grabbing food at fast-food restaurants becomes commonplace. Individuals tend to overeat at one meal because they know that they may not get another chance to eat that day. Consuming fewer than three meals a day causes higher triglyceride and cholesterol levels than eating more frequently than that. Eating more frequent, smaller meals helps satisfy the hunger urge, lessens fatigue, and lowers blood lipid (fat) levels.

The most appropriate diet for athletes is a well-balanced one. I believe the diet must be as low in fat as possible, with the bulk consisting of complex carbohydrates and protein. The protein intake is important and should be especially emphasized during the strength phase of your cycle. Complex carbohydrates are high in fiber, and much has been printed recently about the advantages of a high-fiber diet. Complex carbohydrates are also the best form of energy, which is important for the athlete. Also, remember that carbohydrates have only four calories per gram, so eat up!

Finally, in preparing for a match, what kinds of foods should an athlete eat and when? Does carbohydrate loading help before competition? I personally have had success with this method, but this success could be due to the exclusion of hard-to- digest meats. The old concept of eating meats to make one strong for competition is out. First, meat cannot be used as fuel. Second, the blood flow to the splanchnic region (stomach) in response to the demand for digestion draws away blood from the exercising muscles. The protein associated with meats is essential for rebuilding muscle tissue, but it has no significant place in a pre-competition diet. The pre-competition meal, eaten no later than two-and-a-half to three hours before competition, should be a light meal with easy-to-digest foods, preferably complex carbohydrates.

WEIGHT TRAINING

Not all weight training is identical. Some individuals train for bulk, and others for definition. Some train for strength, and others for speed. In the case of volleyball, strength is needed in the form of speed. This is called *power* and can be defined as force times distance, or the rate at which work is done. In other words, explosive-type movements are desirable in a weight program for volleyballers. Before I get into the types of exercises to perform, I will discuss the major muscle groups of the body which must be worked for volleyball. Since the hips and legs are responsible for jumping and running, they get first priority. Muscle groups involved include the quadriceps, hamstrings, calves, and those associated with the hips, such as the gluteus and adductor muscles. The smaller muscles of the upper body that will be discussed are the deltoids, triceps, biceps, forearm flexors, and pectoralis groups.

Weight training for volleyball should be as specific to the sport as possible. Each exercise movement should correlate highly with the movement involved in the sport. Since volleyball is a very quick and powerful game, the exercises chosen should be of a powerful nature. At the same time, the lifting program should be well-rounded and geared toward a total body strengthening. Dr. John Garhommer, an expert in the field of biomechanics, has shown repeatedly that Olympic-style weightlifters produced the highest power outputs (during the snatch and clean and jerk) of any human movement measured to date. Keeping this in mind, along with the following technical understanding of the lifts, you will understand why I highly recommend these Olympic lifts for any program.

The ingredients to a good lifting program should always include some type of *pull* (Olympic lifts), some type of *push* or *press* (overheads or bench), and the *squat*. These three main categories allow for the development of power while strengthening the upper and lower body simultaneously. Along with these three types of lifts, auxiliary exercises must be performed. They are of less importance but contribute to the development of total body strength.

The Pulls

In my opinion, the Olympic lifts are the most important part of any program. They are explosive, they work the total body, and the movement involved correlates very highly with that of jumping. Also, the body balance and coordination achieved through these lifts is unsurpassed by other exercises.

When lifting for the first time, little or no weight should be used, and technique should be emphasized. The concept of the movement involved is more important than the actual weight lifted. The movement from the floor is the same for all lifts when doing pulls. There may be slight variations in hand spacing or the finish of the lift, for instance, but on the whole the lifts are performed in the same manner.

Olympic lifters, when performing the snatch and clean, drop into a full squat with the weight. This is necessary in order to get under the heavy weights faster. For our purposes, we do not need to full squat the weight because the movement from the floor is more important to us than breaking world lifting records. Therefore, we do variations called the *power clean* and the *power snatch*. These are much safer than the Olympic lifts. In addition, they promote total body conditioning and increase power output.

Power Clean. If there were one exercise I had to choose which worked the entire body while promoting the important power aspect of training, it would be the power clean. The starting position for the clean is shown in Figure 15.5. The feet are about shoulder width apart (depending on the individual's size), with the toes pointing slightly outward, and the shins just barely touching the bar. The back should be flat and tight, with the head position vertical or neutral throughout the lift. The weight should be distributed through the heel-arch portion of the foot when initiating the pull. The arms are straight with the elbows turned out. This causes the shoulders to run forward, which brings the mass of the shoulder girdle forward. This is one of the larger mass areas of the body and can critically affect technique. Curling the wrists in (overhand grip) toward the body can heighten this effect.

From this position, the lifter extends the legs and hips, keeping pressure on the heel-arch of the foot (Figure 15.6). This means the back angle stays the same and the hips rise vertically. The bar must be kept as close to the body as possible throughout the lift. When approaching the knees with the bar, the shoulders should be over the bar with the elbows still pointing outward. If the shoulders are behind the bar, the tendency is to swing the bar up, but this is inefficient and can contribute to injury.

At this point, stretching the hamstrings almost demands an unconscious movement of the hips and legs down and forward (Figure 15.7). This, combined with the thought of scooping or rotating the hips while always maintaining a tight back, will bring the hips down and forward. The downward action is necessary to insure adequate bend in the knees in order to gain the strongest leverage. It also initiates the final extension phase of the legs and hips.

Fig. 15.5   *Fig. 15.6*   *Fig. 15.7*

Fig. 15.8   *Fig. 15.9*

The feet are still flat on the floor at this point, but the weight has begun to shift forward to the toes. This is called the *power position*. As the weight is shifted forward, the legs and hips fully extend until the athlete goes straight up onto his or her toes, and simultaneously shrugs the shoulders (Figure 15.8). At this point, the athlete shuffles his or her feet to the sides in order to lower the center of gravity under the bar. This is where the complete Olympic move (squatting down fully) differs from the power move (catching the bar high with about 45 degrees of knee flexion). While the shuffle is being executed, the ensuing movement is to rack the bar across the deltoids and clavicle for the clean (Figure 15.9). The weight is steadied, the feet return to their initial position, and the bar is returned to the floor with a tight back.

Power Snatch. As mentioned earlier, minor differences separate the power snatch from the power clean, but the movement itself is the same. The grip in the snatch is wider than it is in the clean (Figure 15.10) because the bar must be lifted from the floor to an overhead, arms-locked position in one pauseless move. The wider grip, as opposed to a narrower clean grip, allows for a shorter pulling distance and therefore a quicker lift.

The foot spacing may also be moved out a bit at the start in order for the hips to sit a little lower. This is necessary for a strong bottom position when using a wider snatch grip. Figure 15.10 shows the lifter just before getting into the lower position.

Notice the positions shown in Figures 15.11, 15.12, and 15.13. They are similar to those in Figures 15.6, 15.7, and 15.8, respectively. Figure 15.13 shows the full extension position. Notice how close the bar remains to the body in all the positions and especially in the full extension (Figures 15.8 and 15.13). When shrugging the shoulders, as seen in these two figures, it is important to keep the bar as close to the body as possible for balance and maximum force.

Figure 15.14 depicts the final position of the power snatch. The back should be kept tight and arched and the elbows locked for stability. Shuffling the feet to the sides also makes for a more stable base while simultaneously allowing the center of gravity to drop a bit, making for a quicker lock-out.

The Squats

Contrary to the beliefs of many coaches, squats are not "bad for you." If done properly, the back squat is tremendous for leg and hip strength, and it builds up the back, and develops total body balance and flexibility. There are two variations of squats: the front squat and the back squat.

In the *front squat*, the bar is rested along the clavicle and deltoids (Figure 15.9). The muscles emphasized are the quadriceps, especially those attachments close to the knee. I do not recommend front squats for this type of program because the back squat is easier, safer, and less traumatic to the joints involved.

Fig. 15.10   Fig. 15.11   Fig. 15.12

Fig. 15.13   Fig. 15.14

Figures 15.15, 15.16, and 15.17 illustrate the proper way to *back squat*. The bar is placed on the trapezius muscles of the upper back. The feet should be shoulder width apart, with the toes pointed out slightly. The head is neutral, and the lower back is tightened (Figure 15.15). The back should never round — a tight or arched back should be stressed when coaching.

After the stance is set and stable, the first move is to sit back with the hips, keeping the back tight and the weight distributed through the heel-arch of the foot (Figure 15.16). The head remains neutral or looking straight ahead as the hips continue down. Keeping the chest up aids in keeping the lower back arched. This is a helpful practice when teaching the tight back.

In terms of depth, the bottom position (Figure 15.16) is what I call a parallel squat. In my opinion, anything short of a parallel squat (Figure 15.17) is not efficient, and anything below parallel may be harmful if not done properly.

The key to a proper squat is flexing the hips and knees together. They are made to work together, so they should be trained that way. Figure 15.16 is a prime example of flexing at the two joints without loosening the back or disrupting good shoulder position. The bar should remain directly over the toes, or as close as possible, in the parallel positions. If the knees extend far beyond the toes, knee and lower back problems may result. A simple adjustment of the hips to the rear should prevent this from occurring. Remember, the weight is on the heel-arch of the foot.

I have seen great improvements in flexibility using this type of squat with volleyballers. It has increased their floor position for defense in that they can squat down lower yet remain comfortable. They also showed much greater speed operating from this position. In addition, if done correctly, squats, along with pulls, can increase vertical jumps dramatically.

Fig. 15.17

Fig. 15.15   *Fig. 15.16*

The Presses

The last of the three categories, the press, includes the bench press, the incline press, and the behind-neck push press. All three are designed to develop upper-body strength but in different ways and through different muscle groups.

Bench Press. Almost all gyms have a bench. The bench press works the pectoralis groups, some latissimus dorsi, and the triceps. The starting position (Figure 15.18) is with the feet flat on the floor, and the buttocks and the back of the head flat on the bench. Hand spacing should be comfortable — not too wide and not too narrow. The bar should then be lowered under control to the chest (Figure 15.19) and, without any relaxation, returned to the starting position.

Incline Press. The incline press works the deltoids to a greater extent than the bench does. In addition, the movement of pressing upward parallels the movements in volleyball more closely than does the movement of the bench press. In the initial position, the feet are flat on the floor, the back is flat on the incline bench, and the hands are positioned a little further apart than they are in the bench press (Figure 15.20). The bar is then lowered under control to the highest point on the chest just below the chin (Figure 15.21). Notice that the elbows here are directly under the bar, allowing for a direct line of force to drive the bar up-

Fig. 15.18

Fig. 15.19

Fig. 15.20

Fig. 15.21

ward. If the hands are in too close, the elbows cannot be in their power position, and weakness and the possibility of injury are increased.

Behind-neck Push Press. This is another total-body exercise. It involves balance, coordination and speed. The starting position for this exercise is much the same as the preparation for the back squat (Figure 15.22). The main difference is that the feet should be moved a bit closer together in this exercise to allow room for the shuffle. The back must be tight, the head neutral, the chest up, and the weight distributed through the heel-arch (power position) of the foot.

The ensuing movement is to drop the hips directly downward, and then stop them (Figure 15.23). This movement lowers the body's center of gravity and consequently the bar. By stopping the hips abruptly, the Olympic bar will bend downward and rebound upward (because of the distribution of weight and the length of the bar). As the bar rebounds upward, the lifter should extend the body onto the toes, while maintaining a tight

Fig. 15.22

posture (Figure 15.24). At this point, the bar is accelerated upward and the arms are locked out at the elbows, while the feet are shuffled to the sides (Figure 15.25). The feet, when shuffled, should be returned to the floor flat. This will guarantee a more balanced final position. The feet are then returned to the starting position and the weight is lowered to the shoulders as seen in the first figure.

Fig. 15.23

Fig. 15.24

Fig. 15.25

During the conditioning cycle, I recommend doing behind-the-neck military (seated or standing) presses rather than the aforementioned lift. The military press is similar to the push press except that the lower body is not used. It is strictly meant to strengthen and condition the upper body. The reason for the suggested change is to insure that the upper body is well enough conditioned and strengthened to handle the force exerted by the more explosive move.

Auxiliary Exercises

These auxiliary exercises are not as important as the major lifts already described, but they do contribute to total body strengthening. They are sometimes referred to as "assistance exercises" and can aid in the improvement of the major lifts. The areas covered are the torso, legs, shoulders, and arms. It is important to remember that these are only assistance exercises and that heavy weights should not be used. Instead, the lifter should use light weights with more repetitions.

The Torso. The back and the abdomen must be in a good strength equilibrium to prevent injuries from occurring. Two exercises that I recommend for the back are the *good morning* and the *hyperextension*. The starting position for the good morning is similar to the starting position for the squat pictured earlier. The ensuing movement is to flex the hips backward and continue down with the weight forward (Figure 15.26). The back should remain flat and the hips should stop after a balance position has been reached. I must again stress that heavy weights should not be used — light weights with more repetitions will do the job. The head position must always be neutral, and the feet should stay flat on the floor. After a comfortable position has been reached (back no lower than parallel to the floor), the back is returned to the starting position. Remember, the movement should be slow and controlled.

Fig. 15.26

The second back exercise is the hyperextension. It can be performed on a hyperextension apparatus, as seen in Figure 15.27, or on a regular bench with a partner securing the feet. The hips must be placed just at the end of the bench with the hands clasped behind the head. Keeping the head up, the trunk is lowered, as seen in Figure 15.28. It is important not to drop the torso quickly, but to lower it with a controlled movement. The back is then raised to return to the starting position. In the top position, the back should be nearly parallel to the ground. Too much hyperextension can be counterproductive and harmful to the back. If done with a slow and controlled movement, this exercise is the safest and most productive assistance exercise for the back.

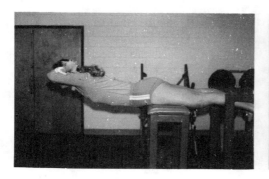

Fig. 15.27   Fig. 15.28

In order to keep an equilibrium of strength, the abdominals, which oppose the back muscles, must also be strengthened. Often, lower back problems stem from weak stomach muscles, hence the importance of the abdominal work. There are two abdominal exercises which work the entire abdominal area. The first is the sit-up. This should be performed with the buttocks as close to the heels as possible (Figure 15.29). The feet should be stabilized and the chin tucked to the chest. The arms should be crossed over the chest to maximize isolation of the abdominals without the use of the latissimus dorsi. The repetitions should be done at a slow and controlled rate, which will fatigue those muscles much more quickly than will rapid sit-ups. These sit-ups will work the upper abdominals and the midsection.

To work the lower abdominals and hip flexors, leg lifts should be performed. The starting position is lying flat on the back, with the feet together, hands clasped behind the head, and the chin tucked. Begin by raising the legs off the ground and pulling the knees toward the chest while keeping the shins parallel to the ground at all times (Figure 15.30). The feet are returned in the same manner but the ground should not be touched until the set is over. Leg lifts should also be done slowly to achieve maximum results.

The Legs. Whenever strengthening exercises are done to work a muscle group on one side of the body, the opposing muscles must also be worked. To counter the quadricep work, which is plentiful, the hamstrings must be worked. Leg curls are the best exercise for this. If a Nautilus leg curl is available, it is recommended because of its constant resistance through a full range of motion. Figure 15.31 shows the initial position for the leg curl, and it is important that the patella (kneecap) is placed just off the end of the bench.

Figure 15.32 shows the movement involved, isolating the hamstrings. Keeping the buttocks down while doing this exercise enables a more efficient working of the hamstrings. Again, repetitions should be controlled, with no jerking movements.

Fig. 15.29

Fig. 15.30

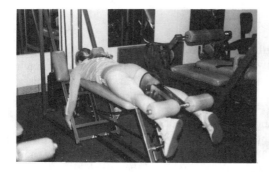

Fig. 15.31

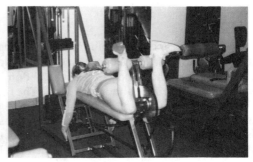

Fig. 15.32

If Nautilus equipment is not practical or available, leg curls may be done on a Universal or other machine, but the important full extension or stretch of the hamstrings as seen in Figure 15.31 will probably be difficult.

Jogging is a good method of building the calves, but a better way to strengthen and stretch this muscle group is through deep raises. These should be done with extra resistance, but with lack of equipment they can be performed with the weight of the body alone as resistance. Figure 15.33 shows the bottom position with the calves in a fully stretched position. Notice how straight the body is maintained. The heels are raised by the contraction of the calves and the body is raised (Figure 15.34). The heels are returned to the bottom position to complete one repetition. Again, the repetitions should be controlled, with no bouncing on the bottom.

The Shoulders. The best auxiliary exercise for the shoulders, especially for volleyball, is the pull-over. The starting position is flat on the bench, with the head hanging slightly off the end of the bench. The bar is held approximately at shoulders' width (Figure 15.35). The bar should be passed over the face and down past the top of the head. In this position (Figure 15.36), the shoulders, triceps, and latissimus dorsi should be stretched in order to increase flexibility and range of motion. Once this point has been reached, the bar is pulled over the head to the starting position in the same manner that it was lowered. You should be able to see the similarity between this exercise and serving or spiking the ball.

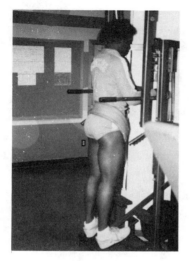

Fig. 15.33

Fig. 15.34

Fig. 15.35

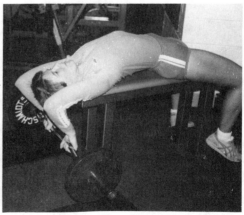

Fig. 15.36

The Arms. Three exercises we will discuss here are the French curl, the bicep curl, and the wrist curl. The *French curl* involves mainly the tricep muscles, which are located on the back of the arm. Strengthening this muscle group will help in the upper body lifts and in any movement requiring extension of the arm. This exercise may be done from either a seated or a standing position. Figure 15.37 pictures the starting position. The arms are fully extended with a close grip. The elbows flex to the outside, not forward, when lowering the bar (Figure 15.38). When the bar reaches the top of the head, the elbows tuck forward next to the ears, and the weight is lowered (Figure 15.39). Notice that the elbows are pointed straight up at this point. This position is excellent for stretching out the shoulders and triceps. The move upward is the same as the move downward. The first move is initiated by the elbows pulling forward, which is similar to the movement of pulling a shirt over one's head. Once the bar is at the back of the head, the elbows move out and the arms extend upward. This may be a variation of what your athletes are accustomed to, but the concept behind it is sound.

Fig. 15.37

Fig. 15.38

Fig. 15.39

The *bicep curl* is performed in the same manner, except a pull rather than a push is involved. Figure 15.40 shows the starting position. The hands are placed a little wider apart now, and the first move is with the elbows out rather than back (Figure 15.41). This allows for other muscle groups (trapezius, deltoids) to aid in the movement, and takes great pressure off the joints. The bar is kept as close to the body as possible at all times. When the bar

Fig. 15.42

Fig. 15.40

Fig. 15.41

cannot be pulled any longer with the elbows out (near the upper abdominal region), the elbows are tucked in close to the body and the bar is lifted to the clavicles (Figure 15.42). To complete one repetition, the bar is returned in the same way it was lifted, only in reverse order. The speed is slow and controlled.

The *wrist curl* works the flexor muscles of the wrist and fingers. This exercise may be done with a barbell or dumbbell. Figure 15.43 shows the arm position for a dumbbell wrist curl.

The wrist should be at the edge of the knee, allowing enough room for full extension. By moving the shoulder over the elbow and holding the forearm down with the other hand, isolation of the forearm flexors is accomplished. The weight should begin at the fingertips and be curled into the hand. The wrist is then flexed as much as possible while keeping the forearm on the thigh (Figure 15.44). The weight is then returned to the starting position for one repetition. Once again, movement is slow and controlled.

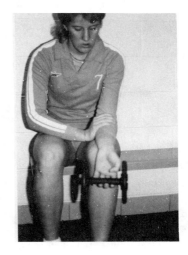

Fig. 15.43

Fig. 15.44

Repetitions

During the *conditioning phase* of your cycle, more repetitions should be used. Briefly:

	Sets	Repetitions	Target (1 Rep) % of Maximum
Back Squat	5	10 or 8	70–75
Pulls	5	5	70–75
Presses	5	8	70–75
Auxiliary Ex.	3	10	no maximum

The *strength phase* should consist of fewer repetitions with an increase in weights.

	Sets	Repetitions	Target (1 Rep) % of Maximum
Back Squat	5	5	80–85
Pulls	5	3	80–85
Presses	5	5	80–85
Auxiliary Ex.	3	10	no maximum

The 1 rep maximums must be tested for at the beginning of the program. If you have beginners, then estimates must be made by you, the coach. Remember, it is better to underestimate than discourage or injure someone with weight they cannot handle. It is also important to do at least three sets in the target percentage range. Auxiliary exercises are always light to moderate weight for three sets of ten repetitions. You may use eight repetitions at some point in order to break up the boredom.

The *competitive cycle* sees a much different program with respect to sets and repetitions.

	Repetitions	Target (1 Rep) % of Maximum
Back Squat	3	80
Pulls	3	83
Presses	2	85
	2	87
	1	90
Auxiliary Ex.	- - same as before - -	

The warm-ups are not included in the above, but are very important for preparing the body for the target percentages. At least three warm-up sets are recommended.

As I mentioned earlier in the planning section, the competitive period is split in two. The above is what I call the minor competitive period. The major competitive period would entail the same set/repetition structure, but with lesser percentages. Namely:

	Repetitions	Target (1 Rep) % of Maximum
Back Squat	3	70
Pulls	3	73
Presses	2	75
	2	77
	1	80

In the event that free weights are not available to you, a universal gym type setup may be your only alternative. Remember that no machine can replace free weights for total body strength development. The human body is made to work as one unit, not in separate parts. Therefore, it is only common sense to train it the same way.

FLEXIBILITY TRAINING

Flexibility may be defined as the range of motion through which the limbs or body parts are able to move. Before any type of flexibility program is composed, we must consider the major limits to flexibility. Muscles are covered with a tough connective tissue which inhibits range of motion. The tendons and the joint capsules are also limiting factors in flexibility. Flexibility exercises gradually lead to minor distentions in the connective tissue mentioned, and in due time these minor changes can result in a dramatically improved range of motion. An increase in the range of motion can significantly reduce the chance of injury to the athlete. Flexibility exercises also play a major role in the rehabilitation of injuries.

In the past, the idea of proper stretching included bounding and jerking movements which were aimed at loosening up the muscles. Today's flexibility concept emphasizes slow and deliberate movements called static stretches. Following are some static flexibility exercises that you can implement into your program. Remember, there is progress in patience. Do not rush through your flexibility exercises. They are extremely important, so take your time.

General Warm-up

This exercise is used in yoga stretching routines and is referred to as the *sun salutation*. It is a tremendous warm-up and should be used at the beginning of a flexibility routine. In the first position, you simply stand with your arms at your sides, and your head down and relaxed. The heels are almost touching with the toes pointed slightly outward.

Breathing during these stretches should be relaxed and no position should be forced. Stretch only as much as you can, and relax. Then, while inhaling, raise the arms reaching outward, upward, and over your head (Figure 15.45). You should bend at the knee and try to reach back while maintaining balance. Exhale while bringing the arms forward, trying to keep the back flat (Figure 15.46). Relax the head down to the knees, or as close as possible, while bending the knees slightly. Place your hands next to your feet and take a long step backward with your right foot (Figure 15.47). Look up while controlling your breathing and push your hips downward and forward. This is great for the groin area, the hamstring, and also the hips. At this point, step back with the left foot and put the feet together. Try to press the heels into the ground while attempting to touch your head to your knees (Figure 15.48). This stretches the calves, hamstrings, shoulders, and back. From here, touch your knees, chest, and forehead to the floor, respectively. Slide yourself forward a bit with your hands and look upward, flexing your back (Figure 15.49). Remember, if it hurts or you get any sharp pains, stop. Only go to where it feels comfortable and then relax. Return your upper body to the floor and lift your buttocks up into the bridged position (Figure 15.49), stretching the calves. Then step forward to your right hand with your right foot. Once again, push your hips downward and forward and look up (Figure 15.50). Return the left foot to the starting position and reach outward, upward, and back over your head while inhaling. Exhale and move the hands and head back to the starting position. Relax. Repeat the same procedure with the left leg.

Fig. 15.45

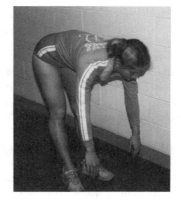

Fig. 15.46

Fig. 15.47

Fig. 15.48

Fig. 15.49

Fig. 15.50

Back Roll

Start by lying flat on your back with your hands at your sides, palms down, and your feet together. Proceed to lift your legs, with the knees straight, directly over your head while keeping your back flat on the floor. Return to the starting position and relax. If there is no problem performing this, then roll all the way up and try to touch the floor with your toes (Figure 15.51). You may want to place your arms over your head to be more comfortable. After relaxing in this position, slowly return to the starting position, trying to touch the floor with one vertebra at a time.

If you have no back problems, try to roll up the same way, but this time bend the knees and try to place them next to your ears (Figure 15.52). Relax. Return to the starting position, one vertebra at a time.

Fig. 15.51

Fig. 15.52

Hurdler Stretch

Everyone knows the hurdler stretch, but this particular one has a few variations. Start with the traditional position of the right leg extended and the left leg flexed and to the side. Now slowly bend over the right leg, trying to touch your chin to your big toe (Figure 15.53). Relax and control your breathing. Then try to relax and let your forehead come down as far as it can without any discomfort. Touch your left knee with your right hand while extending your left hand over your head and then touching your right foot with your left hand (Figure 15.54). Relax. This position stretches the sides while stretching the hamstring on the extended leg.

Fig. 15.53

Fig. 15.54

The third position is similar to the first except that you flex your right foot toward your head and hold while you try to touch your chin to your big toe (Figure 15.55). Then relax and put your forehead down. In the next position, both elbows are placed down on the floor between the legs (Figure 15.56). This stretches the groin and hamstrings very effectively. Look ahead and and point the chin out at first, and then relax by putting the forehead down. Repeat the position shown in Figure 15.54.

Now try to touch your forehead to your left thigh (Figure 15.57). Do not force it. At first you may be very tight through the hip flexors, but stay with it and you will loosen up. Remember to give it time.

The final position is shown in Figure 15.58. Very slowly, lean back on your hands at first. If that feels comfortable, go to the elbows. If that still feels good, ease yourself all the way down and relax. Control your breathing. Sit up and repeat with the other leg. This final position is a good stretch for the hip flexors and quadriceps of the bent leg. Remember, you may only get back on the hands the first day and that is fine. Just keep working at it!

Fig. 15.55

Fig. 15.56

Fig. 15.57

Fig. 15.58

Double Leg

This exercise primarily stretches the quadriceps and the hip flexors (Figure 15.59) and should follow the hurdler sequence. Begin by kneeling down and sitting on your calves, but not before pushing the calves out to the sides so as not to put extra pressure on the knee joints. Be careful here and be aware of any discomfort or pain in the knee. If there is any, stop the exercise immediately.

Calf Stretch

Everyone has seen this one before also. It is the old "lean against the wall, with your legs straight and your heels on the ground" calf stretch (Figure 15.60). This is a good way of stretching the calves if it is not rushed and the individual relaxes.

Arm Stretches

An efficient way to stretch the arms is with a partner. Figure 15.61 shows how a partner can help in stretching the chest, shoulder, and biceps (if the hands are turned out). Another exercise stretches the latissimus dorsi, triceps, and shoulder (Figure 15.62). In both flexes, resistance can be added by the partner. For instance, in Figure 15.61, while the partner holds the arms in one position, the person stretching tries to apply pressure against the resistance, with straight arms. A ten-second count is long enough before relaxation. At this time, the partner tries to stretch the arms a little more until the person stretching feels tightness again. The ten seconds of pressure is then repeated. This is done for three repetitions, and at the end of the third repetition the partner tries to stretch the arms as far as the person stretching will allow. Relaxation is very important during stretching and cannot be emphasized enough.

Fig. 15.59

Fig. 15.60

Fig. 15.61

Fig. 15.62

PLYOMETRICS

Another very efficient mode of conditioning is plyometric training, more commonly referred to as *bounding* or *jumping*. This type of training has been used by the Eastern European countries for many years with much success. The concept behind plyometrics is similar to that discussed previously with weight training. That is, in order to build explosive power, explosive movements must be practiced. More specifically, in order to build fast-twitch muscle fiber response, fast and quick movements must be performed.

Two types of muscular contractions occur during plyometrics. *Concentric contractions* occur during the shortening phase of the muscle, and *eccentric contractions* occur during the lengthening phase of the muscle. An example of an eccentric contraction would be the lengthening of your quadriceps (thigh) muscles when you walk down stairs. This type of contraction can be considered to have a *breaking* action. The concentric contraction can be described by the shortening of the same quadriceps muscle while walking up the stairs.

A concentric contraction is much stronger if it immediately follows an eccentric contraction of the same muscle group. This can be seen when the athlete bounds. The eccentric contraction is seen when the muscle is loaded sufficiently to lengthen it, as when the legs contact the ground just before they push off again. During this push-off, the muscles shorten and the concentric contraction occurs.

A very simple example can help you understand this concept. If you were to drop a rubber ball and observe it striking the ground, the point at which it is deformed is the time when it stores the energy acquired in the drop. As it returns to its original shape, the stored energy is released in the form of kinetic energy and the ball returns to the height from which it was dropped. In the athlete's case, he or she stores the same type of energy during the eccentric contraction and releases it during the concentric phase.

Loading is not recommended while doing plyometrics. Best results are achieved when the body is not loaded. If weights are used with these drills, a decrease in the neuro-muscular response will occur. One of the main principles of plyometric training is that the faster the muscle is forced to lengthen, the greater the tension it is capable of exerting. So you can see that any added weight to the body via ankle, chest, or wrist weights will only defeat the principle just mentioned.

Two-leg Hops (in Place)

This is a good plyometric drill for first timers. Begin in a standing position and drive the legs straight up from the ground, springing equally off both feet. Try to lift the knees into a tuck until they touch the chest. As the feet begin moving downward and out of the tuck, try to return them to the ground at the same time. The key to this drill, as in all plyometric drills, is to spend as little time as possible on the ground.

The athlete should prepare to spring up off the ground before touching down from the previous hop. Often the individual tries to reset the feet between jumps, which defeats the "rapid" concept of the drill. Beginners should start out by doing five sets of five repetitions, with a fifteen-second rest in between sets. More advanced athletes can do three sets of ten repetitions, and they should perform the workout twice a week.

If an athlete is strong enough and has done a great amount of plyometrics, he or she can do one-leg in-place hops. These are performed in the same manner as the two-leg hops but only one leg is used. The athlete should train a minimum of four weeks with two legs before advancing to the one-leg exercise. The same repetition structure may be used. Make sure to use the arms to help thrust the body upward.

Standing Long Jump

This drill is a tremendous preparation for the other plyometric drills. Begin with both feet flat on the ground, flex at the hips and waist as if to squat down, and jump forward. Remember to jump for distance and not for height, and try to use the arms to aid in thrusting the body forward. At the highest point in the jump, the chest should be up and the hips forward. The arms are overhead at this point and the knees bent. As the body descends, pike at the waist and go into a tuck position and maintain that position until landing. I recommend one set of ten jumps with thirty seconds of rest between jumps.

Standing Triple Jump

This exercise promotes not only horizontal and vertical jumping ability, but also leg strength, balance, and coordination. Begin by standing on both feet, jump forward landing first on the right foot, then directly on the left foot, and finally on both feet. The purpose is to try for maximum distance, not height. Remember to alternate the first step, as long as the procedure is followed, to ensure equal work on both legs. I recommend ten jumps per workout with at least thirty seconds of rest between jumps.

Hurdle Hops (Front)

Begin by placing five hurdles, one in front of the other, and about one yard apart from each other. Set each hurdle at its lowest height for beginners and slowly increase the height as the athlete progresses. The more advanced athletes may add more hurdles to this drill.

The athlete starts from a standing position. He jumps over the first hurdle and lands on both feet. Without hesitation, he or she should continue to jump over the other four hurdles in the same manner. It helps if the athlete looks straight ahead rather than down at the hurdle, because this helps the knees to lift and prevents the individual from leaning into the jump. I recommend doing at least five sets of five hurdles to start. Remember, spend as little time on the ground as possible.

Hurdle Hops (Side)

This drill can be performed with a hurdle, as the name describes, or with a bench for a football dummy which is about eighteen inches high. The athlete begins by standing parallel or to the side of the hurdle (or whatever it may be). The feet are together and the athlete's head is straight. Proceed to hop back and forth over the bench or hurdle, landing on both feet. The object of this drill is to cross over and back as quickly as possible while maintaining balance. I recommend doing as many hops as possible in thirty seconds. Keep a record of completions.

Bounding

The most widely used plyometric drill is bounding, when the athlete bounds or leaps from one leg to the other. In order to perform bounding properly, the athlete should concentrate on landing flat-footed. Landing on the toes shifts the center of gravity forward, and this is unwanted. The center of gravity must remain behind each step and then be pulled forward.

Bounding may be varied for each workout. One variation is to bound for 100 m (328 ft.) with a rest period, consisting of a 100-meter walk back to the starting point, and then repeat. Bounding for distance such as this is good for power, whereas taking short, fast bounds is good for developing quickness.

Two other variations of bounding drills include single-leg bounds and combination bounds. The single-leg bounds are initiated with a running start in which the athlete bounds on a single leg over a specific distance. In using only one leg at a time, the athlete is forced to react quickly in order to initiate the next bound with the active leg. I recommend doing ten bounds per

319

set for beginners, whereas the more advanced athletes should exercise at certain distances (e.g., 50 meters).

Combination bounds are different in that they combine both single-leg and alternate (basic) bounding. For example, left foot, left foot, and right foot would be one series combination. Right foot, right foot, and left foot would be another.

The one I like to use is LL-RR-LL-RR. This way, there is less confusion as to which foot is to be next, and the rhythmic coordination of alternate and/or single leg bounds is still maintained. Remember to use the arms to help thrust the body, and try to lift the knee of the active leg while bounding.

Depth Jumping

Sometimes referred to as box jumps, depth jumps are, in my opinion, the most advanced of all plyometric drills. Only the physically well-prepared athletes should perform these drills. Depth jumps are very demanding and if done improperly, or by less conditioned athletes, can prove to be dangerous to the joints of the lower limbs. Most coaches prefer to do depth jumps only once a week, and only in the off-season. This is due to the difficulty of the exercise and the amount of work the athlete must endure in order to perform the exercise well.

Depth jumping is performed by jumping from the top of a sturdy box to a soft surface, such as rubber or grass. The athlete should land in a half squat position and immediately jump straight up as fast as possible. Remember to start with a box no higher than 146 cm (18 ins.). I recommend about fifteen jumps a workout and a workout only one day a week. The more advanced athlete, who is experienced in depth jumping, can do this drill twice per week but must receive at least forty-eight hours of rest in between workout days. Here again, after about three to four weeks at one height, the boxes may be raised to increase the difficulty. Make sure the athlete is jumping comfortably. That is, make certain that the body is always in control and not unbalanced, otherwise injury is more apt to occur.

Box Hops

Similar to the box setup just described, box hops involve two or three boxes which are 46 cm (18 ins.) in height and about 1.8 to 2.4 m (6 to 8 ft.) apart. The athlete starts with both feet together and jumps from the ground to box one, and then back to the ground. Upon landing on the ground, the athlete immediately hops to box two and so on, until he or she has jumped on and off all three boxes. I recommend doing five sets of three to five boxes per workout once a week.

A Composite Plyometric Program

I firmly believe that plyometric drills can greatly benefit any athlete who needs power and speed. Again, the key to making any physical training program work is setting up a program in which the optimal amount of work is done at the proper time in the cycle. It is very easy to overtrain doing plyometrics, especially when combined with other necessary aspects of training. However, I believe that weight training, plyometrics, running, and volleyball itself can be orchestrated into a finely tailored program that will be successful. During the off-season, a general composite could look like this:

MONDAY
- — Jog or jump rope (two to three minutes)
- — Flexibility exercises
- — Weight training
- — 1.6 to 2.4 km (1 to 1 1/2 mi.) easy run
- — Volleyball

TUESDAY
- — Jog or jump rope (two to three minutes)
- — Flexibility exercises
- — Plyometrics
- — Running strides five times 91.4 m (100 yds.) on grass or tartan, half speed.
- — Volleyball

WEDNESDAY
- — Same as Monday

THURSDAY
- — Jog or jump rope (two to three minutes)
- — Flexibility exercises
- — Plyometrics
- — Running strides four times 201.2 m (220 yds.) at three-quarters speed, walk the same distance back.
- — Volleyball

FRIDAY
- — Same as Monday–Wednesday

SATURDAY
- — Flexibility exercises
- — Active rest. Volleyball pick-up game or basketball, etc.

SUNDAY
- — Flexibility exercises
- — 3.2 to 4 km. (2 to 2 1/2 mi.) distance run, at an easy pace.

The physical condition of each athlete will determine the length and number of plyometrics sessions during this period. For beginners, once a week is sufficient. Advanced athletes must endure two per week. The striding on Tuesday and Thursday must accompany this in order to implement some speed work.

In order to be certain that your athletes are ready for this period of major plyometrics, it would be wise to precede it with two to three weeks of skipping (as young children do) or jumping rope. These are a couple of good conditioners for plyometrics. The skipping may also be done after the actual workout to increase the endurance and conditioning.

The weight workout is described in the section on weight training. The volleyball during this period should consist of more instructional, drill type exercises with volume and not intensity being the main concern. Also, notice the one component which is included each day — flexibility. It should become second nature for your athletes to stretch.

You as the coach must adjust the plyometric training accordingly. When doing these drills twice a week, do not perform more than three different drills per workout, unless you cut down on the individual sets and/or repetitions (e.g., one standing jump, one hopping drill, and bounding). Too much will only lead to overtraining, especially in a sport like volleyball where so much jumping is already being performed in the sport itself.

When the strength cycle of your program begins, try to maintain two days of plyometrics per week, but back off the intensity when the weight training increases. Allowing the strength levels to increase in the weight room, while continuing plyometrics at a lower intensity, will make for a more powerful athlete during the competitive phase.

This brings us to the final phase of the cycle. Once in the competitive phase, the plyometrics are cut back to once a week, preferably at the beginning of the week (if the competitions are on weekends). Emphasis here should be on short, fast bounding. In order to prepare for the minor and major peaks, discontinue plyometrics for at least ten days before competition. This will allow maximum recovery time.

ELECTRO-MUSCLE STIMULATION (EMS)

The use of electrical stimulation on muscle tissue is not new. Electrical stimulation has given medical personnel the tool with which to test and treat injured and post-operative muscles. In addition, it has been used to prevent denervation atrophy, decrease muscle spasm and spasticity, and reduce contractures. In animal studies, chronic electrical stimulation showed marked improvements in muscle endurance as evidenced by increased oxidative capacity and capillary density. In human studies, the clinical application of electrical stimulation has been shown to increase succinate dehydrogenase (an enzyme found in oxidative metabolism) in the quadriceps of patients recovering from reconstructive surgery involving ligaments of the knee.

There have been several studies showing varying increases in isometric strength with electrical stimulation. However, in most forms of physical activity, as in volleyball, dynamic strength is much more important than static strength. None of the above studies has shown any increase in the dynamic strength of muscle when treated with electrical stimulation. A recent study, though, showed electrical stimulation to increase the knee extension strength, not only isometrically but also isokinetically at a movement speed of thirty degrees per second. Strength in the latter study was assessed isokinetically with a Cybex II dynamometer at both thirty degrees per second and sixty degrees per second, but showed no significant increase at the faster speed.

Very little research has been done with EMS and dynamic strength. The studies which showed no increases did not use a 2500 Hz frequency stimulator. There are studies being done now (unpublished) which have had much success with strength increases, using the high frequency stimulator. I have used a 2500 Hz stimulator (Electrostim 180) in a human study to determine its effects on the dynamic strength of healthy quadriceps. My study consisted of fifteen healthy male athletes who were on a controlled daily exercise routine. They were divided into three groups of five each. Group A was the control (no stimuli), Group B was stimulated isometrically at one angle of knee flexion and Group C isometrically at two angles of knee flexion. The treatments were given five days per week with weekends off. Each treatment lasted fifteen minutes per subject. Each subject was tested isokinetically (Cybex II dynamometer) before and after the four-week-long study. The final statistics have not been completed, but in reviewing the preliminary data one can see a marked increase in the dynamic strength of Group C (two angles of stimulation) with very little increase in Group B (one angle of stimulation). It must be emphasized that this data is of a preliminary nature only and must be viewed in that fashion. Further research is needed to validate this study and other similar studies dealing with high frequency electrical stimulation.

RESISTANCE TRAINING IN THE POOL

A resistance training program in the pool in conjunction with weight training has produced dramatic improvements in strength and jumping ability. There appear to be several benefits of resistance training in the pool:

- The resistance of the water produces an overload, so strength gain will occur.
- The water has a therapeutic effect in that there is less subsequent muscle soreness, and there is less chance of injury because of the "cushioning" effect of the water.
- The training is movement specific — volleyball movements can be practiced with resistance through the entire range of motion.
- Flexibility may also be enhanced by executing movements through their entire range of motion.
- Training in the pool can also be beneficial for athletes who are recovering from injuries — the water provides a reasonably safe environment for rehabilitation.
- There may also be psychological benefits — the coolness of the water is a relief after a hard practice session.

Listed below are some resistance exercises that are being used in the pool:

- Full squats: In waist-high water, with hands behind the head, go under water and jump explosively. This should be executed repetitively with rhythmic breathing.
- Combination: In waist-high water, with hands behind the head and feet in a front-back stride position, assume a half-squat position, and jump explosively and switch feet on each jump. This should be performed repetitively with rhythmic breathing.
- Arm swings: In shoulder-high water, execute the entire arm swing used in the spiking motion. The heel-toe rock may also be executed to make the movement more specific to the spiking approach.
- Arm circles: In shoulder-high water, with the arms extended at sides, move arms in large and small circular motions, forward and backward.
- Leg circles: In chest-high water, using the side of the pool or a lane divider for support, move each leg in a circular motion.
- Hip diagonal abduction and adduction: In chest-high water, using the side of the pool or a lane divider for support, abduct and then adduct each leg, crossing in front of the body.
- Hip extension and flexion: In chest-high water, using the side of the pool or a lane divider for support, extend and flex straight leg through the entire range of motion.
- Toe raises: In shoulder-high water, using the side of the pool or a lane divider for support, perform toe raises alone or with a partner sitting on shoulders for added resistance.
- Spike approach, blocking movements: Specific volleyball movements can also be performed in the pool.
- Basic movements: Running, skipping, hopping, high knees, etc.
- Specific muscle group exercises: Use kickboards to isolate work on legs or arms.

All movements should be done repetitively and explosively. Perform these exercises in sets of twenty-five to fifty repetitions, using two or three sets for each exercise.

SUMMARY

Physical factors make up the basis of training, and it is very important for a volleyball team to have a well-planned physical training program. There are three things to consider in setting up any physical training program, and they are feasibility, attainability, and specificity. The training itself should consist of an off-season period, a pre-season period, and a competitive period. The program should be such that in each period, the intensity, duration, frequency, and types of drills or workouts can be varied so that the team reaches its physical and mental peak during the competitive period.

A physical training program should also include nutrition instruction, weight training, flexibility training, plyometrics, electro-muscle stimulation, resistance training in the pool, and instruction in nutrition. Nutrition instruction should teach athletes the importance of eating a diet well-balanced in carbohydrates, fats, protein, vitamins, and minerals. Volleyball players should use weight training to develop speed and power. The movements used in weight training should correlate to the movements used in playing volleyball, but should also aid in total body strengthening. For optimal training, flexibility exercizes should emphasize slow and deliberate movements. Plyometrics, or practicing explosive movements, is important in training for many of the movements used in volleyball. Both electro-muscle stimulation and resistance training in water can be used to increase muscle strength.

BIBLIOGRAPHY

Bouman, H. D., and K. J. Shaffer. "Physiological Basis of Electrical Stimulation of Human Muscle and its Clinical Application." *Physical Therapy Review* 37 (1957): 207–223.

Cambell, C. J. "Faradic Stimulation of Muscle." *Journal of Sports: The Coaching Association of Canada.* 1980.

Chase, J. "Elicitation of Periods of Inhibition in Human Muscle by Stimulation of Cutaneous Nerves". *Journal of Bone and Joint Surgery* (AM) 54 (1972): 1737–1744.

Costello, Frank. "Bounding to the Top." Unpublished manuscript.

Edgerton, V. R. "Mammalian Muscle Fiber Types and Their Adaptability." *American Zoology* 18 (1978): 113-125.

Eriksson, E. "Sports Injuries of the Knee Ligaments, Their Diagnosis, Treatment, Rehabilitation and Prevention." *Medicine and Science in Sports* 8 (1976): 133–144.

Garhammer, J. G. *Evaluation of Human Power Capacity through Olympic Weightlifting Analysis.* Ph.D. dissertation. University of California at Los Angeles, 1980.

----------------. "Power Production by Olympic Weightlifters." *Medicine and Science in Sports and Exercise* 12 (1980): 54–60.

----------------. "Equipment for the Development of Athletic Strength and Power." *National Strength and Conditioning Association Journal.* Vol. 3, no. 6. 1981.

Goldberg, A. "Mechanisms of Growth and Atrophy of Skeletal Muscle." In *Muscle Biology,* edited by R. G. Cassens. New York: Dekker, 1972.

Johnson, D. H., and P. J. Ashcroft. "The Russian Technique of Faradism in the Treatment of Chondromalacia Patellae." *Physiotherapy* 29 (1977): 266–268.

Selinger, Dr. Arie, and Joan Ackermann-Blount. *Arie Selinger's Power Volleyball.* New York: St. Martin's Press, 1986.

Weighted rope training can lead to significant increases in vertical jump, speed, endurance, shoulder strength, agility, and explosive power.

SHAPING UP FOR THE ATTACK

Bob Bertucci

Spikes, digs, kills — even the terms for volleyball moves are fierce. To be a top volleyball player, explosive energy, snap coordination, and long-term endurance are all required.

Jump training can be used to build explosive power. There are two stages to jump training. The first stage, which is necessary to provide overall conditioning and to prepare for the second stage, is rope skipping, preferably with a weighted rope such as the ULTRA-ROPE,® made by Garney Inc. of Grand Rapids, Michigan.

Rope skipping can lead to significant increases in vertical jump, speed, endurance, shoulder strength, agility, and explosive power. Because it is so physically strenuous, a player should begin a rope skipping program with light intensity workouts (in terms of their length, revolutions per work interval, or weight of rope) and build from there.

The goal should be to achieve and maintain 80 percent of Maximum Heart Rate (MHR), a point called the Training Heart Rate (THR). Players should monitor themselves after each jumping set. MHR is 220 minus age for women and 204 minus half the age for men. If the pulse rate after a set of skipping rope is more than ten beats over or under 80 percent of the MHR (that is, if it misses the THR by more than ten), the training should be adjusted accordingly.

Players should start skipping with a two-pound rope, and at first they may be able to skip for only one minute. A good initial training regimen would involve skipping with a two-pound rope for six one-minute sessions (with a minute's rest in between) three times a week. At the end of the six weeks, vertical jump, sprint speed, and stamina should show significant improvements. Chest, arm, and shoulder development should occur because turning even a two-pound rope at eighty to 140 turns a minute can generate a centrifugal pull of twenty pounds.

Because jumping a weighted rope requires such a high level of concentrated physical effort over a short period of time — resembling a series of sharp volleys punctuated by brief moments of rest — rope skipping leaves volleyball players with exactly the kind of fitness for explosive performance that their sport requires.

16

PSYCHOLOGICAL FACTORS

Craig Wrisberg and Vanessa Draper

Athletic performance involves more than physical skill — there are important psychological factors as well. Such factors are evident when we witness a superior display of skill by a player on one occasion and then, on a separate occasion, see that same player make error after error. We know the player can physically perform the skills, so when the player fails to perform we usually describe the mistakes as "mental errors" and blame them on a lack of concentration. Many times, our only advice to the player is "relax and concentrate." Unfortunately, we usually do not give our players any clues as to how to do this.

Increasing interest in the psychological factors involved in athletic performance has resulted in the development and implementation of several psychological techniques to help players reduce the stress associated with competition and build the appropriate mental skills for athletic competition. *Relaxation training, mental rehearsal,* and *attentional control training* are important tools for reducing the stress and uncertainty that a player may experience during a point, a game, or a match. An additional psychological edge can be gained through the practice of *goal setting.* When a player becomes actively involved in defining specific goals, motivation is usually increased. This chapter explains these psychological techniques and suggests ways to include such mental training in a competitive volleyball program.

RELAXATION TRAINING

Athletes perform best when they are optimally aroused, both physically and mentally. Physical arousal is defined by the amount of muscle tension that an individual experiences. Too much or too little muscle tension can hinder skill performance, while an optimal amount facilitates coordinated movement. The same is true for mental arousal. Each athlete has a certain level of mental arousal at which he or she performs best. Some athletes need to "psych-up" in order to perform successfully, while others need to "psych-down."

In addition to pre-competition adjustments, performers often need to monitor and alter their arousal levels during competition. What one player perceives as a stressful game situation, another may see as exciting and challenging. For example, an experienced, risk-taking individual might regard a match-point serving situation as an opportunity to shine and win the game single-handedly. However, an inexperienced, less confident player might consider this same situation as a threatening, sure-to-fail proposition. For both of these players, there is a feeling of increased mental arousal and physical tension. If either becomes aroused beyond his or her optimal point, that player can "choke." Therefore, players need to consciously monitor their levels of arousal in order to make the adjustments that will bring their mental and physical tension within an optimal range. If peak arousal can be maintained, peak performance will usually result.

When we realize that a player is over-aroused, we have a tendency to scream "Relax! Concentrate!" More than likely, the player is not comfortable with this tension any more than we are, and our anxious cries do little to remedy the situation. A better strategy would be to address the root of the problem before the problem occurs. The athlete who is trained in muscular relaxation and attentional control techniques can begin to take control of his or her mental state and level of arousal. He or she will then be in a better position to handle competitive anxiety successfully when it occurs.

Muscular relaxation methods are based on two assumptions: that muscular tension can be due to emotional stress, and that learning to reduce one's muscular tension can help in reducing such stress. Relaxation techniques teach the athlete to focus on various muscle groups and help develop control over the amount of tension within the muscle. A typical relaxation session begins with the athlete (or athletes, if in a group session) in a comfortable, reclining position, preferably in a quiet room where there will be no distractions.

Initially, the athlete should be talked through the relaxation procedure by another trained individual. However, with practice, individuals can perform the technique on their own. Most muscular relaxation procedures follow the same general format and use similar terminology. The instructor usually begins the session by having the athletes close their eyes, inhale deeply, and exhale slowly, relaxing completely. The instructor may choose to prepare a monologue which directs the athlete's attention to the various muscle groups, isolating and relaxing each group, and moving systematically through the body from head to toe. Again, the objective is to have the athlete become aware of any isolated muscular tension and become adept at consciously relaxing those muscles.

Being able to achieve a relaxed state spontaneously has two advantages in athletic competition. Not only is it useful prior to competition as a means of relaxing and adjusting arousal levels, but it can also be employed during competition to relieve tension in muscle groups essential to performance. For example, as a player prepares to serve a match point, the last thing needed is tight shoulder and neck muscles because the coordinated effort of these muscles is needed for successful serve execution. Therefore, it would be most beneficial for the player to pause before serving, mentally check those muscle groups to see if excessive tension exists, and consciously relax those muscles before attempting the serve. Muscular relaxation training can enhance a player's ability both to recognize the tension and to do something to relieve it.

MENTAL REHEARSAL

Relaxation methods are sometimes coupled with another psychological technique called mental rehearsal. Mental rehearsal in sport involves mentally practicing specific motor skills, attending to every detail of the skill, and visually imaging successful performance of the skill. Because it requires an internal focus of attention, mental rehearsal is most effective in combination with relaxation sessions. Creating a mental image of a skill is much easier if the athlete has achieved a moderately relaxed state, with a mind relatively clear and free of distractions. For example, a defensive specialist who has achieved a moderate level of relaxation might be instructed to rehearse the following situation mentally:

> Imagine that your team is serving and you are playing left back. You hear your teammate serve the ball and watch it fall deep in the other team's court. The opposing left back plays the ball, and their setter sets the ball to their left front hitter. You watch the hitter closely and notice the body position as the approach is made. As the hitter goes up, he or she is angled toward you and is looking at the inside of the block. The hitter's arm and hand come through and cut the ball around the inside of the block. You position yourself low, with your weight a little forward, and arms outstretched. The ball is coming at you but is falling short. You dive and feel the ball snap off of your hand as you pop the ball to your setter, who sets back to the right front for a down-the-line kill.

Such mental practice of skills has been found to be a very useful addition to physical practice. It will not, however, take the place of physical practice. In order to make mental practice most effective, the following points should be considered:

- Mental practice should be used in conjunction with physical practice, not in place of it.
- Mental practice periods should only last from two to five minutes.
- Mental practice sessions should be as realistic as possible and should always involve a successful performance by the player rehearsing.
- Mental practice is useful both for beginning players and for the rehearsal of intricate skills (e.g., a one-on-one blocking situation).
- Mental practice is most effective when the athlete learns to rehearse in "real time," that is, the time it actually takes to go through the skill physically.

Another important consideration when using mental practice is the basic ability of the athlete to create the mental image of a skill. Not all players are able to create vivid, enduring images of a performance. Some will report quick flashes of figures that are only outlines. But, like any skill, the more mental rehearsal is practiced, the better the performer will get at creating proper images. What is important is that all athletes be encouraged to take the same perspective one would take if actually performing rather than if observing a performance. A player who takes that internalized perspective can create and rehearse the physical feelings that accompany the skill. These feelings are extremely important for successful motor skill learning and performance. Learning to "feel" the skill physically improves the athlete's ability to rehearse in "real time." Being able to associate physical feelings with mental images makes imagery easier, more lifelike, and more effective as a practice method.

Here are some guidelines to follow when incorporating mental rehearsal into the total practice routine:
- Use relaxation procedures first to create the optimal mental state for mental imagery.
- Make sure that each athlete knows precisely what skill or phase of a skill to image (i.e., spiking against an outside block, or blocking a middle hitter).
- Encourage all athletes when they are imaging to take the perspective they would have if they were actually performing the skill, rather than if they were observing as a spectator.
- Emphasize the importance of learning to rehearse mentally in "real time." Have the athletes mentally rehearse an activity as they time it on a stopwatch. Then have them physically rehearse the same activity, also to a stopwatch. Compare the times. If they are not accurate, the athlete does not have a grasp of real time imaging and should practice this exercise until real time rehearsal is achieved.

ATTENTIONAL CONTROL TRAINING

Relaxation procedures and mental rehearsal of skills can be done prior to a competition to help optimize skill and arousal levels. But pre-game preparation and mental readiness will not make a difference unless the athlete can also maintain this readiness throughout the match. To do so, your players must also be able to alter or adjust their attentional focus. It is not much of an advantage to have a player who is physically able to "kill" the ball every time he or she goes up to spike if the player is consistently so distracted by the blocker or by negative thoughts that he or she mis-hits or hits into the block. This type of player can be greatly helped by attentional control training.

Clinical sport psychologist Robert Nideffer categorizes attention according to the dimensions of direction (internal or external) and width (broad or narrow). An internal focus is one in which the individual attends to his or her own thoughts or analysis of a situation. An external focus is one in which the individual concentrates on the activity going on around him or her. For example, in volleyball, the serving player should have an external focus while observing the opposing team's serve-receive positioning. The focus then becomes internal as the player decides which type of serve would be most effective in this situation. Finally, a switch to an external focus occurs as the eyes are fixed on the ball that is to be hit.

Attention can also be described as broad or narrow, depending on how specific the focus is. If a blocker is watching the play unfold on the opposing court, looking for general clues as to the direction the set is headed, then the blocker has a broad focus. However, when it has been determined that the ball is going to the middle hitter, the blocker would then narrow focus to the hitter and concentrate entirely on the ball and the hitter's arm and hand. Thus, both direction and width of focus are important during attentional control.

There are two keys to attentional control: knowing the most appropriate focus for different game situations, and being able to shift from one focus to the other. For example, the server mentioned earlier must shift focus several times before ever hitting the ball. Similarly, if a spiker is aware of when and where the focus should be, potential blockers become another source of information rather then a distraction. As the spiker watches the play develop on his or her court, the attentional focus is broad and external. It should become broad and internal as the spiker realizes that the ball is coming to him or her and begins to determine alternatives for action (e.g., dink, spike cross-court, spike down the line). In order to decide which alternatives to execute, the spiker must again shift to a broad, external focus and assess the opposing blockers' defensive positions. Once a strategy is determined, the spiker must shift to a narrow, internal focus while preparing to approach and hit the ball, concentrating on his or her movement toward the ball. While actually executing the hit, the spiker should have a narrow and external focus, concentrating on the ball and the blocker.

These shifts are neither as complicated nor as difficult to achieve as they may sound. Under non-stressful conditions, these shifts are made rather easily and naturally. But when an athlete becomes tense or anxious, the attentional "flow" can be interrupted. Attentional control training helps the athlete recognize when he or she is losing the "flow" and offers a way to regain control. The first step to regaining control is what Nideffer refers to as "centering."

Centering is a momentary internal check of one's mental and physical state. The athlete checks and adjusts breathing and muscle tension. Being centered can be thought of as feeling balanced and steady. With practice, an athlete can begin to center in the time it takes to inhale and exhale. Nideffer suggests the following technique:

> Take a standing position, feet shoulder-width apart, knees slightly bent. Inhale deeply, from the abdomen. Feel the tension in the chest and shoulders and consciously relax these muscles. As you exhale, relax the muscles of the thighs and calves and feel your body rest more heavily on the ground. You are balanced and steady and ready to direct your attention to the upcoming task or competition.

Centering is a "time-out" that allows the athlete to clear the mind of distracting or negative thoughts and regain a feeling of balance and control. This is not a technique to be used in the middle of a play. Instead, a server may use it while preparing to serve, or any player may center while waiting for the server to serve and play to begin. When the mind is clear and the body balanced, the athlete can then attend to the external cues essential to successful performance (e.g., the ball coming off of the server's hands, the opponents' block, the opponents' spike).

GOAL SETTING

Athletes and coaches alike have aspirations of being "Number One." Early in the season there is often talk of "winning it all come tournament time." Too often this ultimate goal is the only goal. Sometimes we as coaches do not place enough importance on short-term, specific goals that will get a team to the point it wants to be at the end of the season. We also sometimes fail to recognize that each player should be working toward personal goals as well as team goals, for the two go hand in hand. Thus, proper goal setting is an important factor in improving team and individual performances and in enhancing training results. Proper goal setting can also be a source of motivation if handled correctly.

An effective way to insure that goal setting is a positive experience for both individuals and the team is to conduct private coach-athlete sessions in which, together, the coach and player discuss the player's role on the team and the related skill areas and training tasks that that player needs to emphasize. When both player and coach understand and agree on the nature of the player's contribution to the team and the important tasks that player performs, then specific goals and procedures for evaluation can be established. The following sections offer general guidelines for goal setting in a volleyball program.

Goals Must be Realistic: Challenging, but within Reach

Players must honestly assess their abilities and limitations when considering a goal for performance. For a novice hitter with a 50 cm (20 in.) vertical jump to set a goal of putting every middle hit within the 10-foot line is probably unrealistic given that player's experience and jumping ability. That this goal is unrealistic should be pointed out to the player, and the suggestion should be made to revise the goal so that it will be more realistic. For example, this player's goal might instead be to hit progressively closer to the 10-foot line a higher percentage of the time on predesignated evaluation dates throughout the season.

Goals Should be Specific and Have a Time Frame

Evaluation is an important part of goal setting. In order for a goal to be evaluated, it must be specific and include predetermined target dates for evaluation. The player and coach should estimate the level of performance that is desired and attempt to project the amount of time it will take to reach that level. For example, a player who is putting only 50 percent of his or her serves in the court at the beginning of the season might set up the following sequence of serving goals:

> 60 percent by (date)
> 70 percent by (date)
> 80 percent by (date)
> 90 percent by conference tournament (date)

The specificity and the time frame make it easier for players to chart their progress and to see it on paper. Moreover, deadlines tend to be motivating (again, if the goals are realistic).

Leave Room for Revisions

Providing for the revision of goals is not meant to imply that goals should be lowered at the first sign of failure. However, if it becomes obvious that the original goal was not appropriate or realistic, a player needs to feel that it is acceptable to revise the goal and bring it within reach. If a player determines that one training goal is to lose fifteen pounds of body weight, and after several weeks of healthy dieting and workouts is only able to lose eight but is playing the best volleyball ever and feeling good, perhaps the goal weight should be reconsidered. Players need to be given this flexibility because pressure to achieve may become a burden if goals are inflexible and unrealistic.

Put the Goals in Writing

Having something in writing usually adds a seriousness to the player's commitment to goal achievement. Written agreements may take several forms. For example, players may write up contracts that outline their goals, include methods or procedures of evaluation, and establish target dates for evaluation. Coaches might post charts of player and team progress (e.g., graphs charting team serve percentages or individual vertical jump improvements). Making goals visible encourages accountability in each of the individual players, motivating all to do their part to enhance team performance.

Individual Goals Must be Compatible with Player Roles and Team Goals

Volleyball has become extremely specialized at most levels. Players have specific roles on a team, and it is important that they are aware of these roles before setting goals. If a coach intends for a player to play in only a defensive capacity, it is useless to have that player spend time constructing goals for hitting and blocking skills. Put simply, training goals and performance goals should be related to each player's role and responsibility.

A final point to consider when setting goals is the importance of short-term goals. Long-term goals are important, but players need to realize that it takes the achievement of a series of progressive, short-term goals to reach the final goals successfully. Goal-setting and evaluation of progress should be ongoing before, during, after, and in between competitive seasons.

SUMMARY

A number of psychological techniques have been developed to help players reduce stress and gain the mental skills needed for athletic competition. These techniques include: relaxation training, mental rehearsal, attentional control training, and goal setting.

Each athlete has a level of mental and physical arousal at which he or she performs best, and players should monitor and adjust their arousal level accordingly, both before and during play. Relaxation training is used for players who are overly aroused. To perform this training, players recline, close their eyes, and go through a relaxation procedure. Mental rehearsal involves mentally going through specific motor skills and visually imaging a successful performance of the skills. Attentional control training consists of having players adjust their attentional focus, internal or external, broad or narrow. The two keys to attentional control are knowing the most appropriate focus for different game situations, and being able to shift from one focus to another. Goal setting involves setting realistic personal and team goals and working toward reaching them.

BIBLIOGRAPHY

Cratty, Bryant J. *Psychology in Contemporary Sports.* Englewood Cliffs: Prentice-Hall, 1983.

----------------. *Psychological Preparation and Athletic Excellence.* Ithaca: Movement Publications, 1984.

Klavora, P., and Juri V. Daniel. *Coach, Athlete and the Sport Psychologist.* Champaign: Human Kinetics Publishers, 1979.

Nideffer, Robert M. *The Ethics and Practice of Applied Sport Psychology.* Ithaca: Movement Publications, 1981.

----------------. *Athletes' Guide to Mental Training.* Champaign: Human Kinetics Publishers, 1985.